Swift Functional Programming

Second Edition

Build clean, smart, and reliable applications with Swift
Functional Programming

Dr. Fatih Nayebi

BIRMINGHAM - MUMBAI

Swift Functional Programming

Second Edition

First published: June 2016

Second edition: April 2017

Production reference: 1210417

Published by Packt Publishing Ltd.
Livery Place
35 Livery Street
Birmingham
B3 2PB, UK.
ISBN 978-1-78728-450-0

www.packtpub.com

Credits

Author
Dr. Fatih Nayebi

Reviewer
Giordano Scalzo

Commissioning Editor
Ashwin Nair

Acquisition Editor
Dibyajyoti Ghosh

Content Development Editor
Amrita Noronha

Technical Editor
Nilesh Sawakhande

Copy Editor
Safis Editing

Project Coordinator
Shweta H Birwatkar

Proofreader
Safis Editing

Indexer
Pratik Shirodkar

Graphics
Tania Dutta

Production Coordinator
Aparna Bhagat

About the Author

Dr. Fatih Nayebi has more than 15 years of industry experience in software engineering and architecture in various fields. He has developed numerous applications with Visual Basic, C++, C#, Java, MATLAB, Python, Objective-C, and Swift. He has been designing and developing enterprise and consumer iOS applications since the release of first iOS SDK. He is also an enthusiastic Node, Scala, and Haskell developer.

Aside from industry, Fatih earned his Ph.D. degree in software engineering from École de technologie supérieure, Université du Québec by researching on Mobile Human-Computer Interaction, Software Engineering, and Machine Learning.

His specialties include applied predictive and optimization models, human-computer interaction, functional programming, machine learning, and mobile application architecture and development.

Fatih currently works as a Director, Consulting at CGI Group Inc, Montreal, and continues to his academic research and publications as a postdoctoral researcher at École de technologie supérieure.

You can find him talking on Swift and Functional Programming at meetups such as `http://www.meetup.com/swift-mtl/`, on GitHub at `https://github.com/conqueror`, on Twitter as `@thefatih`, and on Instagram as `@thefatih`.

About the Reviewer

Giordano Scalzo is a developer with 20 years of programming experience, since the days of ZXSpectrum. He has worked in C++, Java, .NET, Ruby, Python and in a ton of other languages he has forgotten the names of.

After years of backend development, over the past five years, Giordano has developed extensively for iOS, releasing more than 20 apps, apps that he wrote for clients, enterprise application, or for his own company.

Currently, he is a contractor in London, where, through his company, Effective Code Ltd, `http://effectivecode.co.uk`, he delivers code for iOS aiming at quality and reliability.

In his spare time, when he is not crafting retro game clones for iOS, he writes his thoughts on `http://giordanoscalzo.com`.

I'd like to thank my better half, Valentina, who lovingly supports me in everything I do: without you, none of this would have been possible.

Thanks to my bright future, Mattia and Luca, for giving me lots of smiles and hugs when I needed them.
Finally, my gratitude goes to my mum and dad, who gave my curiosity and the support to follow my passions, begun one day when they bought me a ZXSpectrum.

www.PacktPub.com

For support files and downloads related to your book, please visit www.PacktPub.com.

Did you know that Packt offers eBook versions of every book published, with PDF and ePub files available? You can upgrade to the eBook version at www.PacktPub.com and as a print book customer, you are entitled to a discount on the eBook copy. Get in touch with us at service@packtpub.com for more details.

At www.PacktPub.com, you can also read a collection of free technical articles, sign up for a range of free newsletters and receive exclusive discounts and offers on Packt books and eBooks.

https://www.packtpub.com/mapt

Get the most in-demand software skills with Mapt. Mapt gives you full access to all Packt books and video courses, as well as industry-leading tools to help you plan your personal development and advance your career.

Why subscribe?

- Fully searchable across every book published by Packt
- Copy and paste, print, and bookmark content
- On demand and accessible via a web browser

Customer Feedback

Thanks for purchasing this Packt book. At Packt, quality is at the heart of our editorial process. To help us improve, please leave us an honest review on this book's Amazon page at https://www.amazon.com/dp/1787284506.

If you'd like to join our team of regular reviewers, you can e-mail us at customerreviews@packtpub.com. We award our regular reviewers with free eBooks and videos in exchange for their valuable feedback. Help us be relentless in improving our products!

For Grace,
being a father may make me a better person.

For Necmiye,
because of the love and support throughout the writing of this book.

For Fehiman,
I am grateful for everything you have done for us.

For Negar and Su Tamina,
love you all.

Table of Contents

Preface

Functional programming (FP) is getting a lot of attention as it eases many of the difficulties faced in **object-oriented programming (OOP)**, such as testability, maintainability, scalability, and concurrency. Swift has a lot of functional programming features that can be easily used, but most Objective-C and Swift programmers are not very familiar with these tools.

This book aims to simplify the functional programming paradigms and make it easily usable for Swift programmers, showing you how to use popular functional programming techniques to solve many of your day-to-day development problems. Whether you are new to functional programming and Swift or experienced, this book will provide you with the skills you need to design and develop high quality, easily maintainable, scalable, and efficient applications for iOS Web, macOS, tvOS, and watchOS. Through this book, you'll learn to develop extendable, smart, and maintainable code using functional programming techniques.

What this book covers

Chapter 1, *Getting Started with Functional Programming in Swift*, introduces functional programming paradigms by attempting to answer the questions of *Why functional programming matters?* and *What is functional programming?* It covers topics such as immutability, stateless programming, pure, first-class, and higher-order functions. Also, this chapter will introduce the Swift programming language basics as they are essential for the rest of the book.

Chapter 2, *Functions and Closures*, begins with the definition of functions, continues with other related topics, such as function types, and finally concludes with more advanced topics such as first-class functions, higher-order functions, function composition, custom operator definition, closures, function currying, recursion, and memoization.

Chapter 3, *Types and Type Casting*, takes a look at types in general by introducing different kinds of types such as concrete, abstract, product, and sum. We will cover topics such as value and reference type constants, mixing value and reference types, and copying. Then, we will discuss the characteristics of value types. We will also cover the key differences between value and reference types, and how we should decide which one to use. Finally, we will explore equality, identity, type checking, and casting topics.

Chapter 4, *Enumerations and Pattern Matching*, explains the enumeration definition and usage. We will cover associated and raw values and being introduced to the concept of algebraic data types. We will explore some examples to cover the sum, product, and recursion types. Also, in this chapter, we will explore patterns such as wildcard, value-binding, identifier, tuple, enumeration case, optional, type casting, and expression, along with related pattern matching examples.

Chapter 5, *Generics and Associated Type Protocols*, teaches us how to define and use generics. We will also understand the type of problems generics solve. Moving forward, we will explore type constraints, generic data structures, and associated type protocols with examples. We will explore type erasure by an example and finally we will learn how to extend generic types and how to subclass generic classes.

Chapter 6, *Map, Filter, and Reduce,* introduces the concept of higher-kinded types, Functor, Applicative Functor, and Monad. This chapter covers higher-order functions/methods such as map, flatMap, filter, and reduce in the Swift programming language with examples. The chapter continues by providing implementation of map, filter, flatMap, and flatten in terms of reduce. Then it provides, apply, join, chaining higher-order functions, and zip. Finally, it provides practical examples of higher-order function usage.

Chapter 7, *Dealing with Optionals*, familiarizes us with different techniques to deal with optionals. We will talk about built-in techniques to deal with optionals, such as optional binding, guard, coalescing, and optional chaining. Then, we will explore functional programming techniques to deal with optionals. Finally, this chapter will cover the error handling with an example.

Chapter 8, *Functional Data Structures*, introduces the concept of functional data structures and explores examples of data structures implemented in a functional way, such as Semigroup, Monoid, BST, LinkedList, Stack, and LazyList.

Chapter 9, *Importance of Immutability*, explores the concept of immutability. We will look at its importance and benefits with the help of examples. Then we will consider cases for mutability and go through an example to compare mutability and immutability effects on our code. Finally, we will explore copy constructors and lenses.

Chapter 10, *The Best of Both Worlds - Combining FP Paradigms with OOP*, covers object-oriented programming principles and paradigms. Then, we will be introduced to protocol-oriented programming. Next, we will have an introduction of functional reactive programming and explore how to mix FP with OOP paradigms.

Chapter 11, *Case Study - Developing an iOS Application with the FP and OOP Paradigms,* teaches us to develop a Todo backend with Vapor framework and an iOS application, employing the concepts covered in previous chapters. We will use functional programming techniques to parse and map the data, we will use functional reactive programming to reactively manage events in applications. We will also employ protocol-oriented programming and object-oriented programming techniques as well.

What you need for this book

To follow along with the examples in this book, you'll need to have an Apple computer with macOS 10.10 or higher installed. You'll also need to install Xcode 8.3 or newer with Swift 3.1 or newer.

Who this book is for

This book is for iOS, Web, and macOS developers with basic knowledge of Swift programming who are interested in functional programming techniques. Prior knowledge of object-oriented programming and iOS app development familiarity is assumed.

Conventions

In this book, you will find a number of text styles that distinguish between different kinds of information. Here are some examples of these styles and an explanation of their meaning.

Code words in text, database table names, folder names, filenames, file extensions, pathnames, dummy URLs, user input, and Twitter handles are shown as follows: "The VerboseClass.h file defines an interface as a subclass of the NSObject class."

A block of code is set as follows:

```
let numbers = [9, 29, 19, 79]
// Imperative example
var tripledNumbers: [Int] = []
for number in numbers {
    tripledNumbers.append(number * 3)
}
print(tripledNumbers)
```

New terms and **important words** are shown in bold. Words that you see on the screen, for example, in menus or dialog boxes, appear in the text like this: "Next, we will create a **Single View Application** project in Xcode."

Warnings or important notes appear in a box like this.

Tips and tricks appear like this.

Reader feedback

Feedback from our readers is always welcome. Let us know what you think about this book-what you liked or disliked. Reader feedback is important for us as it helps us develop titles that you will really get the most out of.

To send us general feedback, simply e-mail feedback@packtpub.com, and mention the book's title in the subject of your message.

If there is a topic that you have expertise in and you are interested in either writing or contributing to a book, see our author guide at www.packtpub.com/authors.

Customer support

Now that you are the proud owner of a Packt book, we have a number of things to help you to get the most from your purchase.

Downloading the example code

You can download the example code files for this book from your account at http://www.packtpub.com. If you purchased this book elsewhere, you can visit http://www.packtpub.com/support and register to have the files e-mailed directly to you.

You can download the code files by following these steps:

1. Log in or register to our website using your e-mail address and password.
2. Hover the mouse pointer on the **SUPPORT** tab at the top.
3. Click on **Code Downloads & Errata**.
4. Enter the name of the book in the **Search** box.
5. Select the book for which you're looking to download the code files.
6. Choose from the drop-down menu where you purchased this book from.
7. Click on **Code Download**.

Once the file is downloaded, please make sure that you unzip or extract the folder using the latest version of:

- WinRAR / 7-Zip for Windows
- Zipeg / iZip / UnRarX for Mac
- 7-Zip / PeaZip for Linux

The code bundle for the book is also hosted on GitHub at `https://github.com/PacktPu blishing/Swift-Functional-Programming`. We also have other code bundles from our rich catalog of books and videos available at `https://github.com/PacktPublishing/`. Check them out!

Downloading the color images of this book

We also provide you with a PDF file that has color images of the screenshots/diagrams used in this book. The color images will help you better understand the changes in the output. You can download this file from `https://www.packtpub.com/sites/default/files/down loads/SwiftFunctionalProgramming_ColorImages.pdf`.

Errata

Although we have taken every care to ensure the accuracy of our content, mistakes do happen. If you find a mistake in one of our books-maybe a mistake in the text or the code-we would be grateful if you could report this to us. By doing so, you can save other readers from frustration and help us improve subsequent versions of this book. If you find any errata, please report them by visiting `http://www.packtpub.com/submit-errata`, selecting your book, clicking on the **Errata Submission Form** link, and entering the details of your errata. Once your errata are verified, your submission will be accepted and the errata will be uploaded to our website or added to any list of existing errata under the Errata section of that title.

To view the previously submitted errata, go to `https://www.packtpub.com/books/content/support` and enter the name of the book in the search field. The required information will appear under the **Errata** section.

Piracy

Piracy of copyrighted material on the Internet is an ongoing problem across all media. At Packt, we take the protection of our copyright and licenses very seriously. If you come across any illegal copies of our works in any form on the Internet, please provide us with the location address or website name immediately so that we can pursue a remedy.

Please contact us at `copyright@packtpub.com` with a link to the suspected pirated material.

We appreciate your help in protecting our authors and our ability to bring you valuable content.

Questions

If you have a problem with any aspect of this book, you can contact us at `questions@packtpub.com`, and we will do our best to address the problem.

1
Getting Started with Functional Programming in Swift

Getting onto the functional programming bandwagon needs a mindset shift, and changing our mindset is not an easy task as it takes a considerable amount of time to master a paradigm such as object-oriented programming. It needs a thorough approach, but it should also be easy to grasp. That is why we will be introduced to functional programming paradigms first, before going through each topic in detail.

This chapter introduces immutability, pattern matching, closures, as well as pure, first-class, and higher-order functions with Swift. Although all the topics in this chapter will be covered in detail in upcoming chapters, it is going to be helpful to have a broad view of the paradigms. In addition, this chapter will introduce Swift, as it is important to know the basics of the language to utilize in functional programming.

The following topics will be covered, along with examples:

- Why functional programming matters
- What is FP?
- Swift language basics
- Immutability
- First-class, higher-order, and pure functions
- Optionals and pattern matching
- Closures
- Type aliasing

Why functional programming matters

Software solutions are becoming complex, and it is necessary to structure them very well for future maintenance and extension. Software engineers try to modularize software into smaller pieces and abstract away complexities in different pieces and layers. Dividing the code into smaller pieces makes it possible to tackle each problem individually. This approach improves collaboration because different engineers can take responsibility for different pieces. Also, they can work on specific parts of the software without being concerned about the other parts.

Dividing software into smaller pieces is not the biggest challenge in most projects and programming languages. For instance, in **object-oriented programming** (**OOP**), software is divided into smaller pieces such as packages, classes, interfaces, and methods. Engineers tend to divide the software into these building blocks by domains, logic, and layers. Classes are recipes to create instances and objects. As the name suggests, the most important building blocks in OOP are objects. Engineers deal with objects, and the role and responsibility of them should be clear and understandable.

In OOP, connecting the building blocks to each other is not as easy as dividing them. Connection between different objects may propose strong coupling between them. Coupling is the biggest source of complexity in OOP. A change in a module or class could force change in all coupled modules and classes. Also, a particular module or class might be harder to reuse and test because of coupled modules or classes.

Software engineers try to loosen coupling by structuring the software well and applying different principles and design patterns. For instance, **single responsibility**, **open-closed**, **Liskov substitution**, and **interface segregation and dependency inversion** (**SOLID**) principles, when applied together properly, tend to make software easy to maintain and extend.

Even though it is possible to decrease the coupling and simplify software structures, managing the memory, referencing to instances, and testing of different objects remains difficult because, in OOP, objects are open to change and mutation.

In **Functional Programming** (**FP**), pure functions are the most important building blocks. Pure functions do not rely on data outside of themselves and they do not change data that exists outside of them; in other words, they do not have side effects. Pure functions are easy to test because they will always provide the same results.

Pure functions can be executed on different threads or cores without any mechanisms to handle multithreading and multiprocessing. This is a very important benefit of FP over OOP, as multicore programming mechanisms are very complex to handle in OOP. Also, programming for multicore computers is becoming more important day by day because hardware engineers have finally hit the limit of the speed of light. Computer clocks will not be getting faster in the near future, so in order to have more cycles per second, hardware engineers are adding more processors to chips. There seems to be no end to how many processors we will have in our computers. A larger number of processors to be used for a program means a more complex multithreading and multicore mechanism to handle it. FP eliminates the need for a complex multicore programming mechanism as pure functions are not dependent on any instances or data outside of themselves. It is easy to change pure functions without changing other parts of the software.

FP embraces immutability and stateless programming, and makes applications easy to maintain and extend, as managing states and tracking mutation in code is not a trivial task. In fact, Facebook, in the documentation of `immutable.js`, a framework that brings immutable data structures to JavaScript, states that "*Much of what makes application development difficult is tracking mutation and maintaining state.*"

FP is a declarative programming style, so functionally written code declares the operations, expressions, and what needs to be done. Declarations are easy to trace and less verbose as, opposed to imperative programming, which sends orders to the compiler, it is verbose and hard to trace. Embracing immutability and being declarative makes applications easier to maintain and extend. We will look into examples of declarative versus imperative programming later in this chapter.

What is FP?

We know FP matters, but what is it really? There are a lot of discussions related to FP superiority and different definitions of it, but simply, it is a style of programming that models computations as the evaluation of expressions or declarations. FP is a declarative programming style, as opposed to OOP, which is categorized as imperative programming.

Theoretically, FP employs the concepts of category theory, which is a branch of mathematics. It is not necessary to know the category theory to be able to program functionally, but studying it will help to grasp some of the more advanced concepts, such as Functors, Applicative Functors, and Monads. We will get into category theory and its relationship with FP later, so for now, we are not going to talk math and we will scratch the surface of FP pragmatically.

Let's start with an example to understand the differences between imperative and declarative programming styles. The following example gives two different approaches to array-element multiplication:

```
let numbers = [9, 29, 19, 79]

// Imperative example
var tripledNumbers: [Int] = []
for number in numbers {
    tripledNumbers.append(number * 3)
}
print(tripledNumbers)

// Declarative example
let tripledIntNumbers = numbers.map({ number in number * 3 })
print(tripledIntNumbers)
```

In the imperative example, we create a mutable array of integers. Then, we give a command to go through all items in the array, multiply each item by 3, and add it to our mutable array. Basically, we order the compiler to follow specific steps. As it is written in an imperative style, when we read it, we will need to trace and follow the same steps, like a compiler, which is not very intuitive.

In the declarative example, we declare how numbers should be mapped, multiplying each number by 3. It may not look that intuitive right away if we do not know the map function and closures, but for now we need to understand the differences between commanding and declaration. This example may not be enough to grasp it. Also, understanding a concept is one thing and applying it is another. That is why we will have more examples in upcoming sections and chapters. In fact, everything in this book will be written declaratively, so we will utilize the concept intuitively.

In FP, functions are the fundamental building blocks, so programs are structured by functions. In OOP, programs are composed of classes and objects. This is a fundamental difference because, in OOP, statements can mutate the state of objects when executed, as opposed to FP, which avoids using mutable states.

FP promises that avoiding mutable states makes it easier to test, read, and understand the code. Although it is a well-known fact that state management is hard and error-prone, it is not easy to avoid mutable states in some cases, such as cocoa development and file and database operations. For now, we consider traditional OOP and FP, and we will get into the comparison and combination of different paradigms in an upcoming chapter.

FP requires functions to be first class. First-class functions are going to be treated like any other values, and can be passed to other functions or returned as a result of a function.

FP requires functions to be able to be formed as higher-order functions that take other functions as their arguments. Higher-order functions can be used to refactor code, reduce the amount of repetition, and to implement **domain-specific languages** (DSL).

DSLs are languages that are specialized for a particular application domain. *Domain-Specific Languages*, a book by Martin Fowler, is a great reference for the curious. For more curious readers, declarative Auto Layout DSLs for Swift such as SnapKit and Carthography and a talk given by *Rahul Malik* at Functional Swift conference on writing domain specific languages (`https://github.com/rahul-malik/writing-dsls`) are great resources.

FP requires functions to be pure so they do not depend on any data outside of themselves and do not change any data outside of themselves. Pure functions provide the same result each time they are executed. This property of pure functions is called **referential transparency**, and makes it possible to conduct *equational reasoning* on the code.

Equational reasoning is a way to reason about our code. It enables us to replace code blocks with others without worrying about evaluation order or state. In OOP, generally, the value of a code block depends on object context or state. Having a context and depending on state prevents replacing a code block by another, and therefore makes it impossible to conduct equational reasoning.

First-class, higher-order, and pure functions empower us to compose our applications with functions instead of using classes and objects as building blocks.

In FP, expressions can be evaluated lazily. For instance, in the following code example, only the first element in the array is evaluated:

```
let oneToFour = [1, 2, 3, 4]
let firstNumber = oneToFour.lazy.map({ $0 * 3}).first!
print(firstNumber) // The result is going to be 3
```

The `lazy` keyword is used to get a lazy version of the collection. `lazy` is declared in Swift's Standard Library as a view onto the collection that provides `lazy` implementations of normally eager operations, such as map and filter. In this example, only the first item in the array is multiplied by 3 and the rest of the items are not mapped.

At this point, we should have a very broad view of FP concepts. To be able to get into the detail of these concepts, we will need to cover some of the Swift language basics, which are provided in the following section.

The Swift programming language

Swift is an open-source programming language developed by Apple that combines OOP and protocol-oriented programming (POP) with FP paradigms. Swift is not a pure FP language such as Haskell, Clojure, or F#, but it provides tools that facilitate FP. Swift can be used along with **Objective-C** to develop macOS, iOS, tvOS, and watchOS applications. Swift can also be used on Ubuntu Linux to develop web applications. This book explains Swift 3.1 and utilizes Xcode 8.3.2 compatible source code at a GitHub (`https://github.com/PacktPublishing/Swift-Functional-Programming`) repository, which will be updated frequently to catch up with changes to Swift.

Swift features

Swift has borrowed many concepts from other programming languages, such as Scala, Haskell, C#, Rust, and Objective-C, and has the following features.

Modern syntax

Swift has a modern syntax that eliminates the verbosity of programming languages such as Objective-C. For instance, the following code example shows an Objective-C class with a property and method. Objective-C classes are defined in two separate files (interface and implementation). The `VerboseClass.h` file defines an interface as a subclass of the `NSObject` class. It defines a property, `ourArray`, and a method, `aMethod`.

The implementation file imports the header class and provides an implementation for `aMethod`, as shown in the following code:

```
//  VerboseClass.h
@interface VerboseClass: NSObject
@property (nonatomic, strong) NSMutableArray *ourArray;
- (void)aMethod:(NSMutableArray*)anArray;
@end

//  VerboseClass.m
#import "VerboseClass.h"

@implementation VerboseClass
- (void)aMethod:(NSMutableArray*)anArray {
    self.ourArray = [[NSMutableArrayalloc] initWithArray: @[@"One",
    @"Two", @"Three"]];
}
```

A similar functionality in Swift can be achieved as follows:

```swift
class ASwiftClass {
    var ourArray: [String] = []

    func aMethod(anArray: [String]) {
        self.ourArray  = anArray
    }
}

let aSwiftClassInstance = ASwiftClass()
aSwiftClassInstance.aMethod(anArray: ["one", "Two", "Three"])
print(aSwiftClassInstance.ourArray)
```

As seen from this example, Swift eliminates a lot of unnecessary syntax and keeps code very clean and readable.

Type safety and type inference

Swift has a strong emphasis on types. Classes, enums, structs, protocols, functions, and closures can become types and be used in program composition.

Swift is a type-safe language, unlike languages such as Ruby and JavaScript. As opposed to type-variant collections in Objective-C, Swift provides type-safe collections. Swift automatically deducts types by the type-inference mechanism, a mechanism that is present in languages such as C# and C++ 11. For instance, `constString` in the following example is inferred as `String` during compile time, and it is not necessary to annotate the type:

```swift
let constString = "This is a string constant"
```

Immutability

Swift makes it easy to define immutable values--in other words, constants--and empowers FP, as immutability is one of the key concepts in FP. Once constants are initialized, they cannot be altered or mutated. Although it is possible to achieve immutability in languages such as Java, it is not as easy as Swift. To define any immutable type in Swift, the `let` keyword can be used no matter if it is a custom type, collection type, or a `Struct`/enum type.

Stateless programming

Swift provides very powerful structures and enumerations that are passed by values and can be stateless, and, therefore, very efficient. Stateless programming simplifies the concurrency and multithreading, as pointed out in previous sections of this chapter.

First-class functions

Functions are first-class types in Swift, just as in languages such as Ruby, JavaScript, and Go, and can be stored, passed, and returned. First-class functions empower the FP style in Swift.

Higher-order functions

Higher-order functions can receive other functions as their parameters. Swift provides higher-order functions such as `map`, `filter`, and `reduce`. Also, in Swift, we can develop our own higher-order functions and DSLs.

Closures

Closures are blocks of codes that can be passed around. Closures capture the constants and variables of the context in which they are defined. Swift provides closures with a simpler syntax than Objective-C blocks.

Subscripts

Swift provides subscripts that are shortcuts to access members of collections, lists, sequences, or custom types. Subscripts can be used to set and get values by an index without needing separate methods for the setting and getting.

Pattern matching

Pattern matching is the ability to de-structure values and match different switch cases based on correct value matches. Pattern matching capabilities exist in languages such as Scala, Erlang, and Haskell. Swift provides powerful `switch` cases and `if` cases with `where` clauses as well.

Generics

Swift provides generics that make it possible to write code that is not specific to a type and can be utilized for different types.

Optional chaining

Swift provides optional types that can have some or none values. Swift also provides optional chaining to use optionals safely and efficiently. Optional chaining empowers us to query and call properties, methods, and subscripts on optional types that may be nil.

Extensions

Swift provides extensions that are similar to categories in Objective-C. Extensions add new functionality to an existing class, structure, enumeration, or protocol type, even if it is closed-source.

Objective-C and Swift bridging headers

Bridging headers empower us to mix Swift with Objective-C in our projects. This functionality makes it possible to use our previously written Objective-C code in Swift projects and vice versa.

Automatic Reference Counting

Swift handles memory management through **Automatic Reference Counting** (**ARC**), like Objective-C and unlike languages such as Java and C#, which utilize garbage collection. ARC is used to initialize and de-initialize the resources, thereby releasing memory allocations of the class instances when they are no longer required. ARC tracks, retains, and releases in the code instances to manage the memory resources effectively.

REPL and Playground

Xcode provides the **Read Eval Print Loop** (**REPL**) command-line environment to experiment with the Swift programming language without the need to write a program. Also, Swift provides Playgrounds, which enable us to test Swift code snippets quickly and see the results in real time via a visual interface. Source codes for the first ten chapters of this book are provided as Playgrounds in the GitHub repo and Packt Publishing website.

Language basics

This section will provide a brief introduction to the basics of the Swift programming language. Topics in the upcoming subsections of this chapter will be explained in detail in later chapters.

Types

Types are designated units of composition in Swift. Classes, structs, enums, functions, closures, and protocols can become types.

Swift is a type-safe language. This means that we cannot change the type of a constant, variable, or expression once we define it. Also, the type-safe nature of Swift empowers us to find type mismatches during compile time.

Type inference

Swift provides type inference. Swift infers the type of a variable, constant, or expression automatically, so we do not need to specify the types while defining them. Let's look at the following example:

```
let pi = 3.14159
var primeNumber = 691
let name = "my name"
```

In this example, Swift infers `pi` as `Double`, `primeNumber` as `Int`, and `name` as `String`. If we need special types such as `Int64`, we will need to annotate the type.

Type annotation

In Swift, it is possible to annotate types, or in other words, explicitly specify the type of a variable or expression. Let's look at the following example:

```
let pi: Double = 3.14159
let piAndPhi: (Double, Double) = (3.14159, 1.618)
func ourFunction(a: Int) { /* ... */ }
```

In this example, we define a constant (`pi`) annotated as `Double`, a tuple named `piAndPhi` annotated as `(Double, Double)`, and a parameter of `ourFunction` as `Int`.

Type aliases

Type aliases define an alternative name for an existing type. We define type aliases with the `typealias` keyword. Type aliases are useful when we want to refer to an existing type by a name that is contextually more appropriate, such as when working with data of a specific size from an external source. For instance, in the following example, we provide an alias for an unsigned 32-bit integer that can be used later in our code:

```
typealias UnsignedInteger = UInt32
```

The `typealias` definitions can be used to simplify the closure and function definitions as well.

Type casting

Type casting is a way to check the type of an instance and/or deal with that instance as if it is a different superclass or subclass from somewhere else in its class hierarchy. There are two types of operator to check and cast types as the following:

- **Type check operator (`is`)**: This checks whether an instance is of a definite subclass type.
- **Type cast operator (`as` and `as?`)**: A constant or variable of a definite class type may refer to an instance of a subclass under the hood. If this is the case, we can try to downcast it to the subclass type with `as`.

Type safety, type inference, annotation, aliases and type casting will be covered in detail in `Chapter 3`, *Types and Type Casting*.

Immutability

Swift makes it possible to define variables as mutable and immutable. The `let` keyword is used for immutable declarations and the `var` keyword is used for mutable declarations. Any variable that is declared with the `let` keyword will not be open to change. In the following examples, we define `aMutableString` with the `var` keyword so that we will be able to alter it later on; in contrast, we will not be able to alter `aConstString` that is defined with the `let` keyword:

```
var aMutableString = "This is a variable String"
let aConstString = "This is a constant String"
```

In FP, it is recommended to define properties as constants or immutables with `let` as much as possible. Immutable variables are easier to track and less error-prone. In some cases, such as **CoreData** programming, the **software development kit** (**SDK**) requires mutable properties; however, in these cases, it is recommended to use mutable variables.

Immutability and stateless programming will be covered in detail in Chapter 9, *Importance of Immutability*.

Tuples

Swift provides tuples so that they can be used to group multiple values/types into a single compound value. Consider the following example:

```
let http400Error = (400, "Bad Request")
// http400Error is of type (Int, String), and equals (400, "Bad Request")

// Decompose a Tuple's content
let (requestStatusCode, requestStatusMessage) = http400Error
```

Tuples can be used as return types in functions to implement multi-return functions as well.

Optionals

Swift provides optionals so they can be used in situations where a value may be absent. An optional will have some or none values. The ? symbol is used to define a variable as optional. Consider the following example:

```
// Optional value either contains a value or contains nil
var optionalString: String? = "A String literal"
optionalString = nil
```

The ! symbol can be used to forcefully unwrap the value from an optional. For instance, the following example forcefully unwraps the `optionalString` variable:

```
optionalString = "An optional String"
print(optionalString!)
```

Force unwrapping the optionals may cause errors if the optional does not have a value, so it is not recommended to use this approach as it is very hard to be sure if we are going to have values in optionals in different circumstances. The better approach would be to use the optional binding technique to find out whether an optional contains a value. Consider the following example:

```
let nilName: String? = nil
if let familyName = nilName {
    let greetingfamilyName = "Hello, Mr. \(familyName)"
} else {
    // Optional does not have a value
}
```

Optional chaining is a process to query and call properties, methods, and subscripts on an optional that might currently be `nil`. Optional chaining in Swift is similar to messaging `nil` in Objective-C, but in a way that works for any type and can be checked for success or failure. Consider the following example:

```
class Residence {
    var numberOfRooms = 1
}

class Person {
    var residence: Residence?
}

let jeanMarc = Person()
// This can be used for calling methods and subscripts through optional
chaining too
if let roomCount = jeanMarc.residence?.numberOfRooms {
    // Use the roomCount
}
```

In this example, we were able to access `numberOfRooms`, which was a property of an optional type (`Residence`) using optional chaining.

Optionals and optional binding and chaining will be covered in detail in `Chapter 7`, *Dealing with Optionals*.

Basic operators

Swift provides the following basic operations:

- The = operator for assignments, similar to many different programming languages.
- The + operator for addition, – for subtraction, * for multiplication, / for division, and % for remainders. These operators are functions that can be passed to other functions.
- The -i operator for unary minus and +i for unary plus operations.
- The +=, -=, and *= operators for compound assignments.
- The a == b operator for equality, a != b for inequality, and a>b, a<b, and a<=b for greatness comparison.
- The ternary conditional operator, question ? answer1: answer2.
- nil coalescing a ?? b unwraps optional a if it has a value and returns a default value b if a is nil.
- Range operators:
  - Closed range (a...b) includes the values a and b
  - Half-open range (a..<b) includes a but does not include b
- Logical operators:
  - The !a operator is NOT a
  - The a && b operator is logical AND
  - The a || b operator is logical OR

Strings and characters

In Swift, String is an ordered collection of characters. String is a structure and not a class. Structures are value types in Swift; therefore, any String is a value type and passed by values, not by references.

Immutability

Strings can be defined with let for immutability. Strings defined with var will be mutable.

String literals

String literals can be used to create an instance of String. In the following code example, we define and initialize aVegetable with the String literal:

```
let aVegetable = "Arugula"
```

Empty Strings

Empty Strings can be initialized as follows:

```
// Initializing an Empty String
var anEmptyString = ""
var anotherEmptyString = String()
```

These two strings are both empty and equivalent to each other. To find out whether a String is empty, the isEmpty property can be used as follows:

```
if anEmptyString.isEmpty {
    print("String is empty")
}
```

Concatenating strings and characters

Strings and characters can be concatenated as follows:

```
let string1 = "Hello"
let string2 = " Mr"
var welcome = string1+string2

var instruction = "Follow us please"
instruction += string2

let exclamationMark: Character = "!"
welcome.append(exclamationMark)
```

String interpolation

String interpolation is a way to construct a new `String` value from a mix of constants, variables, literals, and expressions by including their values inside a `String` literal. Consider the following example:

```
let multiplier = 3
let message = "\(multiplier) times 7.5 is \(Double (multiplier) * 7.5)"
// message is "3 times 2.5 is 22.5"
```

String comparison

Strings can be compared with `==` for equality and `!=` for inequality.

The `hasPrefix` and `hasSuffix` methods can be used for prefix and suffix equality checking.

Collections

Swift provides typed collections such as array, dictionaries, and sets. In Swift, unlike Objective-C, all elements in a collection will have the same type, and we will not be able to change the type of a collection after defining it.

We can define collections as immutable with `let` and mutable with `var`, as shown in the following example:

```
// Arrays and Dictionaries
var cheeses = ["Brie", "Tete de Moine", "Cambozola", "Camembert"]
cheeses[2] = "Roquefort"
var cheeseWinePairs = [
    "Brie":"Chardonnay",
    "Camembert":"Champagne",
    "Gruyere":"Sauvignon Blanc"
]

cheeseWinePairs ["Cheddar"] = "Cabarnet Sauvignon"
// To create an empty array or dictionary
let emptyArray = [String]()
let emptyDictionary = Dictionary<String, Float>()
cheeses = []
cheeseWinePairs = [:]
```

The `for-in` loops can be used to iterate over the items in collections.

Control flows

Swift provides different control flows that are explained in the following subsections.

for loops

Swift provides `for` and `for-in` loops. We can use the `for-in` loop to iterate over items in a collection, a sequence of numbers such as ranges, or characters in a string expression. The following example presents a `for-in` loop to iterate through all items in an `Int` array:

```
let scores = [65, 75, 92, 87, 68]
var teamScore = 0

for score in scores {
    if score > 70 {
        teamScore = teamScore + 3
    } else {
        teamScore = teamScore + 1
    }
}
```

and over dictionaries:

```
for (cheese, wine) in cheeseWinePairs{
    print("\(cheese): \(wine)")
}
```

As C styles for loops with incrementers/decrementers are removed from Swift 3.0, it is recommended to use `for-in` loops with ranges instead, as follows:

```
var count = 0
for i in 0...3 {
    count + = i
}
```

while loops

Swift provides `while` and `repeat-while` loops. A `while` or `repeat-while` loop performs a set of expressions until a condition becomes false. Consider the following example:

```
var n = 2
while n < 100 {
    n = n * 2
}
var m = 2
```

```
repeat {
    m = m * 2
} while m < 100
```

The while loop evaluates its condition at the beginning of each iteration. The repeat-while loop evaluates its condition at the end of each iteration.

The stride functions

stride functions enable us to iterate through ranges with a step other than one. There are two stride functions: the stride to function, which iterates over exclusive ranges, and stride through, which iterates over inclusive ranges. Consider the following example:

```
let fourToTwo = Array(stride(from: 4, to: 1, by: -1)) // [4, 3, 2]
let fourToOne = Array(stride(from:4, through: 1, by: -1)) // [4, 3, 2, 1]
```

if

Swift provides if to define conditional statements. It executes a set of statements only if the condition statement is true. For instance, in the following example, the print statement will be executed because anEmptyString is empty:

```
var anEmptyString = ""
if anEmptyString.isEmpty {
    print("An empty String")
} else {
    // String is not empty.
}
```

Switch

Swift provides the switch statement to compare a value against different matching patterns. The related statement will be executed once the pattern is matched. Unlike most other C-based programming languages, Swift does not need a break statement for each case and supports any value types. Switch statements can be used for range matching, and where clauses in switch statements can be used to check for additional conditions. The following example presents a simple switch statement with additional conditional checking:

```
let aNumber = "Four or Five"
switch aNumber {
    case "One":
```

```
        let one = "One"
    case "Two", "Three":
        let twoOrThree = "Two or Three"
    case let x where x.hasSuffix("Five"):
        let fourOrFive = "it is \(x)"
    default:
        let anyOtherNumber = "Any other number"
}
```

Guard

A `guard` statement can be used for early exits. We can use a `guard` statement to require that a condition must be `true` in order for the code after the `guard` statement to be executed. The following example presents the `guard` statement usage:

```
func greet(person: [String: String]) {
    guard let name = person["name"] else {
        return
    }
    print("Hello Ms\(name)!")
}
```

In this example, the `greet` function requires a value for a person's `name`; therefore, it checks whether it is present with the `guard` statement, otherwise it will return and not continue to execute. As can be seen from the example, the scope of the guarded variable is not only the `guard` code block, so we were able to use `name` after the `guard` code block in our `print` statement.

Functions

Functions are self-contained blocks of code that perform a specific task.

In Swift, functions are first-class citizens, meaning that they can be stored, passed, and returned. Functions can be curried and defined as higher-order functions that take other functions as their arguments.

Functions in Swift can have multiple input parameters and multiple returns using tuples. Let's look at the following example:

```
func greet(name: String, day: String) ->String {
    return "Hello \(name), today is \(day)"
}

greet(name: "Francois", day:"Saturday")
```

Functions can have variadic parameters. Consider the following example:

```
// Variable number of arguments in functions - Variadic Parameters
func sumOf(numbers: Int...) -> (Int, Int) {
    var sum = 0
    var counter = 0
    for number in numbers {
        sum += number
        counter += 1
    }
    return (sum, counter)
}

sumOf()
sumOf(numbers: 7, 9, 45)
```

Functions can have `in-out` parameters. Consider the following example:

```
func swapTwoInts ( a: inout Int, b: inout Int) {
    let temporaryA = a
    a = b
    b = temporaryA
}
```

The `in-out` parameters are not favorable in functional Swift as they mutate states and make functions impure.

In Swift, we can define nested functions. The following example presents a function named add nested inside another function. Nested functions can access the data in scope of their parent function. In this example, the add function has access to the y variable:

```
func returnTwenty() ->Int {
    var y = 10
    func add() {
        y += 10
    }
    add()
    return y
}
```

```
returnTwenty()
```

In Swift, functions can return other functions. In the following example, the `makeIncrementer` function returns a function that receives an `Int` value and returns an `Int` value (`Int ->Int`):

```
func makeIncrementer() -> ((Int) ->Int) {
    func addOne(number: Int) ->Int {
        return 1 + number
    }
    return addOne
}

var increment = makeIncrementer()
increment(7)
```

Closures

Closures are self-contained blocks of code that provide a specific functionality and can be stored, passed around, and used in the code. Closures are the equivalent of blocks in C and Objective-C. Closures can capture and store references to any constants and variables from the context in which they are defined. Nested functions are special cases of closures.

Closures are reference types that can be stored as variables, constants, and type aliases. They can be passed to and returned from functions.

The following examples present different declarations of closures in Swift from the website, `http://goshdarnclosuresyntax.com`:

```
// As a variable:
var closureName: (parameterTypes) -> (returnType)

//As a type alias:
typealias closureType = (parameterTypes) -> (returnType)

//As an argument to a function call:
func Name({ (ParameterTypes) -> (ReturnType) in statements })
```

Closures and first-class, higher-order, and pure functions will be covered in detail in `Chapter 2`, *Functions and Closures*.

The map, filter, and reduce functions

Swift provides `map`, `filter`, and `reduce` functions, which are higher-order functions.

The map function

The `map` function is a higher-order function that solves the problem of transforming the elements of an array using a function. Consider the following example:

```
let numbers = [10, 30, 91, 50, 100, 39, 74]
var formattedNumbers: [String] = []

for number in numbers {
    let formattedNumber = "\(number)$"
    formattedNumbers.append(formattedNumber)
}

let mappedNumbers = numbers.map{ "\($0)$" }
```

The filter function

The `filter` function is a higher-order function that takes a function that, given an element in the array, returns `Bool`, indicating whether the element should be included in the resulting array. Consider the following example:

```
let evenNumbers = numbers.filter { $0 % 2 == 0 }
```

The reduce function

The `reduce` function is a higher-order function that reduces an array to a single value. It takes two parameters: a starting value and a function, which takes a running total and an element of the arrays as parameters and returns a new running total. Consider the following example:

```
let total = numbers.reduce(0) { $0 + $1 }
```

The `map`, `filter`, and `reduce` functions accept a closure as the last parameter, so we were able to use the trailing closure syntax. These higher-order functions will be covered in detail in Chapter 6, *Map, Filter, and Reduce*.

Enumerations

In Swift, an enumeration defines a common type for related values and enables us to work with those values in a type-safe way. Values provided for each enumeration member can be a `String`, `Character`, `Int`, or any floating-point type. Enumerations can store associated values of any given type, and the value types can be different for each member of the enumeration, if needed. Enumeration members can come pre-populated with default values (called raw values), which are all of the same type. Consider the following example:

```
enum MLSTeam {
    case montreal
    case toronto
    case newYork
    case columbus
    case losAngeles
    case seattle
}

let theTeam = MLSTeam.montreal
```

Enumeration values can be matched with a `switch` statement, which can be seen in the following example:

```
switch theTeam {
case .montreal:
    print("Montreal Impact")
case .toronto:
    print("Toronto FC")
case .newYork:
    print("NewyorkRedbulls")
case .columbus:
    print("Columbus Crew")
case .losAngeles:
    print("LA Galaxy")
case .seattle:
    print("Seattle Sounders")
}
```

Enumerations in Swift are actually algebraic data types that are types created by combining other types. Consider the following example:

```
enum NHLTeam { case canadiens, senators, rangers, penguins, blackHawks,
capitals }

enum Team {
    case hockey(NHLTeam)
    case soccer(MLSTeam)
```

```
    }

    struct HockeyAndSoccerTeams {
        var hockey: NHLTeam
        var soccer: MLSTeam
    }
```

The `MLSTeam` and `NHLTeam` enumerations each have six potential values. If we combine them, we will have two new types. A `Team` enumeration can be either `NHLTeam` or `MLSTeam`, so it has 12 potential values that are the sum of `NHLTeam` and `MLSTeam` potential values. Therefore, `Team`, an enumeration, is a sum type.

To have a `HockeyAndSoccerTeams` structure, we need to choose one value for `NHLTeam` and one for `MLSTeam` so that it has 36 potential values that are the product of `NHLTeam` and `MLSTeam` values. Therefore, `HockeyAndSoccerTeams` is a product type.

In Swift, an enumeration's option can have multiple values. If it happens to be the only option, then this enumeration becomes a product type. The following example presents an enumeration as a product type:

```
    enum HockeyAndSoccerTeams {
        case value(hockey: NHLTeam, soccer: MLSTeam)
    }
```

As we can create sum or product types in Swift, we can say that Swift has first-class support for algebraic data types.

Enumerations and pattern matching will be covered in detail in `Chapter 4`, *Enumerations and Pattern Matching*.

Generics

Generic code enables us to write flexible and reusable functions and types that can work with any type, subject to requirements that we define. For instance, the following function that uses `in-out` parameters to swap two values can only be used with `Int` values:

```
    func swapTwoIntegers(a: inout Int, b: inout Int) {
        let tempA = a
        a = b
        b = tempA
    }
```

To make this function work with any type, generics can be used, as shown in the following example:

```
func swapTwoValues<T>(a: inout T, b: inout T) {
    let tempA = a
    a = b
    b = tempA
}
```

Generics will be covered in detail in Chapter 5, *Generics and Associated Type Protocols*.

Classes and structures

Classes and structures are general-purpose, flexible constructs that become the building blocks of a program's code. They have the following features:

- Properties can be defined to store values
- Methods can be defined to provide functionality
- Subscripts can be defined to provide access to their values using subscript syntax
- Initializers can be defined to set up their functionality beyond a default implementation
- They can conform to protocols to provide standard functionality of certain kinds

Classes versus structures

This section compares classes and structures:

- Inheritance enables one class to inherit the characteristics of another
- Type casting enables us to check and interpret the type of a class instance at runtime
- De-initializers enable an instance of a class to free any resources it has assigned
- Reference Counting allows more than one reference to a class instance
- Structures are value types so they are always copied when they are passed around in code
- Structures do not use Reference Counting
- Classes are reference types

Choosing between classes and structures

Consider creating a structure when one or more of the following conditions apply:

- The structure's primary purpose is to encapsulate a few relatively simple data values
- It is reasonable to expect that the encapsulated values will be copied rather than referenced when you assign or pass around an instance of the structure
- Any properties stored by the structure are themselves value types, which would also be expected to be copied rather than referenced
- The structure does not need to inherit properties or behavior from another existing type

Examples of good candidates for structures include the following:

- The size of a geometric shape
- A point in a 3D coordinate system

Identity operators

As classes are reference types, it is possible for multiple constants and variables to refer to the same single instance of class behind the scenes. To find out if two constants or variables refer to the same instance of a class exactly, Swift provides the following identity operators:

- Identical to (===)
- Not identical to (!==)

Properties

Properties associate values with a particular class, structure, or enumeration. Swift enables us to set sub-properties of a structure property directly without needing to set the entire object property to a new value. All structures have an automatically generated member-wise initializer, which can be used to initialize the member properties of new structure instances. This is not true for class instances.

Property observers

Property observers are used to respond to change in a property's value. Property observers are called every time a property's value is set, even if the new value is the same as the property's current value. We have the option to define either or both of the following observers on a property:

- The `willSet` observer is called just before the value is stored
- The `didSet` observer is called immediately after the new value is stored

The `willSet` and `didSet` observers are not called when a property is set in an initializer before delegation takes place.

Methods

Methods are functions that are associated with a particular type. Instance methods are functions that are called on an instance of a particular type. Type methods are functions that are called on the type itself.

The following example presents a class containing a type method that is named `someTypeMethod()`:

```
class AClass {
    class func someTypeMethod() {
        // type method body
    }
}
// We can call this method as follows:
AClass.someTypeMethod()
```

Subscripts

Subscripts are shortcuts to access the member elements of a collection, list, sequence, or any custom type that implement subscripts. Consider the following example:

```
struct TimesTable {
    let multiplier: Int
    subscript(index: Int) ->Int {
        return multiplier * index
    }
}

let fiveTimesTable = TimesTable(multiplier: 5)
```

```
print("six times five is \(fiveTimesTable[6])")
// prints "six times five is 30"
```

Inheritance

A class can inherit methods, properties, and other characteristics from another class:

```
class SomeSubClass: SomeSuperClass
```

Swift classes do not inherit from a universal base class. Classes that we define without specifying a superclass automatically become base classes for us to build on. To override a characteristic that would otherwise be inherited, we prefix our overriding definition with the `override` keyword. An overridden method, property, or subscript can call the superclass version by calling `super`. To prevent overrides, the `final` keyword can be used.

Initialization

The process of preparing an instance of a class, structure, or enumeration for use is called initialization. Classes and structures must set all of their stored properties to an appropriate initial value by the time an instance of that class or structure is created. Stored properties cannot be left in an intermediate state. We can modify the value of a constant property at any point during initialization as long as it is set to a definite value by the time initialization finishes. Swift provides a default initializer for any structure or base class that provides default values for all of its properties and does not provide at least one initializer itself. Consider the following example:

```
class ShoppingItem {
    var name: String?
    var quantity = 1
    var purchased = false
}
var item = ShoppingItem()
```

The `struct` types automatically receive a member-wise initializer if we do not define any of our own custom initializers, even if the struct's stored properties do not have default values.

Swift defines two kinds of initializers for class types:

- **Designated initializers**: Methods that are able to fully initialize the object
- **Convenience initializers**: Methods that rely on other methods to complete initialization

De-initialization

A de-initializer is called immediately before a class instance is deallocated. Swift automatically deallocates instances when they are no longer needed in order to free up resources.

Automatic Reference Counting

Reference Counting only applies to instances of classes. Structures and enumerations are value types, not reference types, and are not stored and passed by reference.

Weak references can be used to resolve strong reference cycles and can be defined as follows:

```
weak var aWeakProperty
```

An unowned reference does not keep a strong reference hold on the instance it refers to. Unlike a weak reference, however, an unowned reference is always defined as a non-optional type. A closure capture list can be used to resolve closure strong-reference cycles.

A capture in a closure can be defined as an unowned reference when the closure and the instance that it captures will always refer to each other and be deallocated at the same time.

A capture as a weak reference can be defined when the capture's reference may become nil at some point in the future. Weak references are always of an optional type. Consider the following example:

```
class AClassWithLazyClosure {
    lazy var aClosure: (Int, String) -> String = {
      [unowned self] (index: Int, stringToProcess: String) -> String in
      // closure body goes here
        return ""
    }
}
```

Classes, objects, and reference types will be covered in detail in Chapter 10, *The Best of Both Worlds - Combining FP Paradigms with OOP.*

Any and AnyObject

Swift provides two special type aliases to work with non-specific types:

- `AnyObject` can represent an instance of any class type
- `Any` can represent an instance of any type, including structs, enumerations, and function types

The `Any` and `AnyObject` type aliases must be used only when we explicitly require the behavior and capabilities that they provide. Being precise about the types we expect to work with in our code is a better approach than using the `Any` and `AnyObject` types as they can represent any type and pose dynamism instead of safety. Consider the following example:

```
class Movie {
    var director: String
    var name: String
    init(name: String, director: String) {
        self.director = director
        self.name = name
    }
}

let objects: [AnyObject] = [
    Movie(name: "The Shawshank Redemption", director: "Frank Darabont"),
    Movie(name: "The Godfather", director: "Francis Ford Coppola")
]

for object in objects {
    let movie = object as! Movie
    print("Movie: '\(movie.name)', dir. \(movie.director)")
}

// Shorter syntax
for movie in objects as! [Movie] {
    print("Movie: '\(movie.name)', dir. \(movie.director)")
}
```

Nested types

Enumerations are often created to support a specific class or structure's functionality. Likewise, it can be convenient to declare utility classes and structures purely to use within the context of a complex type.

Swift enables us to declare nested types, whereby we nest supporting enumerations, classes, and structures within the definition of the type that they support. The following example, borrowed from *The Swift Programming Language* by *Apple Inc.*, presents nested types:

```swift
struct BlackjackCard {
    // nested Suit enumeration
    enum Suit: Character {
        case spades = "♠",
        hearts = "♡",
        diamonds = "◊",
        clubs = "♣"
    }

    // nested Rank enumeration
    enum Rank: Int {
        case two = 2, three, four, five, six, seven, eight, nine, ten
        case jack, queen, king, ace

        // nested struct
        struct Values {
            let first: Int, second: Int?
        }

        var values: Values {
            switch self {
            case .ace:
                return Values(first: 1, second: 11)
            case .jack, .queen, .king:
                return Values(first: 10, second: nil)
            default:
                return Values(first: self.rawValue, second: nil)
            }
        }
    }

    let rank: Rank, suit: Suit

    var description: String {
        var output = "suit is \(suit.rawValue),"
        output += "value is \(rank.values.first)"
        if let second = rank.values.second {
            output += " or \(second)"
        }
        return output
    }
}
```

Protocols

A protocol defines signatures or types of methods, properties, and other requirements that fit to a specific task or piece of functionality. The protocol doesn't actually implement any functionality. It only describes what an implementation will look like. A class, structure, or enumeration that provides an actual implementation of requirements can adopt the protocol. Protocols use the same syntax as normal methods but are not allowed to specify default values for method parameters.

The `is` operator can be used to check whether an instance conforms to a protocol. We can check for protocol conformance only if our protocol is marked with `@objc` for classes. The `as` operator can be used to cast to a specific protocol.

Protocols as types

Any protocol that we define will become a fully-fledged type to use in our code. We can use a protocol as follows:

- A parameter type or return type in a function, method, or initializer
- The type of a constant, variable, or property
- The type of items in an array, dictionary, or another container

Let's look at the following example:

```
protocol ExampleProtocol {
    var simpleDescription: String { get }
    mutating func adjust()
}

// Classes, enumerations and structs can all adopt protocols.
class SimpleClass: ExampleProtocol {
    var simpleDescription: String = "A very simple class example"
    var anotherProperty: Int = 79799

    func adjust() {
        simpleDescription += "Now 100% adjusted..."
    }
}

var aSimpleClass = SimpleClass()
aSimpleClass.adjust()
let aDescription = aSimpleClass.simpleDescription

struct SimpleStructure: ExampleProtocol {
```

```
    var simpleDescription: String = "A simple struct"
    // Mutating to mark a method that modifies the structure - For
    classes we do not need to use mutating keyword
    mutating func adjust() {
        simpleDescription += "(adjusted)"
    }
}

var aSimpleStruct = SimpleStructure()
aSimpleStruct.adjust()
let aSimpleStructDescription = aSimpleStruct.simpleDescription
```

Extensions

Extensions add new functionality to an existing class, structure, enumeration, or protocol. This includes the ability to extend types for which we do not have access to the original source code.

Extensions in Swift enables us to perform the following:

- Define instance methods and type methods
- Provide new initializers
- Define and use new nested types
- Define subscripts
- Add computed properties and computed static properties
- Make an existing type conform to a new protocol

Extensions enable us to add new functionality to a type, but we will not be able to override the existing functionality.

In the following example, we extend `AType` by making it conform to two protocols:

```
extension AType: AProtocol, BProtocol { }
```

The following example presents an extension to `Double` by adding computed properties:

```
extension Double {
    var mm: Double{ returnself / 1_000.0 }
    var ft: Double{ returnself / 3.2884 }
}

let threeInch = 76.2.mm
let fiveFeet = 5.ft
```

Protocol extensions

Protocol extensions allow us to define behavior on protocols rather than in each type's individual conformance or global function. By creating an extension on a protocol, all conforming types automatically gain this method implementation without any additional modification. We can specify constraints that conforming types must satisfy before the methods and properties of the extensions are available when we define a protocol extension. For instance, we can extend our `ExampleProtocol` to provide default functionality as follows:

```
extension ExampleProtocol {
    var simpleDescription: String {
        get {
            return "The description is: \(self)"
        }
        set {
            self.simpleDescription = newValue
        }
    }

    mutating func adjust() {
        self.simpleDescription = "adjusted simple description"
    }
}
```

Access control

Access control restricts access to parts of our code from code in other source files and modules. Access levels are as follows:

- **Open** and **Public** accesses enable entities to be used within any source file from their defining module and also in a source file from another module that imports the defining module. **Open** access enables subclassing, as opposed to **Public** access, which disallows subclassing.
- **Internal** access enables entities to be used within any source file from their defining module, but not in any source file outside of this module.
- **File-private** access restricts the use of an entity to its defining source file.
- **Private** access restricts the use of an entity to its enclosing declaration.

Swift evolution proposals *SE-0025* and *SE-0117* explain the motivation, proposed solution, and provide code examples for access levels.

Error handling

Swift provides support to throw, catch, propagate, and manipulate recoverable errors at runtime.

Value types should conform to the `Error` protocol to be represented as errors. The following example presents some 4xx and 5xx HTTP errors as `enum`:

```
enum HttpError: Error {
    case badRequest
    case unauthorized
    case forbidden
    case requestTimeOut
    case unsupportedMediaType
    case internalServerError
    case notImplemented
    case badGateway
    case serviceUnavailable
}
```

We will be able to throw errors using the `throw` keyword and mark functions that can throw errors with the `throws` keyword.

We can use a `do-catch` statement to handle errors by running a block of code. The following example presents JSON parsing error handling in a `do-catch` statement:

```
protocol HttpProtocol{
    func didRecieveResults(results: Any)
}

struct WebServiceManager {
    var delegate:HttpProtocol?
    let data: Data
    func test() {
        do {
            let jsonResult = try JSONSerialization.jsonObject(with:
            self.data, options: JSONSerialization.ReadingOptions
            .mutableContainers)
            self.delegate?.didRecieveResults(results: jsonResult)
        } catch let error {
            print("json error" + error.localizedDescription)
        }
    }
}
```

We can use a `defer` statement to execute a set of statements just before code execution leaves the current code block, regardless of how the execution leaves the current block of code.

Summary

This chapter began by explaining why FP matters, and then it introduced the key paradigms of FP in general. Furthermore, it introduced the basics of the Swift programming language with code examples. At this point, we should have a broad view of FP concepts and the Swift programming language. All the topics in this chapter will be covered in detail in the upcoming chapters.

We will begin to dive deeper into these topics with functions, as they are the most essential building blocks in FP. Therefore, the following chapter will explain functions and give examples for pure, first-class, higher-order, and nested functions. Also, it will explain slightly more advanced topics such as memoization, function currying, and composition.

2
Functions and Closures

In the previous chapter, we had an overview of **Functional Programming** (**FP**) and the Swift programming language. It introduced some of the key concepts of functions. As functions are the fundamental building blocks in FP, this chapter dives deeper into the subject and explains all the aspects related to the definition and usage of functions in Swift and FP, together with coding examples.

This chapter starts with the Swift function and method syntax, continues with other related topics such as function types and tuples, and finally concludes with FP topics such as first-class functions, higher-order functions, function composition, closures, currying, recursion, and memoization.

This chapter will cover the following topics by coding examples:

- General syntax of functions
- Defining and using function parameters
- Setting internal and external parameters
- Setting default parameter values
- Defining and using variadic functions
- Returning values from functions
- Defining and using nested functions
- Function types
- Pure functions
- First class functions
- Higher-order functions
- Function composition
- Custom operator definition
- Defining and using closures

- Function currying
- Recursion
- Memoization

What is a function?

Object-oriented programming (**OOP**) looks very natural to most developers as it simulates a real-life situation of classes or, in other words, blueprints and their instances. However, it brings a lot of complexities and problems such as instance and memory management, complex multithreading, and concurrency programming.

Before OOP became mainstream, we were used to developing in procedural languages. In the C programming language, we did not have objects and classes, and we would use structs and function pointers. FP relies mostly on functions, just as procedural languages relied on procedures. We can develop very powerful programs in C without classes; in fact, most operating systems are developed in C. There are other multipurpose programming languages, such as Go by Google. This is not object-oriented and is getting very popular because of its performance and simplicity.

So, are we going to be able to write very complex applications without classes in Swift? We might wonder why we should do this. Generally, we cannot because of language and SDK limitations, but attempting it will introduce us to the capabilities of FP. This is why we will have a whole chapter on functions before talking about other building blocks such as types, classes, structs, and enums.

A function is a block of code that executes a specific task, can be stored, can persist data, and can be passed around. We define functions in standalone Swift files as **global functions**, or inside other building blocks such as classes, structs, enums, and protocols as **methods**.

They are called methods if they are defined in other building blocks; but, in terms of definition, there is no difference between a function and method in Swift.

Defining them in other building blocks enables methods to use the scope of the parent or to be able to change it. They can access the scope of their parent and they have their own scope. Any variable that is defined inside a function is not accessible outside of it. The variables defined inside them and the corresponding allocated memory go away when the function terminates.

Functions are very powerful in Swift. We can compose a program with only functions as functions can receive and `return` functions, capture variables that exist in the context they were declared, and can persist data inside themselves. To understand the FP paradigms, we need to understand the capability of functions in detail. We need to consider whether we can avoid classes and only use functions. We will cover all the details related to functions within this chapter.

Syntax

In this section, we will deep dive into Swift function and method syntax. Boring stuff alert! To make it a little more interesting, revisit or remember the function definition in mathematics and compare the functions and methods you write to math functions.

If you think that you already know the details or if it is not that interesting for you now, you can fast read or skip this first section, and go to the *Return values from functions* section of this chapter as it is directly related to FP.

Let's get it over with! We define functions or methods as the following:

```
accessControl methodForm func functionName(parameter: ParameterType) throws
-> ReturnType { }
```

As we know already, when functions are defined in objects they become methods.

The first step to define a method is to tell the compiler where it can be accessed. This concept is called *access control* in Swift and there are five levels of access control. We are going to explain them for methods as follows:

- **open and public access**: Any entity can access a method that is defined as public if it is in the same module. If the entity is not in the same module, we will need to import the module to be able to call the method. We need to mark our methods as `open`/`public` when we develop frameworks in order to enable other modules to use them. `open` access level enables subclasses to override the methods while `public` access level restricts the ability to override.
- **internal access**: Any method that is defined `internal` can be accessed from other entities in a module but cannot be accessed from other modules.
- **fileprivate access**: Any method that is defined `fileprivate` can be accessed only from the defining source file.
- **private access**: Any method that is defined `private` can be accessed only from its enclosing declaration.

By default, if we do not provide the access modifier, a variable or method becomes internal. Using these access modifiers, we can structure our code properly; for instance, we can hide details from other modules if we define an entity as `internal`. We can even hide the details of a method from other files if we define them as private.

Before Swift 2.0, we had to define everything as public or add all source files to the testing target. Swift 2.0 introduced the `@testable import` syntax that enables us to define `internal` or `private` methods that can be accessed from testing modules.

The second step to method definition is to declare the method form. In Swift, methods can be generally in three forms:

- **Instance methods**: We need to obtain an instance of an object (in this book we will refer to classes, `struct`s and `enum`s as **objects**) to be able to call the method defined in it; then we will be able to access the scope and data of the object.
- **Static methods**: Swift names these type methods also. They do not need any instances of objects and they cannot access the instance data. They are called by putting a dot after the name of the object type (for example, `Person.sayHi()`). `Static` methods cannot be overridden by the subclasses of the object they reside in.
- **Class methods**: Class methods are like static methods but they can be overridden by subclasses.

We have covered the keywords that are required for method definitions; now we will concentrate on the syntax that is shared among functions and methods. There are other concepts related to methods that are out of the scope of this book because we are concentrating on functional programming in Swift.

Continuing to cover the function definition, now comes the `func` keyword that is mandatory and is used to tell the compiler that it is going to deal with a function.

Then comes the `functionName` that is mandatory and is recommended to be camel-cased with the first letter as lowercase. The function name should be stating what the function does and is recommended to be in the form of a verb when we define our methods in objects.

Basically, our classes will be named nouns, and methods will be verbs that are in the form of orders to the class. In pure functional programming, as the function does not reside in other objects, they can be named by their functionalities.

Parameters follow the `func` name. They will be defined in parentheses to pass arguments to the function. Parentheses are mandatory even if we do not have any parameters. We will cover all aspects of parameters in the *Defining and using function parameters* section of this chapter.

Then comes *throws*, which is not mandatory. A function or method that is marked with the *throws* keyword may or may not throw errors. We will cover error handling mechanisms in upcoming chapters. At this point, it is enough to know what they are when we see them in a function or method signature.

The next entity in a function type declaration is the `return` type. If a function is not `Void`, the `return` type will come after the `->` sign. The return type indicates the type of entity that is going to be returned from a function.

We will cover `return` types in detail in the *Returning values from functions* section of this chapter, so now we can move on to the last piece of the function that is present in most programming languages, our beloved { }. We defined functions as blocks of functionality and { } defines the borders of the block so that the function body is declared and execution happens within them. We will write the functionality inside { }.

Best practices in function definition

There are proven best practices for function and method definition provided by amazing software engineering resources, such as *Clean Code: A Handbook of Agile Software Craftsmanship,* by *Robert C. Martin, Code Complete: A Practical Handbook of Software Construction, Second Edition,* by *Steve McConnell,* and *Coding Horror* (`https://blog.codingh orror.com/code-smells/`), that we can summarize as follows:

- Try not to exceed 8-10 lines of code in each function as shorter functions or methods are easier to read, understand, and maintain.
- Keep the number of parameters minimal because the more parameters a function has, the more complex it is.
- Functions should have at least one parameter and at least one `return` value.
- Avoid using type names in function names since they are going to be redundant.
- Aim for one and only one functionality in a function.
- Name a function or method in a way that it describes its functionality properly and is easy to understand.

- Name functions and methods consistently. For instance, if we have a connect function, we can have a disconnect one.
- Write functions to solve the current problem and generalize it when needed. Try to avoid what-if scenarios as probably **You Aren't Going to Need It (YAGNI)**.

It is important to follow these best practices. After all, we are talking about FP and you know, functions are important!

Calling functions

We have covered a general syntax to define a function and method if it resides in an object. Now it is time to talk about how we call our defined functions and methods. That should not be difficult, right? There were complexities with parameters in previous versions of Swift but v3.0 solves the issues and streamlines it.

To call a function, we will use its name and provide its required parameters. For now, we are going to cover the most basic type of parameter, as follows:

```
funcName(firstParam: firstParamName, secondParam: secondParamName)
```

To call a method, we need to use the dot notation provided by Swift. The following examples are for instance and class methods:

```
class AClass {
    func instanceMethod(param1: String, param2: String) {
        // function body
    }

    class func classMethod(param1: String, param2: String) {
        // function body
    }
}

let aClassInstance = AClass()
aClassInstance.instanceMethod(param1: "first string", param2: "second
string")
AClass.classMethod(param1: "first string", param2: "second string")
```

Defining and using function parameters

In function definition, parameters follow the function name and they are constants by default so we will not be able to alter them inside the function body.

Parameters should be inside parentheses. If we do not have any parameters, we simply put open and close parentheses without any characters between them as follows:

```
func functionName() { }
```

In FP, it is important to have functions that have at least one parameter. Remember, a function in mathematics is a relation between a set of inputs and outputs. So, we always have at least an input in a function and the same principle applies to FP.

As you'll already know or have guessed, we can have multiple parameters in function definition. Parameters are separated by commas and are named, so we need to provide the parameter name and type after a colon (:), as shown in the following example:

```
func functionName(param1: ParamType, param2: ParamType) { }
// To call:
functionName(param1: parameter, param2: secondParam)
```

`ParamType`, which is an example type, can also be an optional type so the function becomes the following if our parameters need to be optionals:

```
func functionName(param1: ParamType?, param2: ParamType?) { }
```

Swift enables us to provide external parameter names that will be used when functions are called. The following example presents the syntax:

```
func functionName(externalParamName localParamName: ParamType)
// To call:
functionName(externalParamName: parameter)
```

Only a local parameter name is usable in the function body.

It is possible to omit parameter names with the _ syntax; for instance, if we do not want to provide any parameter name when the function is called, we can use _ as the `externalParamName` for the second or subsequent parameters.

If we want to have a parameter name for the first parameter name in function calls, we can basically provide the local parameter name as external also. In this book, we are going to use the default function parameter definition.

Parameters can have default values as follows:

```
func functionName(param: Int = 3) {
    print("\(param) is provided.")
}
functionName(5) // prints "5 is provided."
functionName() // prints "3 is provided"
```

Parameters can be defined as `inout` to enable function callers obtaining parameters that are going to be changed in the body of a function. As we can use tuples for function returns, it is not recommended to use `inout` parameters unless we really need them.

We can define function parameters as tuples. For instance, the following example function accepts a tuple of the `(Int, Int)` type:

```
func functionWithTupleParam(tupleParam: (Int, Int)) {}
```

In Swift, parameters can be of a generic type. The following example presents a function that has two generic parameters. In this syntax, any type (for example, `T` or `V`) that we put inside <> should be used in parameter definition:

```
func functionWithGenerics<T, V>(firstParam: T, secondParam: V)
```

We will cover generics in `Chapter 5`, *Generics and Associated Type Protocols*; at this point, knowing the syntax should be enough.

We are almost over with function parameters, finally! Last but not least, we are going to look into variadic functions in the next section.

Defining and using variadic functions

Swift enables us to define functions with variadic parameters. A variadic parameter accepts zero or more values of a specified type. Variadic parameters are similar to array parameters but they are more readable and can only be used as the last parameter in multi-parameter functions.

As variadic parameters can accept zero values, we will need to check whether they are empty.

The following example presents a function with variadic parameters of the `String` type:

```
func greet(names: String...) {
    for name in names {
        print("Greetings, \(name)")
    }
}

// To call this function
greet(names: "Josee", "Jorge") // prints twice
greet(names: "Josee ", "Jorge ", "Marcio") // prints three times
```

The most boring part of the chapter is almost over. Seriously, we needed to master the Swift function/method syntax and we will see the benefits in upcoming chapters. If you speed read or skipped previous sections, it is okay. The upcoming sections are going to be essential for FP so they need more attention.

Returning values from functions

Swift functions can `return` a value, tuple, closure, or another function. The ability of a function to `return` a closure or function is an essential concept for FP as it empowers us to compose with functions. We will get into the use of it when we talk about first-class and higher-order functions.

Syntax-wise, we can specify that a function returns by providing `ReturnType` after ->. For instance, the following example returns `String`:

```
func functionName() -> String { }
```

Any function that has `ReturnType` in its definition should have a `return` keyword with the matching type in its body.

`return` types can be optionals in Swift, so the function becomes as follows for our previous example:

```
func functionName() -> String? { }
```

Tuples can be used to provide multiple `return` values. For instance, the following function returns a tuple of the (Int, String) type:

```
func functionName() -> (code: Int, status: String) { }
```

Tuple `return` types can be optional too, so the syntax becomes as follows:

```
func functionName() -> (code: Int, status: String)? { }
```

This syntax makes the entire tuple optional. If we want to make only `status` optional, we can define the function as follows:

```
func functionName() -> (code: Int, status: String?) { }
```

In Swift, functions can `return` functions. The following example presents a function with the `return` type of a function that takes two `Int` values and returns an `Int` value:

```
func funcName() -> (Int, Int)-> Int {}
```

If we do not expect a function to `return` any value, tuple, or function, we simply do not provide `ReturnType`:

```
func functionName() { }
```

We could also explicitly declare it with the `Void` keyword as follows:

```
func functionName() -> Void { }
```

In FP, it is important to have `return` types in functions. In other words, it is good practice to avoid functions that have `Void` as a `return` type. A function with the `Void` `return` type typically is a function that changes another entity in the code; otherwise, why would we need to have a function?

OK, we might have wanted to log an expression to the `console`, save a file or write data to a database or a file to a filesystem. In these cases, it is also preferable to have a `return` or feedback related to the success of the operation. As we try to avoid mutability and stateful programming in FP, we can assume that our functions will have returns in different forms.

This requirement is in line with the mathematical underlying bases of FP. In mathematics, a simple function is defined as follows:

```
y = f(x) or f(x) -> y
```

Here, f is a function that takes x and returns y. Therefore, a function receives at least one parameter and returns at least a value. In FP, following the same paradigm makes reasoning easier, function composition possible, and code more readable.

Defining and using nested functions

In Swift, it is possible to define functions inside other functions. In other words, we can nest functions inside other functions. Nested functions are only accessible inside their enclosing functions and are hidden from the outside world by default. The enclosing function can `return` the nested function in order to allow the nested function to be used in other scopes. The following example presents a function that contains two nested functions and returns one of them according to the value of its `isPlus` parameter:

```
func choosePlusMinus(isPlus: Bool) -> (Int, Int) -> Int {
    func plus(a: Int, b: Int) -> Int {
```

```
        return a + b
    }
    func minus(a: Int, b: Int) -> Int {
        return a - b
    }
    return isPlus ? plus : minus
}
```

Pure functions

Pure functions are functions that do not possess any side effects; in other words, they do not change or alter any data or state outside of themselves. Additionally, they do not access any data or state except their provided parameters. Pure functions are like mathematical functions that are pure by nature.

Pure functions `return` a value that is only determined by its parameter values. Pure functions are easy to test as they rely only on their parameters and do not change or access any data or state outside of themselves. Pure functions are suitable for concurrency as they do not access and change global data or states.

The following list presents examples of pure and not pure functions:

- Printing a `String` literal to a console is not pure as it modifies an external state.
- Reading a file is not pure as it depends on the external state at different times.
- The length of a `String` is pure as it does not rely on a state. It only takes a `String` as input and returns the length as output.
- Getting the current date is not pure as it returns different values when called on different dates.
- Getting a random number is not pure as it returns different values each time it is called.

Using pure functions may sound very restrictive and impossible to utilize in real-world scenarios. For instance, file and database development in Swift cannot be perfectly pure but there are lots of other functionalities that can be developed using pure functions. We will see the benefits of pure functions in more detail and examples in upcoming chapters.

Function types

Along with, classes, structs, enums, and protocols, functions can also be used as types in Swift. In this section, we will explore how we can define functions as types and how we can use function types. Let's first discover what the type of the function is and how it is defined.

A function parameter type along with its `return` type defines the type of the function. For instance, the function type for the following coding example is `(Int, Double) -> String`:

```
func functionName(firstParam: Int, secondParam: Double) -> String
```

We will be able to use function types in the way we use other types. The following code example presents a function type:

```
var simpleMathOperator: (Double, Double) -> Double
```

Here, `simpleMathOperator` is a variable of a function of the `(Double, Double) -> Double` type. In other words, `simpleMathOperator` stores a function that accepts two `Double` parameters and returns a `Double` value.

To make it a little easier to read, we could define `typealias` for the function type as follows:

```
typealias SimpleOperator = (Double, Double) -> Double
```

We can use this `typealias` in the `simpleMathOperator` definition as follows:

```
var simpleMathOperator: SimpleOperator
```

We can define functions with the same type and assign them to our `simpleMathOperator`. The type of function in the following code snippet is `(Double, Double) -> Double`, which is in fact `SimpleOperator`:

```
func addTwoNumbers(a: Double, b: Double) -> Double { return a + b }

func subtractTwoNumbers(a: Double, b: Double) -> Double { return a - b }

func divideTwoNumbers(a: Double, b: Double) -> Double { return a / b }

func multiplyTwoNumbers(a: Double, b: Double) -> Double { return a * b }
```

Therefore, we are able to assign these functions to `simpleMathOperator` as follows:

```
simpleMathOperator = multiplyTwoNumbers
```

This means that `simpleMathOperator` refers to the `multiplyTwoNumbers` function:

```
let result = simpleMathOperator(3.0, 4.0) // result is 12
```

As the other three functions also have the same function type, we will be able to assign them to the same variable:

```
simpleMathOperator = addTwoNumbers
let result2 = simpleMathOperator(3.5, 5.5) // result is 9
```

We can use `SimpleOperator` as a parameter type of other functions:

```
func calculateResult(mathOperator: SimpleOperator,
                     a: Double,
                     b: Double) -> Double {
    return mathOperator(a, b)
}

print("The result is \(calculateResult(mathOperator: simpleMathOperator, a:
3.5, b: 5.5))") // prints "The result is 9.0"
```

Here, the `calculateResult` function has three parameters. The `mathOperator` parameter is a type of function type. The a and b parameters are `Double`. When we call this function, we pass a `simpleMathOperator` function and two `Double` values for a and b.

It is important to know that we pass only a reference to `simpleMathOperator` and this is not going to execute it. In the function body, we use this function and call it with a and b.

We can use `SimpleOperator` as a `return` type of a function as follows:

```
func choosePlusMinus(isPlus: Bool) -> SimpleOperator {
    return isPlus ? addTwoNumbers : subtractTwoNumbers
}

let chosenOperator = choosePlusMinus(isPlus: true)
print("The result is \(chosenOperator(3.5, 5.5))") // prints "The result is
9.0"
```

Here, the `choosePlusMinus` function has a `Bool` parameter; in its body, it checks for this parameter and returns `addTwoNumbers` or `subtractTwoNumbers` that have the same type, `SimpleOperator`.

It is important to understand that calling `choosePlusMinus(true)` does not execute the returned function and in fact only returns the reference to `addTwoNumbers`. We save this reference in `chosenOperator`. The `chosenOperator` variable becomes the following:

```
func addTwoNumbers(a: Double, b: Double) -> Double { return a + b }
```

When we call `chosenOperator(3.5, 5.5)`, we pass these two numbers to the `addTwoNumbers` function and execute it.

The capability to define function types makes functions first-class citizens in Swift. Function types are used for first-class and higher-order functions that are going to be explained in upcoming sections.

First-class functions

In the *Function types* section of this chapter, we saw that we can define function types and store and pass functions around. In practice, this means that Swift treats functions as values. To explain this, we will need to examine a couple of examples:

```
let name: String = "Grace"
```

In this code example, we create a constant of the `String` type `name` and store a value (`"Grace"`) into it.

When we define a function, we need to specify the type of parameter, as follows:

```
func sayHello(name: String) {
    print("Hello, \(name)")
}
```

In this example, our `name` parameter is of the `String` type. This parameter could be any other value type or reference type. Simply, it could be `Int`, `Double`, `Dictionary`, `Array`, `Set`, or it could be an object type such as an instance of `class`, `struct`, or `enum`.

Now, let's call this function:

```
sayHello(name: "Your name") // or
sayHello(name: name)
```

Here, we pass a value for this parameter. In other words, we pass one of the previously mentioned types with their respective values.

Swift treats functions like the other aforementioned types so we can store a function in a variable as we were able to do with other types:

```
var sayHelloFunc = sayHello
```

In this example, we saved the `sayHello` function in a variable that can be used later and passed around as a value.

In pure OOP, we do not have functions; instead, we have methods. In other words, functions can only reside in objects and then they are called methods. In OOP, classes are first-class citizens and methods are not. Methods are not solely reachable and cannot be stored or passed around. In OOP, methods access the object's data that they are defined in.

In FP, functions are **first-class** citizens. Just like other types, they can be stored and passed around. In contrast to OOP, that method can only access their parent object's data and change it; in FP, they can be stored and passed to other objects.

This notion enables us to compose our applications with functions as they are just another type that can be used. We will talk about this in more detail; for now, it is important to understand why we define functions as first-class citizens in Swift.

Higher-order functions

As we have seen in the *Defining and using function parameters* and *Function types* sections of this chapter, functions can accept functions as parameters in Swift. Functions that can accept other functions as parameters are called **higher-order** functions. This concept, along with first-class functions, empowers FP and function decomposition.

As this topic is essential in FP, we will go through another simple example.

Suppose that we need to develop two functions that add and subtract two Int values as follows:

```
func subtractTwoValues(a: Int, b: Int) -> Int {
    return a - b
}

func addTwoValues(a: Int, b: Int) -> Int {
    return a + b
}
```

Also, we need to develop functions to calculate the square and triple of two `Int` values as follows:

```
func square(a: Int) -> Int {
    return a * a
}

func triple(a: Int) -> Int {
    return a * a * a // or return square(a) * a
}
```

Suppose we need another function that subtracts the two squared values:

```
func subtractTwoSquaredValues(a: Int, b: Int) -> Int {
    return (a * a) - (b * b)
}
```

In case we needed to add two squared values:

```
func addTwoSquaredValues(a: Int, b: Int) -> Int {
    return (a * a) + (b * b)
}
```

Let's say that we need another function that triples a value and multiplies it with another tripled value:

```
func multiplyTwoTripledValues(a: Int, b: Int) -> Int {
    return (a * a * a) * (b * b * b)
}
```

This way, we had to write a lot of redundant and inflexible functions. Using higher-order functions, we could write a flexible function as follows:

```
typealias AddSubtractOperator = (Int, Int) -> Int
typealias SquareTripleOperator = (Int) -> Int

func calculate(a: Int,
               b: Int,
               funcA: AddSubtractOperator,
               funcB: SquareTripleOperator) -> Int {
    return funcA(funcB(a), funcB(b))
}
```

This higher-order function takes two other functions as parameters and uses them. We can call it for different scenarios as follows:

```
print("The result of adding two squared values is: \(calculate(a: 2, b: 2,
funcA: addTwoValues, funcB: square))")
// prints "The result of adding two squared value is: 8"

print("The result of subtracting two tripled value is: \(calculate(a: 3, b:
2, funcA:  subtractTwoValues, funcB: triple))")
// prints "The result of adding two tripled value is: 19"
```

This simple example presented the utility of higher-order functions in function composition and subsequently in program modularity.

Function composition

In the previous section, we saw an example of higher-order functions that could accept two different functions and execute them in a predefined order. This function was not so flexible in the sense that it would break if we wanted to combine two accepted functions differently. Function composition can solve this issue and make it even more flexible. To present this concept, we will examine an example of non-functional composition first, and then we will introduce functional composition.

Suppose that, in our application, we need to interact with a backend RESTful API and receive a String value that contains a list of prices in order. The backend RESTful API is being developed by a third-party and is not designed properly. Unfortunately, it returns a String with numbers in it separated by commas, as follows:

```
"10,20,40,30,80,60"
```

We need to format the content that we receive before using it. We will extract elements from String and create an array, and then we will append $ as currency to each item to use it in a table view. The following code example presents an approach to this problem:

```
let content = "10,20,40,30,80,60"

func extractElements(_ content: String) -> [String] {
    return content.characters.split(separator: ",").map { String($0) }
}

let elements = extractElements(content)

func formatWithCurrency(content: [String]) -> [String] {
    return content.map {"\($0)$"}
```

```
    }

    let formattedElements = formatWithCurrency(content: elements)
```

In this code example, we treated each function individually. We could use the result of the first function as an input parameter for the second function. Either approach is verbose and not functional. Additionally, we used the map function, which is a higher-order function, but our approach is still not functional.

Let's approach this problem in a functional way.

The first step will be to identify function types for each function:

- `extractElements - String -> [String]`
- `formatWithCurrency - [String] -> [String]`

If we pipe these functions, we will get the following:

```
extractElements: String -> [String] | formatWithCurrency: [String] ->
[String]
```

We can combine these functions with a functional composition and the composed function will be of type of `String -> [String]`. The following code snippet shows the composition:

```
let composedFunction = {
    data in
    formatWithCurrency(content: extractElements(data))
}

composedFunction(content)
```

In this example, we define `composedFunction`, which is composed of two other functions. We can compose functions like this as each function has at least one parameter and `return` value.

This composition is like the mathematical composition of functions. Suppose that we have a function `f(x)` that returns `y` and a `g(y)` function that returns `z`. We can compose the `g` function as `g(f(x)) -> z`. This composition makes our `g` function take `x` as a parameter and `return z` as a result. This is exactly what we have done in our `composedFunction`.

Custom operators

Although `composedFunction` is less verbose than the non-functional version, it does not look great. Also, it is not easy to read as we need to read it inside out. Let's make this function simpler and more readable. One solution will be to define a custom operator that will be used instead of our composed function. In the following sections, we will examine what the standard operators are that are allowed to define a custom operator. We will also explore the custom operator definition technique. It is important to learn this concept as we will be using it in the rest of the book.

Allowed operators

The Swift standard library provides a number of operators that can be used to define custom operators. Custom operators can begin with one of the ASCII characters -/, =, -, +, !, *, %, <, >, &, |, ^, ?, ~, or one of the Unicode characters. After the first character, combining Unicode characters is allowed.

We can also define custom operators that begin with a dot. If an operator does not start with a dot, it cannot contain a dot elsewhere. Although we can define custom operators that contain a question mark (?), they cannot consist of a single question mark character only. Additionally, although operators can contain an exclamation point (!), postfix operators cannot begin with either a question mark or an exclamation point.

Custom operator definition

We can define custom operators using the following syntax:

```
operatorType operator operatorName { }
```

Here, `operatorType` can be one of the following:

- prefix
- infix
- postfix

Custom `infix` operators can also specify a precedence and an associativity:

```
infix operator operatorName { associativity left/right/none precedence}
```

The possible values for associativity are `left`, `right`, and `none`. Left-associative operators associate to the left if written next to other left-associative operators of the same precedence. Similarly, right-associative operators associate to the right if written next to other right-associative operators of the same precedence. Non-associative operators cannot be written next to other operators with the same precedence.

The associativity value defaults to `none` if it is not specified. The precedence value defaults to `100` if it is not specified.

Any custom operator defined with the preceding syntax will not have an existing meaning in Swift; therefore, a function with `operatorName` as its name should be defined and implemented. In the following section, we will examine an example of custom operator definition with its respective function definition.

A composed function with custom operator

Let's define a new custom operator to use instead of our composed function:

```
precedencegroup AssociativityLeft {
    associativity: left
}

infix operator |> : AssociativityLeft
func |> <T, V>(f: @escaping (T) -> V, g: @escaping (V) -> V ) -> (T) -> V {
    return { x in g(f(x)) }
}

let composedWithCustomOperator = extractElements |> formatWithCurrency
composedWithCustomOperator("10,20,40,30,80,60")
// The result will be: ["10$", "20$", "40$", "30$", "80$", "60$"]
```

In this example, we have defined a new operator, `|>`, that takes two generic functions and combines them, returning a function that has the first function's input as the parameter and the second function's `return` as the `return` type.

As this new operator is going to combine two functions and is binary, we defined it as `infix`. Then we need to use the `operator` keyword. The next step will be to choose the notation for our new custom operator. As we will group functions to the left, we need to specify it as `associativity left`.

To be able to use this operator, we need to define a corresponding function. Our function takes two functions as follows:

- f: This function takes a generic type of T and returns a generic type of V
- g: This function takes a generic type of V and returns a generic type of V

In our previous example, we had the following functions:

- extractElements – String -> [String]
- formatWithCurrency – [String] -> [String]

So T becomes String and V becomes [String].

Our |> function returns a function that takes a generic type of T and returns a generic type of V. We need to receive the String -> [String] from the composed function so, again, T becomes String and V becomes [String].

Using our |> custom operator makes our code more readable and less verbose. Do not worry about @escaping for now, we will talk about it in the *Closures--Capturing values* section of this chapter.

Closures

Closures are great tools for FP as they are functions without the func keyword and name. Like functions, closures are self-contained blocks of code that provide a specific functionality and can be stored, passed around, and used in the code. Closures capture the constants and variables of the context in which they are defined. Although closures are the equivalent of blocks in Objective-C, they have a simpler syntax in Swift compared to the C and Objective-C block syntax. Nested functions, which we have covered in a previous section, are special cases of closures. Closures are reference types that can be stored as variables, constants, and type aliases. They can be passed to and returned from functions.

Closure syntax

A general closure syntax is as follows:

```
{ (parameters) -> ReturnType in // body of closure }
```

A closure definition starts with {, then we define the closure type, and finally we use the in keyword to separate the closure definition from its implementation.

After the `in` keyword, we write the body of the closure and finish our closure by closing }.

Closures can be used to define variables or stored as variables. The following closure defines a variable of a type closure that accepts `Int` and returns `Int`:

```
let closureName: (Int) -> (Int) = { _ in 10 }
```

Closures can be stored as optional variables. The following closure defines a variable of a type closure that accepts `Int` and returns Optional `Int`

```
var closureName: (Int) -> (Int)?
```

Closures can be defined as `typealiases`. The following example presents `typealias` of a closure that has two `Int` parameters and returns `Int`.

```
typealias closureType = (Int, Int) -> (Int)
```

The same `typealias` could be used for a function type definition as functions are named closures in Swift.

Closures can be used as an argument to a function call. For instance, the following example presents a function that is called with a closure that receives `Int` and returns `Int`:

```
func aFunc(closure: (Int) -> Int) -> Int  {
    // Statements, for example:
    return closure(5)
}

let result = aFunc(closure: {
    number in
    // Statements, for example:
    return number * 3
})

print(result) // prints 15
```

Closures can be used as function parameters. The following example shows an array sort method that receives a closure:

```
var anArray = [1, 2, 5, 3, 6, 4]

anArray.sort(by: {
    (param1: Int, param2: Int) -> Bool in
    return param1 < param2
})
```

This syntax can be simplified with implied types as the Swift compiler has the ability to infer the types for parameters from the context as follows:

```
anArray.sort(by: {
    (param1, param2) -> Bool in
    return param1 < param2
})
```

The syntax can be further simplified with implied `return` types using the Swift type inference:

```
anArray.sort(by: {
    (param1, param2) in
    return param1 < param2
})
```

Swift enables us to eliminate the parameter name and open and close parentheses if we need to pass the closure as the last parameter of a function, in other words, if our closure is a trailing closure:

```
anArray.sort {
    (param1, param2) in
    return param1 < param2
}
```

Also, Swift provides a shorthand argument notation that can be used instead of using arguments:

```
anArray.sort {
    return $0 < $1
}
```

We can simplify this syntax even further by eliminating the `return` keyword as we have only one line of expression, as follows:

```
anArray.sort { $0 < $1 }
```

Using the Swift type inference, we were able to shorten the closure syntax drastically. Shorter syntax does not mean a simpler code to read and understand. It is recommended to find the optimum syntax that suits you and your team and adapt it consistently.

Capturing values

Closures can capture variables and constants from the surrounding context in which they are created. Closures can refer to these variables and modify them within their body, even if the original scope that defined variables no longer exists.

A closure is said to escape a function when the closure is passed as an argument to the function but is called after the function returns. One way that a closure can escape is by being stored in a variable that is defined outside the function.

The following is an example of escaping closures, in other words, completion handlers:

```
func sendRequest(completion: @escaping (_ response: String?, _ error:
Error?) -> Void) {
    // execute some time consuming operation, if successfull {
    completion("Response", nil)
    //}
}

sendRequest {
    (response: String?, error: Error?) in
    if let result = response {
        print(result)
    } else if let serverError = error {
        // Error
    }
}
```

We have a function named `sendRequest` that has a parameter of type of closure, `completion` which it takes an `OptionalString`, and an `Optional Error` parameters, and does not `return` any value.

Suppose that we execute some asynchronous time-consuming operations in the body of the function, such as reading from a file, reading from a database, or calling a web service.

To call this function, we provide a closure as argument. Our closure has two variables in it: a variable named `response` of the `Optional String` type and an `error` variable of the `Optional Error` type. As our function does not have any `return` type, it does not `return` any value to its caller. Here comes the concept of **escaping a function**.

Our passed closure escapes our function as it will be called after our time-consuming asynchronous operation finishes with success and the following call happens:

```
completion("Response", nil)
```

If a closure is going to be passed as an argument to a function and it is going to be invoked after the function returns, the closure is `escaping`. In other words, the closure argument escapes the function body. In Swift 3, we need to use the `@escaping` keyword in the function definition to tell our function users that closure can escape the function body.

In this call, we pass the `response` and `error` and call back the `completion` closure. Then the body of closure in the caller function is executed with passed variables. This concept is a very powerful concept that eases all asynchronous operations. It is very readable and easy to follow compared with mechanisms such as delegation and notification.

Function currying

Function currying translates a single function with multiple arguments into a series of functions each with one argument. Let's examine an example.

Suppose that we have a function that combines `firstName` and `lastName` to `return` the full name as follows:

```
func extractFullName(firstName: String, lastName: String) -> String {
    return "\(firstName) \(lastName)"
}
```

This function could be translated into a curried function as follows:

```
func curriedExtractFullName(firstName: String)(lastName: String) -> String
{
    return "\(firstName) \(lastName)"
}
```

As seen from this example, we replace the comma with `)` `(` parentheses. So now we can use this function as follows:

```
let fnIncludingFirstName = curriedExtractFullName("John")
let extractedFullName = fnIncludingFirstName(lastName: "Doe")
```

Here, `fnIncludingFirstName` will already have `firstName` in it so that, when we use it, we can provide `lastName` and extract the full name.

Starting with Swift 2.2, Apple deprecated function currying and removed it from Swift 3.0. We can convert the function currying to returning a closure explicitly:

```
// Before:
func curried(x: Int)(y: String) -> Float {
    return Float(x) + Float(y)!
}

// After:
func curried(x: Int) -> (String) -> Float {
    return {
        (y: String) -> Float in
        return Float(x) + Float(y)!
    }
}
```

Let's convert our curried function to `return` the closure version explicitly:

```
func explicityRetunClosure(firstName: String) -> (String) -> String {
    return {
        (lastName: String) -> String in
        return "\(firstName) \(lastName)"
    }
}
```

We can use this function as follows and the result is going to be identical:

```
let fnIncludingFirstName = explicityRetunClosure(firstName: "John")
let extractedFullName = fnIncludingFirstName("Doe")
```

Recursion

Recursion is one of the most used techniques in FP and it is the process of calling a function inside itself. The function that calls itself is a recursive function.

Recursion is best used for problems where a large problem can be broken down into a repetitive subproblem. As a recursive function calls itself to solve these subproblems, eventually the function will come across a subproblem that it can handle without calling itself. This is known as a *base case*, and it is needed to prevent the function from calling itself over and over again without stopping.

In the base case, the function does not call itself. However, when a function does have to call itself in order to deal with its subproblem, then this is known as a *recursive* case. So, there are two types of cases when using a recursive algorithm: base cases and recursive cases. It is important to remember that, when using recursion and when we are trying to solve a problem, we should ask ourselves: what is my base case and what is my recursive case?

To apply this simple process, let's start with an example of recursion: the factorial function. In mathematics, an exclamation mark after a number (n!) presents the factorial of the number. A factorial of a number n is the product of all integers between 1 and n. So, if n is equal to 3, then the factorial of n would be 3 * 2 * 1, which equals 6. We could also say that the factorial of 3 is equal to 3 multiplied by the factorial of 2, which would be 3 * 2! or 3 * 2 * 1.

So, the factorial of any number n could also be defined as follows:

```
n! = n * (n - 1)!
```

We also need to know the following:

```
0! = 1! = 1
```

Note how we defined the factorial of a number as that number multiplied by the factorial of the integer that is 1 less than the number (n * (n - 1)!). So, what we have done is essentially broken the problem into a subproblem and, in order to find the factorial of a number, we keep finding the factorials of the integers below that number and multiplying. So, the factorial of 3 is equal to 3 multiplied by the factorial of 2 and the factorial of 2 is equal to 2 multiplied by the factorial of 1. So, if we have a function to find the factorial of a given number, then our code for the recursive case would look something like the following:

```
func factorial(n: Int) -> Int {
    return n * factorial(n: n - 1)
}
```

Here, we want to find n number's factorial.

In this example, we divided the problem into a subproblem. There is still one problem that we need to solve. We need to check for the base case in order to be able to stop the function from calling itself infinitely.

Therefore, we can modify our factorial example as follows:

```
func factorial(n: Int) -> Int {
    return n == 0 || n == 1 ? 1 : n * factorial(n: n - 1)
}

print(factorial(n: 3))
```

As seen in this example, we check for n; if it is 0 or 1, we `return1` and stop the recursion. Another example of a simple recursive function is as follows:

```
func powerOfTwo(n: Int) -> Int {
    return n == 0 ? 1 : 2 * powerOfTwo(n: n - 1)
}

let fnResult = powerOfTwo(n: 3)
```

The non-recursive version of this example is as follows:

```
func power2(n: Int) -> Int {
    var y = 1
    for _ in 0...n - 1 {
        y *= 2
    }
    return y
}

let result = power2(n: 4)
```

As we can see from this example, the recursive version is more expressive and shorter. The following example presents a function that repeats a given `String` for a desired time:

```
func repateString(str: String, n: Int) -> String {
    return n == 0 ? "" : str + repateString(str: str , n: n - 1)
}

print(repeatString(str: "Hello", n: 4))
```

The following code snippet presents the same functionality without using recursion, in other words, in the imperative programming style:

```
func repeatString(str: String, n: Int) -> String {
    var ourString = ""
    for _ in 1...n {
        ourString += str
    }
    return ourString
}

print(repeatString(str: "Hello", n: 4))
```

The non-recursive, imperative version is slightly longer and we need to use a `for` loop and variable to be able to achieve the same result. Some functional programming languages, such as Haskell, do not have `for` loop mechanisms and we have to use recursion; in Swift, we have `for` loops but as we have seen here, it is better to use recursive functions whenever we can.

Tail recursion

Tail recursion is a special case of recursion where the calling function does no more execution after making a recursive call to itself. In other words, a function is named **tail recursive** if its final expression is a recursive call. The previous recursion examples that we have been introduced to were not tail recursive functions.

To be able to understand tail recursion, we will develop the factorial function that we developed before with the tail recursion technique. Then we will talk about the differences:

```
func factorial(n: Int, currentFactorial: Int = 1) -> Int {
    return n == 0 ? currentFactorial : factorial(n: n - 1,
    currentFactorial: currentFactorial * n)
}

print(factorial(n: 3))
```

Note that we provide a default argument of 1 for `currentFactorial`, but this only applies to the very first call of the function. When the factorial function is called recursively, the default argument is overridden with whatever value is passed by the recursive call. We need to have that second argument there because it will hold the current factorial value that we intend on passing to the function.

Let's try to understand how it works and how it is different from the other factorial functions:

```
factorial(n: 3, currentFactorial: 1)
return factorial(n: 2, currentFactorial: 1 * 3) // n = 3
return factorial(n: 1, currentFactorial: 3 * 2) // n = 2
return 6 // n = 1
```

In this function, each time the factorial function is called, a new value for `currentFactorial` is passed to the function. The function basically updates `currentFactorial` with each call to itself. We are able to save the current factorial value as it accepts `currentFactorial` as a parameter.

All of the recursive calls to the factorial, such as `factorial(2, 1 * 3)`, do not actually need to `return` in order to get the final value. We can see that we actually arrive at the value of 6 before any of the recursive calls actually `return`.

Therefore, a function is tail-recursive if the final result of the recursive call, in this example 6, is also the final result of the function itself. The non-tail-recursive function is not in its final state in the last function call because all of the recursive calls leading up to the last function call must also `return` in order to actually come up with the final result.

Memoization

In previous sections, we talked about functions as building blocks and explained that we can compose our applications with functions. If functions can be building blocks in our programs, then they should be cacheable! But how do we cache them? The answer is **memoization**.

Memoization is the process of storing the result of functions, given their input, in order to improve the performance of our programs. We can memoize pure functions as pure functions do not rely on external data and do not change anything outside themselves. Pure functions provide the same result for a given input every time. Therefore, we can save or cache the results (in other words, memoize the results) given their inputs and use them in the future without going through the calculation process.

To be able to understand the concept, let's look at the following example in which we will manually memoize the `power2` function:

```
var memo = Dictionary<Int, Int>()

func memoizedPower2(n: Int) -> Int {
    if let memoizedResult = memo[n] {
        return memoizedResult
    }
    var y = 1
    for _ in 0...n-1 {
        y *= 2
    }
    memo[n] = y
    return y
}
print(memoizedPower2(n: 2))
print(memoizedPower2(n: 3))
print(memoizedPower2(n: 4))
print(memo) // result: [2: 4, 3: 8, 4: 16]
```

As we can see from the example, we define a dictionary of the `[Int, Int]` type. We save the result of the function given its input to this dictionary.

This approach works properly but we need to manually modify and maintain a collection outside of the function to be able to memoize the results of the function. Also, it adds a lot of boilerplate code to each function that we need memoization for.

The advanced Swift session presented at the **Worldwide Developers Conference (WWDC) 2014** (https://developer.apple.com/videos/play/wwdc2014-404/) provides a convenient function for memoization that can be used with any pure function.

Watching the video is highly recommended. Let's see if we can automatize this functionality and reuse it using the memoize function from that session:

```
func memoize<T: Hashable, U>(fn: @escaping ((T) -> U, T) -> U) -> (T) -> U
{
    var memo = Dictionary<T, U>()
    var result: ((T) -> U)!
    result = {
        x in
        if let q = memo[x] { return q }
        let r = fn(result, x)
        memo[x] = r
        return r
    }
    return result
}
```

The function looks complex but don't worry, we will go through it in detail.

First of all, it is a generic function. Do not worry about generics, we will cover generics in detail in Chapter 5, *Generics and Associated Type Protocols*. Secondly, Hashable is used because we need to store T as a key in a dictionary.

If we look at the signature of the function, we see that the memoize function takes a function (fn) with two parameters and a return type. So the signature of fn, which is a function, is as follows:

```
((T) -> U, T) -> U
```

The first parameter of fn is a function of the (T) -> U type and the second parameter is of the T type and finally fn returns U.

OK, the memoize function received fn, which is described in the preceding code snippet.

At the end, the memoize function returns a function of the (T) -> U type; in other words, the memoized version of the function that takes a T type and returns U type.

Now let's look at the body of the memoize function. First, we need to have a dictionary to cache the results. Second, we need to define the result type, which is a closure. In the closure body, we check whether we already have the key in our dictionary. If we do, we return it, otherwise, we call the function and save the result in our memo dictionary.

Now we can use this function to memoize the results of different function calls and improve the performance of our programs.

The following example presents the *memoized* version of the factorial function:

```
let factorial = memoize {
    factorial, x in
    x == 0 ? 1 : x * factorial(x - 1)
}

print(factorial(5))
```

The `memoize` function expects a closure as input; therefore, we can use the trailing closure syntax. In the preceding example, we provided the `factorial` function and x parameters as input to the closure and the line after the `in` keyword is the body of the closure. In the previous example, we used memoize for a recursive function and it works properly. Let's look at another example:

```
let powerOf2 = memoize {
    pow2, x in
    x == 0 ? 1 : 2 * pow2(x - 1)
}

print(powerOf2(5))
```

In this example, we use the `memoize` function to have a memoized version of the `powerOf2` function.

Writing the `memoize` function once, we will be able to use it for any pure functions to cache the data and improve the performance of our programs.

Summary

This chapter started by explaining function definition and usage in detail by giving examples for parameter and `return` types. Then it continued to cover FP-related concepts such as pure, first-class, higher-order, and nested functions. Finally, it covered function composition, closures, currying, and memoization.

At this point, we should be familiar with different types of functions and closures and their usages. In the following chapter, we will cover types and explore the concept of value types versus reference types. Also, we will look at value type characteristics in detail and cover type equality, identity, and casting.

3
Types and Type Casting

In the previous chapter, we talked about functions and closures and covered topics such as function types. We know that functions are first-class citizens in Swift and they can be stored and passed around like any type. It is the time to look into types in detail.

This chapter starts with explaining types, touching on the concept of types in the category theory very briefly. Then it explains value and reference types and compares them in detail. Finally, it talks about equality, identity, and type casting.

This chapter will cover the following topics with coding examples:

- Types
- Different categories of types
- Value versus reference types
    - Value and reference type constants
    - Mixing value and reference types
    - Copying
    - Value type characteristics
- Equality, identity, and comparing
- Type checking and casting

Kinds of types

You may have heard that **Functional Programming** (**FP**) uses concepts of the category theory and type theory. This link is the reason why some people find FP closer to mathematics. Theoretically, category refers to a collection that contains the following:

- A collection of objects (types in Swift)
- A collection of morphisms, each of which ties two objects together (functions in Swift)
- A notion of composition of the morphisms (function composition in Swift)

We have already discussed functions and function composition and now we are going to explore types.

It is possible to categorize types in four different ways:

- Named versus compound types
- Sum versus product types
- Abstract versus concrete types
- Value versus reference types

Any type that we can give a name to while we define it, is a **named** type. For instance, if we create a class named `OurClass`, any instance of `OurClass` will be of the `OurClass` type.

Function types and tuple types are **compound** types. A compound type may contain named types and other compound types. For instance, `(String, (Double, Double))` is a compound type and in fact it is a tuple of `String` and another tuple of the `(Double, Double)` type. We can use named types and compound types in type annotation, identification, and aliasing.

`Tuples` and `structs` are **product** types or `AND` types. For instance, to create a `User` entity we will need to have `name` and `age` properties. `Enums` are **sum** types or `OR` types. For instance, a web API can either return a `2XX` or `4XX` or `5XX` HTTP status code. We will talk about sum, product, and recursive types when we talk about algebraic data types in `Chapter 4`, *Enumerations and Pattern Matching*.

Types that the compiler can figure out their size at compile time and we can instantiate them are **concrete**. For instance, `String`, `Int`, and `Double` are concrete types. On the other hand, types that the compiler cannot figure out their size at compile time and we cannot instantiate them are **abstract**. Generics and protocols are examples of abstract types. Then there is type erasure that is a process to make abstract types concrete. We will talk about *abstract types* and *type erasure* in `Chapter 5`, *Generics and Associated Type Protocols*.

So far, we did not talk a lot about reference versus value types and type casting. In the following sections of this chapter, we will explore these concepts.

Also, in previous chapters, we saw that we can use Swift inference that infers the types unless we want to specify the type explicitly. We annotate the type in case we need to specify the type explicitly.

Value versus reference types

In Swift, there are two kinds of types in terms of memory allocation: value and reference.

Value type instances keep a copy of their data. Each type has its own data and is not referenced by another variable. Structures, enums, and tuples are value types; therefore, they do not share data between their instances. Assignments copy the data of an instance to the other and there is no reference counting involved. The following example presents a struct with copying:

```
struct OurStruct {
    var data: Int = 3
}

var valueA = OurStruct()
var valueB = valueA // valueA is copied to valueB
valueA.data = 5 // Changes valueA, not valueB
print("\(valueA.data), \(valueB.data)") // prints "5, 3"
```

As seen from the preceding example, changing valueA.data does not change valueB.data.

In Swift, arrays, dictionaries, strings, and sets are all value types.

On the other hand, reference type instances share the same copy of the data. Classes and closures are reference types, so assignment only adds a reference, but it does not copy the data. In fact, initialization of a reference type creates a shared instance that will be used by different instances of a reference type such as class or closure. Two variables of the same class type will refer to a single instance of the data, so if we modify the data in one of the variables, it will also affect the other variable. The following example presents a class with referencing:

```
class OurClass {
    var data: Int = 3
}
```

```
var referenceA = OurClass()
var referenceB = referenceA // referenceA is copied to referenceB
referenceA.data = 5 // changes the instance referred to by referenceA and
referenceB
print("\(referenceA.data), \(referenceB.data)") // prints "5, 5"
```

As seen from the preceding example, changing `referenceA.data` also changes `referenceB.data` as they refer to the same shared instance.

This fundamental difference between value and reference types can have a huge impact on our system architecture. In functional programming, it is recommended to prefer value types over reference types as it is easier to trace and reason about value types. As we always get a unique copy of data and the data is not shared among instances, we can reason that no other part of our program is going to change the data. This feature of value types makes them especially helpful in multithreaded environments where a different thread will be able to change our data without informing us. This can create bugs that are very hard to debug and fix.

To be able to use this feature in Swift with `classes`, we can develop immutable `classes` using only immutable stored properties and avoiding exposing any APIs that can alter the state. However, Swift does not provide any language mechanism to enforce class immutability the way it enforces immutability for `struct` and `enum`. Any API user can subclass our provided class and make it mutable unless we define them as `final` and avoid `open` definitions. This is not the case with `struct`, `enum`, and `tuples` as basically we cannot subclass them.

Value and reference type constants

Constants behave differently if they are value or reference types. We will be able to change the variables in a constant class, but we cannot change them for structs.

Let's examine the following example:

```
class User {
    var name: String
    init(name: String) {
        self.name = name
    }
}

let grace = User(name: "Grace")
let tamina = User(name: "Tamina")

struct Student {
```

```
    var user: User
}

let student = Student(user: grace)
student.user = tamina // compiler error - cannot assign to property:
'student' is a 'let' constant
```

In this example, we have a class named `User` and two constants that point to the instance of the class. Also, we have a `Student struct` that has a variable of the `User` type.

We create `student` using the `Student` structure. If we try to change the `user` variable in `student`, the compiler gives us an error telling us that `student` is a constant even though we defined `user` as a variable.

So we cannot change any variable in `struct` if we instantiate it as a constant. In other words, `let student = Student(user: grace)` makes the whole `struct` immutable.

Let's try the same operation with `classes`. In the following code, we change the name of `tamina`, which is defined as a constant. The compiler does not give us an error and accepts the following assignment:

```
tamina.name = "Su Tamina"
print(tamina.name) // prints "Su Tamina"
```

Even though we defined `tamina` as a constant, we could change the `name` variable as it was a `class`.

From the preceding examples, we have seen that we can change the value of a variable on a constant that is an instance of a `class` (reference type), but we cannot change the value of a variable on a constant that is an instance of a `struct` (value type).

As `tamina` is an instance of a reference type, it refers to the instance of `User`. When we change `name`, we are not actually changing what `tamina` is, which is a reference to `User`. We change the `name` that we made mutable by defining it as a variable. This is not the case for our `student` constant as it is a value type. Defining it as a constant makes its variables constant too.

This property of reference types makes them hard to track and since we are defining them as constants, it is not going to make them immune to changes. To be able to make them immutable, we will need to define their properties as constants.

Mixing value and reference types

In real-world problems, we may need to mix reference types with value types. For instance, we may need to have a reference to class in struct like our previous example or we may need to have a struct variable in class. How would we reason about the assignments and copying in these circumstances?

Let's examine the following example:

```
class User {
    var name: String
    init(name: String) {
        self.name = name
    }
}
let julie = User(name: "Julie")

struct Student {
    var user: User
}

let student = Student(user: julie)
student.user.name // prints "Julie"
let anotherStudent = student
julie.name = "Julie Jr."
anotherStudent.user.name // prints "Julie Jr."
```

In this example, we have a User class and a Student struct that has the user variable. We define a constant, student with julie, which is of the class type. If we print student.user.name, the result will be julie.

Now if we define anotherStudent and copy student to it by assignment, changing the name of Julie will change the name of anotherStudent too.

We would expect anotherStudent to have a copy of student, but name has been changed. It is changed because the user variable is of the User type, which is class and therefore a reference type.

This example presents the complexity of using reference types in value types. To avoid these complications, it is recommended to avoid using reference type variables inside value types. If we need to use reference types in our value types, as we stated before, we should define them as constants.

Copying

Assignment operations on value types copy values from one value type to another value type. There are two types of copying in different programming languages, shallow and deep copying.

Shallow copying duplicates as little as possible. For instance, a shallow copy of a collection is a copy of the collection structure, not its elements. With a shallow copy, two collections share the same individual elements.

Deep copying duplicates everything. For instance, a deep copy of a collection results in another collection with all of the elements in the original collection duplicated.

Swift does the shallow copying and does not provide a mechanism for deep copying. Let's examine an example to understand shallow copying:

```
let julie = User(name: "Julie")
let steve = User(name: "Steve")
let alain = User(name: "Alain")
let users = [alain, julie, steve]
```

In the preceding example, we created a new User named alain and added three users to a new array named users. In the following example, we copy the users array to a new array named copyOfUsers. Then we change the name of one of our users in the users array as follows:

```
let copyOfUsers = users
users[0].name = "Jean-Marc"

print(users[0].name) // prints "Jean-Marc"
print(copyOfUsers[0].name) // prints "Jean-Marc"
```

Printing users and copyOfUsers will show us that changing the name of Alain to Jean-Marc in the users array has changed the name of Alain in copyOfUsers to Jean-Marc too. The users and copyOfUsers are arrays, and we would expect assignment expression to copy the values from users to copyOfUsers as arrays are value types, but as we have seen from the preceding example, changing the name of user in one array changed the username in the copied array. There are two reasons for this behavior. First of all, User is a type of class. So it is a reference type. Secondly, Swift does the shallow copying.

Shallow copying does not provide a distinct copy of an instance, as we have seen in this example. Shallow copying duplicates the references to the same elements of the instance. So again, this example presents complications with using reference types in value types as Swift does not provide deep copying to overcome these complications.

Copying reference types

Two variables can point to the same object, so changing one variable changes the other too. Having lots of objects point to the same data can be useful in some circumstances, but mostly we will want to modify copies so that modifying one object doesn't have an effect on the others. The foundation framework provides us the means to copy reference types. To make it work, we need to do the following:

- Our class should be of the NSObject type
- Our class should conform to the NSCopying protocol (which is not mandatory, but makes our intent clear for our API user)
- Our class should implement the copy(with: NSZone) method
- To copy the object, we will need to call the copy() method on the object

Here's an example of a Manager class that conforms fully to the NSCopying protocol:

```
class Manager: NSObject, NSCopying {
    var firstName: String
    var lastName: String
    var age: Int

    init(firstName: String, lastName: String, age: Int) {
        self.firstName = firstName
        self.lastName = lastName
        self.age = age
    }

    func copy(with: NSZone? = nil) -> Any {
        let copy = Manager(firstName: firstName, lastName: lastName,
        age: age)
        return copy
    }
}
```

The copy(with: NSZone) function is implemented by creating a new Manager object using the information of the current Manager. To test our class, we create two instances and copy one instance over the other as follows:

```
let john = Manager(firstName: "John", lastName: "Doe", age: 35)
let jane = john.copy() as! Manager

jane.firstName = "Jane"
jane.lastName = "Doe"
jane.age = 40
```

```
print("\(john.firstName) \(john.lastName) is \(john.age)")
print("\(jane.firstName) \(jane.lastName) is \(jane.age)")
```

The result will be as follows:

```
"John Doe is 35"
"Jane Doe is 40"
```

Value type characteristics

We have examined the notion of value types and reference types. We have looked into simple scenarios of value type versus reference type usage. We understand that using value types makes our code simpler and easier to trace and reason. Now let's look into the characteristics of value types in more detail.

Behaviour

Value types do not behave. A value type stores data and provides methods to use its data. A value type can only have a single owner and it does not have deinitializers as there are no references involved. Some of the value type methods may cause the value type to mutate itself, but control flow is rigidly controlled by the single owner of the instance. As the code will only execute when directly invoked by a single owner and not from many sources, it is easy to reason about the value type code execution flow.

On the other hand, a reference type might subscribe itself as a target of other systems. It might receive notifications from other systems. These sorts of interactions require reference types as they can have multiple owners. It's unnecessarily difficult to develop value types that perform side effects on their own in most cases.

Isolation

A typical value type has no implicit dependencies on the behavior of any external system. Therefore, a value type is isolated. It interacts only with its owner and it is easy to understand how it interacts in comparison to a reference type's interactions with a multiple number of owners.

If we access a reference to a mutable instance, we have an implicit dependency on all its other owners and they could change the instance at any time without notifying us.

Interchangeability

As a value type is copied when it is assigned to a new variable, all of those copies are completely interchangeable.

We can safely store a value that is passed to us, and then later utilize this value as if it were a new value. It will not be possible to compare the instance with another instance using anything but its data.

Interchangeability also means that it does not matter how a given value was defined. Two value types are equal by all means if comparing them via == results in equality.

Testability

There is no need for a mocking framework to write unit tests that deal with value types. We can directly define values indistinguishable from the instances in our applications.

If we use reference types that behave, we have to test the interactions between the reference type that we will test and the rest of the system. This typically means a lot of mocking or extensive setup code to establish the required relationships.

In contrast, value types are isolated and interchangeable, so we can directly define a value, call a method, and examine the result. Simpler tests with greater coverage yield a code that is easier to change and maintain.

Threats

While the structure of value types encourages testability, isolation, and interchangeability, one can define value types that diminish these advantages. Value types containing code that executes without being called by its owner are generally hard to track and reason about, and should often be avoided.

Also, value types containing reference types are not necessarily isolated. Using reference types in value types should generally be avoided as they are dependent on all other owners of that referent. These kinds of value types are also not easily interchangeable as the external reference might interact with the rest of the system and cause some complications.

Using value and reference types

The Swift Programming Language by *Apple Inc.* has a section on comparing *structs* (value type) and `classes` (reference type) and how to prefer one over the other. It is highly recommended to read that section to understand why we prefer one over the other. Although we touched on the topic briefly in `Chapter 1`, *Getting Started With Functional Programming in Swift*, we will explore this topic further as the distinction between reference and value types is very important in FP.

In OOP, we model real-world objects as `classes` and `interfaces`. For instance, to model an Italian restaurant with different types of pizzas, we may have a `Pizzaclass` and subclasses of it such as `Margherita`, `Napoletana`, or `Romana`. Each of these pizzas will have different ingredients. Different restaurants may make them slightly differently, and whenever we read their recipes in different books or websites, we may understand it differently. This level of abstraction enables us to refer to a specific pizza without caring about how other people really imagine that pizza. Whenever we talk about that pizza, we do not transfer it, we just refer to it.

On the other hand, in our Italian restaurant, we will need to provide bills to our customers. Whenever they ask for the bill, we are going to provide real information about quantity and prices. Everyone has the same perception about quantities, prices in dollars, and, in fact, values. Our customers can calculate the invoice total. If our customers modify the bill, it is not going to modify the source that we used to provide the bill. No matter whether they write something on the bill or spill wine on it, the value and bill total amount is not going to change.

The preceding example presents a simple real-world usage of reference versus value types. Value types and reference types have their own usages in the Swift programming language and in web, mobile, or desktop application programming.

Value types enable us to make architectures clearer, simpler, and more testable. Value types typically have fewer or no dependencies on the outside state, so there's less that we have to consider when reasoning about them. Also, value types are essentially more reusable because they are interchangeable. As we use more value types and immutable entities, our system will become easier to test and maintain over time.

In contrast, reference types are acting entities in the system. They have identity. They can behave. Their behavior is often complex and hard to reason about, but some of the details can usually be represented by simple values and isolated functions involving those values. Reference types maintain a state defined by values, but these values can be considered independently of the reference type. Reference types perform side effects such as I/O, file and database operations, and networking. Reference types can interact with other reference types, but they generally send values, not references, unless they truly plan to create a persistent connection with the external system.

It is important to use value types (`enums`, `tuples`, or `structs`) as much as possible unless we need to create a shared mutable state. There are cases where we have to use `classes`. For instance, when we work with `Cocoa`, many APIs expect subclasses of `NSObject`, so we have to use `classes` in these cases. Whenever we need to use `classes`, we avoid variables; we define our properties as constants and avoid exposing any APIs that can alter states.

Equality versus identity

Two instances are equal if they have the same value. Equality is used to determine the equality of two value types. For instance, two strings are equal if they have the same text value. The == operator is used to check for equality. The following example presents equality checking for two `Int` numbers (`Int` is a value type):

```
let firstNumber = 1
let secondNumber = 1

if firstNumber == secondNumber {
    print("Two numbers are equal") // prints "Two numbers are equal\n"
}
```

On the other hand, two instances are identical if they refer to the same instance of memory. Identity is used to determine whether two reference types are identical. The === operator is used to check for identity. The following example presents identity checking for two instances of the `User` class that we defined earlier:

```
let tarang = User(name: "Tarang")
let sangeeth = User(name: "Sangeeth")

if tarang === sangeeth {
    print("Identical")
} else {
    print("Not identical")
}
```

The preceding code example prints `Not identical`.

The identity checking operator is available only for reference types.

Equatable and Comparable

We are able to compare two value types such as `String`, `Int`, and `Double`, but we cannot compare two custom value types that we have developed. To make our custom value types comparable, we need to implement `Equatable` and `Comparable` protocols. Let's first examine an example of equality checking without conforming to protocols:

```
struct Point {
    let x: Double
    let y: Double
}

let firstPoint = Point(x: 3.0, y: 5.5)
let secondPoint = Point(x: 7.0, y: 9.5)

let isEqual = (firstPoint == secondPoint)
```

In this example, the compiler will complain that binary operator == cannot be applied to two `Point` operands. Let's fix this problem by conforming to the `Equatable` protocol:

```
struct Point: Equatable {
    let x: Double
    let y: Double
}

func ==(lhs: Point, rhs:Point) -> Bool {
    return (lhs.x == rhs.x) && (lhs.y == lhs.y)
}

let firstPoint = Point(x: 3.0, y: 5.5)
let secondPoint = Point(x: 7.0, y: 9.5)

let isEqual = (firstPoint == secondPoint)
```

The value for `isEqual` is going to be `false` as they are not equal. To be able to compare two points, we need to conform to the `Comparable` protocol. Our example becomes as follows:

```
struct Point: Equatable, Comparable {
    let x: Double
    let y: Double
```

```
    }

    func ==(lhs: Point, rhs:Point) -> Bool {
        return (lhs.x == rhs.x) && (lhs.y == rhs.y)
    }

    func <(lhs: Point, rhs: Point) -> Bool {
        return (lhs.x < rhs.x) && (lhs.y < rhs.y)
    }

    let firstPoint = Point(x: 3.0, y: 5.5)
    let secondPoint = Point(x: 7.0, y: 9.5)

    let isEqual = (firstPoint == secondPoint)
    let isLess = (firstPoint < secondPoint)
```

The result of the comparison will be `true`.

Type checking and casting

Swift provides type checking and type casting. We can check the type of a variable with the `is` keyword. It is most commonly used in `if` statements, as shown in the following code:

```
    let aConstant = "String"

    if aConstant is String {
        print("aConstant is a String")
    } else {
        print("aConstant is not a String")
    }
```

As `String` is a value type and the compiler can infer the type, the Swift compiler will issue a warning because it already knows that `aConstant` is `String`. Another example can be the following, where we check whether `anyString` is `String`:

```
    let anyString: Any = "string"

    if anyString is String {
        print("anyString is a String")
    } else {
        print("anyString is not a String")
    }
```

Using the `is` operator is useful to check the type of a class instance, specifically, the ones that have subclasses. We can use the `is` operator to determine if an object is an instance of a specific class.

Similarly, we can use the `as` operator to actually coerce an object to a type other than what the compiler has inferred it to be. The `as` operator comes in two flavors: the `as!` (forced form) operator and `as?` (conditional form). The former casts the object into the desired type without asking. If the object cannot be cast to that type, a runtime error is thrown. The `as?` operator asks an object if it can be cast to a given type. If the object can be cast, then some value is returned; otherwise, `nil` is returned. The `as?` operator is most often used as part of an `if` statement.

Obviously, it's best to use `as?` whenever possible. We should use `as` only if we know it will not result in a runtime error.

Summary

In this chapter, we looked into types in general and explored reference versus value types in detail. We covered topics such as value and reference type constants, mixing value and reference types, and copying. Then we learned the characteristics of value types, key differences between value and reference types, and how we should decide which one to use. We continued by exploring equality, identity, type checking, and casting topics. Even though we explored the topic of value types, we did not explore a related topic-immutability, in this chapter. `Chapter 9`, *Importance of Immutability* will cover the importance of immutability. Furthermore, for in depth coverage of these concepts it is recommended to watch the following videos: *WWDC 2015--Building Better Apps with Value Types in Swift* (`https://developer.apple.com/videos/play/wwdc2015/414/`), and *WWDC 2016--Protocol and Value Oriented Programming in UIKit Apps* (`https://developer.apple.com/videos/play/wwdc2016/419/`).

In the following chapter, we will explore the enumeration and pattern matching topics. We will familiarize ourselves with associated and raw values. We will be introduce to algebraic data types and finally, we will cover patterns and pattern matching.

4
Enumerations and Pattern Matching

In `Chapter 1`, *Getting Started with Functional Programming in Swift*, we were introduced to enumerations briefly. In the previous chapter we got familiar with types and we learned that enums are *sum* types.

In this chapter, we will cover enumerations and algebraic data types in detail. Also, we will explore patterns and pattern matching in Swift.

This chapter will cover the following topics with coding examples:

- Defining enumerations
- Associated values
- Raw values
- Nesting and containing enumerations
- Using enumerations
- Algebraic data types
- Patterns and pattern matching

Defining enumerations

In Swift, an enumeration defines a common type for related values and enables us to work with those values in a type-safe way. Values provided for each enumeration member can be a `String`, `Character`, `Integer`, or any `floating-point` type.

The following example presents a simple definition of an `enum`:

```
enum MLSTeam {
    case montreal
    case toronto
    case newYork
    case columbus
    case losAngeles
    case seattle
}

let theTeam = MLSTeam.montreal
```

`enum MLSTeam` provides options for MLS teams. We can choose only one of the options each time; in our example, `montreal` is chosen.

Multiple cases can be defined and separated by a comma on a single line:

```
enum MLSTeam {
    case montreal, toronto, newYork, columbus, lA, seattle
}
var theTeam = MLSTeam.montreal
```

The type of `theTeam` is inferred when it is initialized with `MLSTeam.montreal`. As `theTeam` is already defined, we can change it with a shorter syntax as follows:

```
theTeam = .newYork
```

In Swift, enums are very powerful sum types that can have associated and raw values. We will look into these concepts in the upcoming sections of this chapter.

Associated values

Enumerations can store associated values of any given type, and the value types can be different for each member of the enumeration, if required. Enumerations similar to these are known as discriminated unions, tagged unions, or variants in other programming languages. The following example presents a simple usage of associated values:

```
enum Length {
    case us(Double)
    case metric(Double)
}

let lengthMetric = Length.metric(1.6)
```

The enumeration type Length can either take a value of us with an associated value of the Double type or a value of metric with an associated value of the Double type.

The lengthMetric is a variable that gets assigned as a value of Length; metric with an associated value of 1.6.

As seen in the preceding example, associated values are set when we create a new constant or variable based on one of the enumeration's cases and can be different each time we do so.

Raw values

Enumeration members can come prepopulated with default values (called **raw** values), which are all the same type. The following example presents an incomplete HttpErrorenum with raw values:

```
enum HttpError: Int {
    case badRequest = 400
    case unauthorized = 401
    case forbidden = 403
}
```

In the preceding example, the raw values for enum called HttpError are defined to be of the Int type and are set to some of their integer code.

Raw values can be of String, Character, Int, or any floating number types. Each raw value must be unique within its enumeration declaration.

Raw values are set to prepopulated values when we first define the enumeration such as HttpError in the preceding example; therefore, the raw value for an enumeration case is always the same and it is not going to change, unlike associated values.

If we define an enumeration with a raw-value type, the enumeration automatically receives an initializer that takes a value of the raw value's type and returns either an enumeration case or nil. We can use this initializer to try to create a new instance of the enumeration. The following example presents the initialization of an HttpError instance:

```
let possibleError = HttpError(rawValue: 400)
print(possibleError?.rawValue ?? 404) // prints 400
```

Nesting and containing enumerations

Enums are so powerful in Swift that we can have enums, structs, computed properties, and methods in our enums.

We can logically nest an `enum` in another `enum` or `struct` and we can add additional information or context to our `enum` cases using computed properties, nested enums, or methods.

Let's look at an example:

```swift
struct NAAthlete {

    enum Conference {
        case eastern, western

        static func conferenceFrom(division: String) -> Conference {
            if division.contains("Metropolitan") ||
                division.contains("Atlantic") {
                return .eastern
            } else {
                return .western
            }
        }
    }

    enum League {
        case nhl
        case mls
        case nba
        case mlb

        enum Team {
            case montreal
            case anaheim
            var conference: Conference {
                switch self {
                case .montreal: return .eastern
                case .anaheim: return .western
                }
            }
        }
    }

    let league: League
    let team: League.Team
```

```
    func properties() -> (League, League.Team) {
        return (self.league, self.team)
    }
}

let player = NAAthlete(league: .nhl, team: .montreal)
print(player.team.conference) // prints eastern
print(player.properties()) // prints (NAAthlete.League.nhl,
NAAthlete.League.Team.montreal)
print(NAAthlete.Conference.conferenceFrom(division: "Metropolitan")) //
prints eastern
```

In this example, we have a `NAAthlete` `struct` that contains `Conference` and `League` enums, `league` and `team` variables, and a `properties` method. A `League` enum nests a `Team` enum.

By adding a conference computed property, we could add specific information to our `Team` enum. As computed properties and methods exist for all `enum` cases, we can `switch-case` for specific cases. In our example we returned the `conference` of teams in our `Team` enum. We will talk more about this concept in the *Pattern matching* section of this chapter.

Also, we had a static method, `conferenceFrom(division: String)`, to find out the conference from division.

Finally, Swift empowers us to have `mutating` methods in enums that we are not going to recommend.

Algebraic data types

Enumerations in Swift are actually algebraic data types that are types created by combining other types. Algebraic data types are essential to many functional programming languages, such as Haskell.

An algebraic data type is based on the idea of algebraic structures, which are a set of possible values and one or more operators to combine a finite number of these values into a single one. An example structure is (Z, +, -), a set of all integers (in math, Z refers to set of all positive and negative integer numbers) with the plus and minus operations on them.

So an algebraic data type is a data type that is created by algebraic operations, specifically, with sum and product as our operations.

Additionally, algebraic data types are composite data types that may contain multiple values such as a data type with multiple fields, or they may consist of variants or multiple finite different values.

Simple types

The `Boolean` type is a simple algebraic data type as it may take one of two values: `true` or `false`. An instance of a `Boolean` type should be either `true` or `false`, but the instance cannot be both at once; it has to be one or the other, unlike the `struct/class` properties and variables.

Composite types

Algebraic data types can also be composite types. For instance, a `tuple` of two `Double` values is a simple algebraic data type. Such a tuple could be expressed as having the `(Double, Double)` type, and an example value for this type could be `(1.5, 3.2)`.

Composite types with variants

Algebraic data types can be composite types with variants as well. We could create an `enum` named `Dimension` to hold the `length` and `width`. We can express this `enum` in both `us` `feet` and `metric` meters. In Swift, we can define such an `enum` as follows:

```
enum Dimension {
    case us(Double, Double)
    case metric(Double, Double)
}
```

Then we can use the `Dimension` enumeration to create a variable as follows:

```
let sizeMetric = Dimension.metric(5.0, 4.0)
```

The algebra of data types

We have seen that enums in Swift are actually algebraic data types. Let's explore some examples to get more familiar with the topic.

The following example presents a simple enum NHLTeam with different options. Playing hockey is the second biggest sport after snow shoveling in Canada so don't get bored by the NHL examples!

The enum Team uses NHLTeam along with MLSTeam that we defined before to combine Hockey and Soccer teams. Team can be either a Hockey NHL team or a Soccer MLS team:

```
enum NHLTeam {
    case canadiens
    case senators
    case rangers
    case penguins
    case blackHawks
    case capitals
}

enum MLSTeam {
    case montreal
    case toronto
    case newYork
    case columbus
    case losAngeles
    case seattle
}

enum Team {
    case Hockey(NHLTeam)
    case Soccer(MLSTeam)
}

struct HockeyAndSoccerTeams {
    var hockey: NHLTeam
    var soccer: MLSTeam
}
```

MLSTeam and NHLTeam each have six potential values. If we combine them, we will have two new types. Team can be either NHLTeam or MLSTeam, so *it has 12 potential values that is the sum* of NHLTeam and MLSTeam potential values. Therefore, the Team enum is a sum type.

To have a `HockeyAndSoccerTeams` structure, we need to choose one value for `NHLTeam` and one for `MLSTeam` so *it has 36 potential values that are the products of* `NHLTeam` and `MLSTeam` values. Therefore, `HockeyAndSoccerTeams` is a product type.

In Swift, an enumeration's option can have multiple values. If it happens to be the only option, then this enumeration becomes a `product` type. The following example presents an enum as a `product` type:

```
enum HockeyAndSoccerTeams {
    case value(hockey: NHLTeam, soccer: MLSTeam)
}
```

Recursion types are another class of algebraic data types.

A recursive data type is a data type for values that may contain other values of the same type. An important application of recursion in computer science is in defining dynamic data structures such as arrays. Recursive data structures can dynamically grow to a theoretically infinite size in response to runtime requirements.

Operations used to do simple integer arithmetic can be modeled with `enums`. These operations let us combine simple arithmetic expressions. *The Swift Programming Language* by *Apple Inc.* provides an example of simple integer arithmetic:

```
enum ArithmeticExpression {
    case number(Int)
    indirect case addition(ArithmeticExpression, ArithmeticExpression)
    indirect case multiplication(ArithmeticExpression, ArithmeticExpression)
}
```

This enumeration can store three kinds of arithmetic expressions: a plain number, the addition of two expressions, and the multiplication of two expressions. The addition and multiplication cases have associated values that are also arithmetic expressions--these associated values make it possible to nest expressions. For example, the expression (5 + 4) * 2 has a number on the right-hand side of the multiplication and another expression on the left-hand side of the multiplication. Because the data is nested, the enumeration used to store the data also needs to support nesting--this means the enumeration needs to be recursive. The code below shows the `ArithmeticExpression` recursive enumeration being created for (5 + 4) * 2:

```
let five = ArithmeticExpression.number(5)
let four = ArithmeticExpression.number(4)
let sum = ArithmeticExpression.addition(five, four)
let product = ArithmeticExpression.multiplication(sum,
ArithmeticExpression.number(2))
```

Another example of recursive data structures is a `Tree` that is implemented as a recursive data type:

```
enum Tree {
    case empty
    case leaf(Int)
    indirect case node(Tree, Tree)
}

let ourTree = Tree.node(Tree.leaf(1), Tree.node(Tree.leaf(2),
Tree.leaf(3)))
print(ourTree) // prints node(Tree.leaf(1), Tree.node(Tree.leaf(2),
Tree.leaf(3)))
```

`Tree` can be empty, it can have a `leaf`, or another `Tree` as `node`.

As the data is nested, the enumeration used to store the data also needs to support nesting, which means that the enumeration needs to be recursive.

The compiler has to insert a layer of indirection when it works with recursive enumerations. We indicate that an enumeration case is recursive by writing `indirect` before it.

The following example presents the search function on `Tree`:

```
func searchInTree(_ search: Int, tree: Tree) -> Bool {
    switch tree {
    case .leaf(let x):
        return x == search
    case .node(let l, let r):
        return searchInTree(search, tree:l) || searchInTree(search, tree:r)
    default:
        return false
    }
}

let isFound = searchInTree(3, tree: ourTree)
print(isFound) // prints true
```

As we can create `sum`, `product`, or `recursion` types in Swift, we can say that Swift has first-class support for algebraic data types.

Pattern matching

Programming languages that support algebraic data types often support a set of features to work with fields of composite types or variants of a type. These features are essential in defining functions to operate on different fields or variants in a type-safe manner.

One such feature is called **pattern matching**, that enables us to define functions that operate differently on each of a type's variants and extract individual fields from a composite type while maintaining the language's type safety guarantees.

In fact, the compilers of many languages with pattern matching will issue warnings or errors if we do not handle all of a type's fields or variants properly. These warnings help us write safer and more robust code.

The following example presents simple pattern matching with a switch statement:

```
let theTeam = MLSTeam.montreal

switch theTeam {
case .montreal:
    print("Montreal Impact")
case .toronto:
    print("Toronto FC")
case .newYork:
    print("Newyork Redbulls")
case .columbus:
    print("Columbus Crew")
case .losAngeles:
    print("LA Galaxy")
case .seattle:
    print("Seattle Sounders")
}
```

In this example, the Swift compiler infers `theTeam` as `MLSTeam`; therefore, we do not need to write `MLSTeam` for each case.

We use the `switch case` to match the pattern as it is a basic way of pattern matching for enumerations in Swift. This code block will `print Montreal Impact` as it matches the `.montreal` case.

To further explore pattern matching, we can look at an other example, the `Dimension` enumeration. Using pattern matching, it is easy to write a `function`, convert that will take `Dimension` as a parameter and convert it to the other variant (us measurements to metric and vice versa):

```
func convert(dimension: Dimension) -> Dimension {
    switch dimension {
    case let .us(length, width):
        return .metric(length * 0.304, width * 0.304)
    case let .metric(length, width):
        return .us(length * 3.280, width * 3.280)
    }
}

let convertedDimension = convert(dimension: Dimension.metric(5.0, 4.0))
print(convertedDimension)
```

In this function, we check for the `dimension` type with a `switch case` code block. We extract the associated values with our `let` statement and use `length` and `width` in our return statement.

To test our function, we provide a `metric` dimension of `5.0` and `4.0` so that the resulting `us length` will be approximately `16.4` and the `us width` will be approximately `13.12`.

Swift requires us to handle all the cases of an enumerated type; if we do not cover all the cases, the Swift compiler will warn us and prevent us from introducing runtime errors. For instance, if we remove the second case, the compiler will warn us, as shown in the following screenshot:

```
enum Dimension {
    case us(Double, Double)
    case metric(Double, Double)
}

func convert(dimension: Dimension) -> Dimension {
    switch dimension {
    case let .us(length, width):
        return .metric(length * 0.304, width * 0.304)
    }                                    ❶ Switch must be exhaustive, consider adding a default clause
}

let convertedDimension = convert(dimension: Dimension.metric(5.0, 4.0))
print(convertedDimension)
```

If we have a lot of cases that we want to handle generically, we can use the `default` keyword. As an example, let's add a `default` case to our `convert` function:

```
func convert(dimension: Dimension) -> Dimension {
    switch dimension {
    case let .us(length, width):
        return .metric(length * 0.304, width * 0.304)
    default:
        return .us(0.0, 0.0)
    }
}
```

The preceding example serves only as a `default` usage example and we should avoid a `default` case as much as possible.

Patterns and pattern matching

In the previous section, we looked at simple pattern matching examples for enumerations. In this section, we will examine patterns and pattern matching in detail.

The wildcard pattern

The wildcard pattern matches and ignores any value. It consists of an underscore, `_`. We use a wildcard pattern when we do not care about the values being matched against.

For instance, the following code example ignores the matched values:

```
for _ in 1...5 {
    print("The value in range is ignored")
}
```

We use _ to ignore the value in the iteration.

The wildcard pattern can be used with optionals as follows:

```
let anOptionalString: String? = nil

switch anOptionalString {
case _?: print ("Some")
case nil: print ("None")
}
```

As seen from the preceding example, we matched an optional by _?.

The wildcard pattern can be used to ignore data that we do not need and values that we do not want to match against. The following code example presents the way in which we use the wildcard pattern to ignore the data:

```
let twoNumbers = (3.14, 1.618)

switch twoNumbers {
case (_, let phi): print("phi: \(phi)")
}
```

The value-binding pattern

A value-binding pattern binds matched values to variable or constant names. The following example presents the value binding pattern by binding x to 5 and y to 7:

```
let position = (5, 7)

switch position {
case let (x, y): print("x:\(x), y:\(y)")
}
```

The identifier pattern

An identifier pattern matches any value and binds the matched value to a variable or constant name. For instance, in the following example, ourConstant is an identifier pattern that matches the value of 7:

```
let ourConstant = 7

switch ourConstant {
case 7: print("7")
default: print("a value")
}
```

An identifier pattern is a sub-pattern of the value-binding pattern.

The tuple pattern

A tuple pattern is a comma-separated list of zero or more patterns, enclosed in parentheses. Tuple patterns match values of corresponding tuple types.

We can constrain a tuple pattern to match certain kinds of tuple types using type annotations. For instance, the tuple pattern `(x, y): (Double, Double)` in the declaration, `let (x, y): (Double, Double) = (3, 7)`, matches only tuple types in which both elements are of the `Double` type.

In the following example, we match the pattern by binding the `name`, checking whether `age` has a value, and finally, if the `address` is of the `String` type. We use only the `name` that we need and, for `age` and `address`, we use the wildcard pattern to ignore the values:

```
let name = "John"
let age: Int? = 27
let address: String? = "New York, New York, US"

switch (name, age, address) {
case (let name, _?, _): print(name)
default: ()
}
```

The enumeration case pattern

An enumeration `case` pattern matches a `case` of an existing enumeration type. Enumeration case patterns appear in a `switch` statement's `case` labels and `case` conditions of `if`, `while`, `guard`, and `for-in` statements.

If the enumeration `case` that we are trying to match has any associated values, the corresponding enumeration case pattern must specify a tuple pattern that contains one element for each associated value. The following example presents the enumeration case pattern:

```
let dimension = Dimension.metric(9.0, 6.0)

func convert(dimension: Dimension) -> Dimension {
    switch dimension {
    case let .us(length, width):
        return .metric(length * 0.304, width * 0.304)
    case let .metric(length, width):
        return .us(length * 3.280, width * 3.280)
    }
}
```

```
print(convert(dimension: dimension))
```

In the preceding example, we use *tuple pattern* for each associated value (`length` and `width`).

The optional pattern

An optional pattern matches values wrapped in a `Some (Wrapped)` case of an `Optional<Wrapped>` or `ImplicitlyUnwrappedOptional<Wrapped>` enumeration. Optional patterns consist of an identifier pattern followed immediately by a question mark and appear in the same places as enumeration case patterns. The following example presents optional pattern matching:

```
let anOptionalString: String? = nil

switch anOptionalString {
case let something?: print("\(something)")
case nil: print ("None")
}
```

Type casting patterns

There are two types of casting patterns as follows:

- `is`: This matches the type against the right-hand side of the expression
- `as`: This casts the type to the left-hand side of the expression

The following example presents the `is` and `as` type casting patterns:

```
let anyValue: Any = 7

switch anyValue {
case is Int: print(anyValue + 3)
case let ourValue as Int: print(ourValue + 3)
default: ()
}
```

The `anyValue` variable is type of `Any` storing, an `Int` value, then the first case is going to be matched but the compiler will complain, as shown in the following screenshot:

```
let anyValue: Any = 7

switch anyValue {
case is Int: print(anyValue + 3)                    ⊘ Binary operator '+' cannot be applied to operands of type 'Any' and 'Int'
case let ourValue as Int: print(ourValue + 3)
default: ()
}
```

We could cast `anyValue` to `Int` with `as!` to resolve the issue.

The first case is already matched. The second case will not be reached. Suppose that we had a non-matching case as the first case, as shown in the following example:

```
let anyValue: Any = 7

switch anyValue {
case is Double: print(anyValue)
case let ourValue as Int: print(ourValue + 3)
default: ()
}
```

In this scenario, the second case would be matched and cast `anyValue` to `Int` and bind it to `ourValue`, then we will be able to use `ourValue` in our statement.

The expression pattern

An expression pattern represents the value of an expression. Expression patterns appear only in a `switch` statement's `case` labels. The expression represented by the expression pattern is compared with the value of an input expression using the `~=` operator.

The matching succeeds if the `~=` operator returns `true`. By default, the `~=` operator compares two values of the same type using the `==` operator. The following example presents an example of the expression pattern:

```
let position = (3, 5)

switch position {
case (0, 0):
    print("(0, 0) is at the origin.")
case (-4...4, -6...6):
    print("(\(position.0), \(position.1)) is near the origin.")
default:
```

```
        print("The position is:(\(position.0), \(position.1)).")
    }
```

We can overload the ~= operator to provide custom expression matching behavior.

For instance, we can rewrite the preceding example to compare the position expression with a `String` representation of positions:

```
func ~=(pattern: String, value: Int) -> Bool {
    return pattern == "\(value)"
}

switch position {
case ("0", "0"):
    print("(0, 0) is at the origin.")
default:
    print("The position is: (\(position.0), \(position.1)).")
}
```

Summary

This chapter explained the enumeration definition and usage. We covered associated and raw values and an introduction to the concept of algebraic data types. We explored some examples to cover the sum, product, and recursion types. We will use the concept of algebraic data types in Chapter 8, *Functional Data Structures* when we talk about functional data structures. In this chapter, we explored patterns such as wildcard, value-binding, identifier, tuple, enumeration case, optional, type casting, and expressions, along with related pattern matching examples.

The next chapter will cover generics and associated type protocols that are very useful tools in functional programming, generic programming, and protocol-oriented programming.

5
Generics and Associated Type Protocols

Generics enable us to write flexible and reusable functions, methods, and types that can work with any type. This chapter explains how to define and use Generics and introduces the problems that can be solved with Generics in the Swift programming language with examples.

This chapter will cover the following topics with coding examples:

- Generic functions and methods
- Generic parameters
- Generic type constraints and `where` clauses
- Generic data structures
- Associated type protocols
- Type erasure
- Extending Generic types
- Subclassing Generic classes

What are Generics and what kind of problems do they solve?

Swift is a type-safe language. Whenever we work with types, we need to specify them. For instance, a function can have specific parameters and return types. We cannot pass any types but the ones that are specified. What if we need a function that can handle more than one type?

We already know that Swift provides `Any` and `AnyObject`, but it is not good practice to use them unless we have to. Using `Any` and `AnyObject` will make our code fragile as we will not be able to catch type mismatching during compile time. Generics are the solution to our problem. Let's examine an example first. The following function simply swaps two values (a and b). The values a and b are of the `Int` type. We should pass only `Int` values to this function to be able to compile the application:

```
func swapTwoValues(a: inout Int, b: inout Int) {
    let tempA = a
    a = b
    b = tempA
}
```

Type safety is supposed to be a good thing, but it makes our code less generic in this case. What if we want to swap two `Strings`? Should we replace this function with a new one?

```
func swapTwoValues(a: inout String, b: inout String) {
    let tempA = a
    a = b
    b = tempA
}
```

The bodies of these two functions are identical. The only difference is the function type, more specifically, the parameter types. Some may think it is a good idea to change these parameter types to `Any` or `AnyObject`. Remembering that `AnyObject` can represent an instance of any class type and `Any` can represent an instance of any type, excluding function types, let's assume that we change the types to `Any`:

```
func swapTwoValues(a: Any, b: Any) -> (a: Any, b: Any) {
    let temp = a
    let newA = b
    let newB = temp
    return (newA, newB)
}
```

Our API user can go ahead and send any types as parameters. They may not match. The compiler is not going to complain. Let's examine the following example:

```
var name = "John Doe"
var phoneNumber = 5141111111

let (a, b) = swapTwoValues(a: name, b: phoneNumber)
```

Our function is called by `String` and `Int` parameters. Our function swaps two values so the returned a becomes `Int` and b becomes `String`. This will make our code easily breakable and very hard to follow.

We do not want to be that flexible! We do not want to use `Any` and `AnyObject`, but we still need some level of flexibility. Generics are the solution to our problem. We can make this function generic and robust using Generics. Let's examine the following example:

```
func swapTwoValues<T>(a: T, b: T) -> (a: T, b: T) {
    let temp = a
    let newA = b
    let newB = temp
    return (newA, newB)
}
```

In this example, we replaced `Any` with `T`. It could be anything that is not defined already in our code or that is not a part of the SDK. We put this type inside <> after the function name and before its parameters. Then we use this type in the parameter or return type. This way, we tell the compiler that our function accepts a Generic type. Any type can be passed to this function, but both parameters and return types have to be of the same type. So, our API user is not going to be able to pass `String` and `Int` as follows:

```
let (a, b) = swapTwoValues(a: name, b: phoneNumber)
```

As seen in the following screenshot, the compiler complains about the type mismatch:

```
var name = "John Doe"
var phoneNumber = 5141111111

let (a, b) = swapTwoValues(a: name, b: phoneNumber)
                                    Cannot invoke 'swapTwoValues' with an argument list of type '(a: @lvalue String, b: @lvalue Int)'
```

The use of Generics makes our code type-safe and flexible so that we can use it for different types without worrying about type mismatching problems.

Generics are great tools in FP because with them we can develop powerful, multipurpose, and generic functions and types. Let's examine a functional example of Generic usage.

In `Chapter 2`, *Functions and Closures*, we had an example like the following one. Suppose that we need to develop a function that adds two `Int` values, as follows:

```
func addTwoValues(a: Int, b: Int) -> Int {
    return a + b
}
```

Also, we need to develop a function to calculate the square of an `Int` value:

```
func square(a: Int) -> Int {
    return a * a
}
```

Suppose that we need to add two squared values:

```
func addTwoSquaredValues(a: Int, b: Int) -> Int {
    return (a * a) + (b * b)
}
```

What if we needed to develop functions to multiply, subtract, or divide two squared values?

The answer is to use higher-order functions to write a flexible function, as follows:

```
typealias AddSubtractOperator = (Int, Int) -> Int
typealias SquareTripleOperator = (Int) -> Int

func calculate(a: Int,
               b: Int,
               funcA: AddSubtractOperator,
               funcB: SquareTripleOperator) -> Int {

    return funcA(funcB(a), funcB(b))
}
```

This higher-order function takes two other functions as parameters and uses them. We can call it for different scenarios, such as the following one:

```
print("The result of adding two squared values is: \(calculate(a: 2, b: 2,
funcA: addTwoValues, funcB: square))") // prints "The result of adding two
squared value is: 8"
```

Using higher-order functions makes them flexible and more generic but still not that generic! These functions work only with `Int` values. Using Generics, we can make them work with any numerical type. Let's make our `calculate` function even more generic:

```
func calculate<T>(a: T,
                  b: T,
                  funcA: (T, T) -> T,
                  funcB: (T) -> T) -> T {

    return funcA(funcB(a), funcB(b))
}
```

The calculate function accepts two values of the same type (T) and two functions. The funcA function accepts two values of the T type and returns a value of the T type. The funcB function accepts one value of the T type and returns a value of the same T type.

We can use the `calculate` function with any type now. For instance, we can pass any number and the function will calculate it for that specific type.

There are two things to notice here. Firstly, the same techniques can be applied to methods, and secondly, we can define `typealiases` with Generic types directly in Swift 3.0:

```
typealias AddSubtractOperator<T> = (T, T) -> T
typealias SquareTripleOperator<T> = (T) -> T

func calculate<T>(a: T,
                  b: T,
                  funcA: AddSubtractOperator<T>,
                  funcB: SquareTripleOperator<T>) -> T {

    return funcA(funcB(a), funcB(b))
}

print("The result of adding two squared values is: \(calcualte(a: 2, b: 2,
funcA: addTwoValues, funcB: square))") // prints "The result of adding two
squared value is: 8"
```

Type constraints

It is great that our function works with any type, but what if our API user tries to use the `calculate` function on types that cannot be used in arithmetic calculations?

To mitigate this problem, we can use type constraints. Using type constraints, we will be able to enforce the use of a certain type. Type constraints specify that a type parameter must inherit from a specific class or conform to a particular protocol or protocol composition. Collections are examples of type constraints that we are already familiar with in the Swift programming language. Collections are Generics in Swift, so we can have arrays of Int, Double, String, and so on.

Unlike Objective-C, where we could have different types in a collection, in Swift we need to have the same type that complies to the type constraint. For instance, the keys of a dictionary must conform to the Hashable protocol.

We can specify type constraints with either of the following two syntaxes:

```
<T: Class> or <T: Protocol>
```

Let's go back to our `calculate` example and define a numerical type constraint. There are different protocols, such as `Hashable` and `Equatable`. However, none of these protocols are going to solve our problem. The easiest solution would be defining our protocol and extending the types that we want to use by conforming to our protocol. This is a Generic approach that can be used to solve similar problems:

```
protocol NumericType {
    static func +(lhs: Self, rhs: Self) -> Self
    static func -(lhs: Self, rhs: Self) -> Self
    static func *(lhs: Self, rhs: Self) -> Self
    static func /(lhs: Self, rhs: Self) -> Self
    static func %(lhs: Self, rhs: Self) -> Self
}
```

We define a protocol for numeric types with related basic math operators. We will require the types that we want to use to conform to our protocol. So we extend them as follows:

```
extension Double : NumericType { }
extension Float  : NumericType { }
extension Int    : NumericType { }
extension Int8   : NumericType { }
extension Int16  : NumericType { }
extension Int32  : NumericType { }
extension Int64  : NumericType { }
extension UInt   : NumericType { }
extension UInt8  : NumericType { }
extension UInt16 : NumericType { }
extension UInt32 : NumericType { }
extension UInt64 : NumericType { }
```

Finally, we need to define the type constraint in our function as follows:

```
func calculate<T: NumericType>(a: T,
                               b: T,
                               funcA: (T, T) -> T,
                               funcB: (T) -> T) -> T {

    return funcA(funcB(a), funcB(b))
}

func addTwoValues(a: Int, b: Int) -> Int {
    return a + b
}
```

```
func square(a: Int) -> Int {
    return a * a
}

print("The result of adding two squared values is: \(calculate(a: 2, b: 2,
funcA: addTwoValues, funcB: square))") // prints "The result of adding two
squared value is: 8"
```

Thus, we have a function that only accepts numerical types. Let's test it with a non-numeric type to ensure its correctness:

```
func format(a: String) -> String {
    return "formatted \(a)"
}

func appendStrings(a: String, b: String) -> String {
    return a + b
}

print("The result is: \(calculate(a: "2", b: "2", funcA: appendStrings, funcB: format))")
```
Cannot convert value of type '(String, String) -> String' to expected argument type '(_, _) -> _'

This code example does not compile because of our type constraint.

The where clauses

The where clause can be used to define more complex type constraints, for instance, to conform to more than one protocol with some constraints.

We can specify additional requirements on type parameters and their associated types by including a where clause after the Generic parameter list. A where clause consists of the where keyword, followed by a comma-separated list of one or more requirements.

For instance, we can express the constraints that a Generic type T inherits from a C class and conforms to a V protocol as <T where T: C, T: V>.

We can constrain the associated types of type parameters to conform to protocols. Let's consider the following Generic parameter clause:

```
<Seq: SequenceType where Seq.Generator.Element: Equatable>
```

Here, it specifies that Seq conforms to the SequenceType protocol and the associated Seq.Generator.Element type conforms to the Equatable protocol. This constraint ensures that each element of the sequence is Equatable.

We can also specify that two types should be identical using the == operator. Let's consider the following Generic parameter clause:

```
<Seq1: SequenceType, Seq2: SequenceType where Seq1.Generator.Element ==
Seq2.Generator.Element>
```

Here, it expresses the constraints that `Seq1` and `Seq2` conform to the `SequenceType` protocol and the elements of both sequences must be of the same type.

Any type argument substituted for a type parameter must meet all the constraints and requirements placed on the type parameter.

We can overload a Generic function or initializer by providing different constraints, requirements, or both on the type parameters in the Generic parameter clause. When we call an overloaded Generic function or initializer, the compiler uses these constraints to resolve which overloaded function or initializer to invoke.

Generic data structures

In addition to Generic functions, Swift empowers us to define our own Generic types and data structures. In Chapter 4, *Enumerations and Pattern Matching*, we developed a simple tree with enumeration. Let's make it Generic so that it can take different types as its `leaf` and `node`:

```
enum GenericTree <T> {
    case empty
    case leaf(T)
    indirect case node(GenericTree, GenericTree)
}

print(GenericTree.node(GenericTree.leaf("First"),
GenericTree.node(GenericTree.leaf("Second"), GenericTree.leaf("Third"))))
// prints node(GenericTree<Swift.String>.leaf("First"),
GenericTree<Swift.String>.node(GenericTree<Swift.String>.leaf("Second"),
GenericTree<Swift.String>.leaf("Third")))
```

With Generics, our tree, which could accept only `Int` as a `leaf`, became a Generic tree that can accept any type.

Using Generics, it is possible to develop simple and Generic types or data structures such as graphs, linked lists, stacks, and queues.

Let's examine a **queue** data structure example by making a `struct` Generic. Queue is a well-known data structure in computer science that provides a means to store items in the **First In First Out** (**FIFO**) order. A Generic queue will be able to store any type in the FIFO order. The following example is not a complete implementation of a queue, but it gives an idea about how Generics can help develop Generic data structures. Also, it is not a functional data structure as it has mutable variables and functions. In `Chapter 8`, *Functional Data Structures*, we will explore the functional data structures in detail:

```
struct Queue<Element> {
    private var elements = [Element]()
    mutating func enQueue(newElement: Element) {
        elements.append(newElement)
    }

    mutating func deQueue() -> Element? {
        guard !elements.isEmpty else {
            return nil
        }
        return elements.remove(at: 0)
    }
}
```

Associated type protocols

So far, have to made functions, methods, and types Generic. Can we make protocols Generic too? The answer is no, we cannot, but protocols support a similar feature named **associated types**. Associated types give placeholder names or aliases to types that are used as part of the protocol. The actual type to use for an associated type is not specified until the protocol is adopted. Associated types are specified with the `associatedtype` keyword. Let's examine the following example:

```
protocol CustomView {
    associatedtype ViewType
    func configure(view with: ViewType)
}
```

This protocol defines a `configure` method that takes any item of the `ViewType` type. This protocol does not specify how the items in the `CustomView` should be configured or what type they should be. The protocol only specifies a `configure` method that any type must provide to be considered a `CustomView`.

Any type that conforms to the `CustomView` protocol should be able to specify the type of view that it configures. Specifically, it must ensure that only items of the right type are configured.

To define these requirements, the `CustomView` protocol requires a placeholder to refer to the type of view that a `CustomView` will configure, without knowing what that type is for a specific custom view. The `CustomView` protocol needs to specify that any object passed to the `configure` method must have the same type as the `ViewType` of the `CustomView`.

To achieve this, the `CustomView` protocol declares an associated type called `ViewType`, written as `associatedtype ViewType`.

The protocol does not define what `ViewType` is an `associatedtype` for, and this information is left for any conforming type to provide. Nonetheless, `ViewType` `associatedtype` provides us with a way to refer to the type of the view and define a type to use with `configure`.

The following example shows how we will conform to a protocol with an associated type:

```
struct Button {}

struct CustomEnabledButton: CustomView {
    typealias ViewType = Button
    func configure(view with: ViewType) {
        // configure the view
        print("Enabled button")
    }
}

var customEnabledButton = CustomEnabledButton()
customEnabledButton.configure(view: Button())
print(customEnabledButton)
```

Here, we define a new `struct` that conforms to the `CostumView` protocol and takes `Button` as `ViewType`.

Type erasure

In `Chapter 3`, *Types and Type Casting* we talked about **Abstract** versus **Concrete** types. Type erasure is a process to make abstract types such as Generics concrete.

Why we would want to do it? The answer is because we want to write code against contracts; in other words, we want to prefer composition over inheritance. Also, sometimes we would want to be more flexible with the types. This concept may sound complicated, so let's continue our example from the previous section to understand why and how we would create type-erased structures.

First, we want to examine if we can use `CustomView` type and create an array with `CustomView` elements. We will create a `CustomView`:

```
struct CustomDisabledButton: CustomView {
    typealias ViewType = Button
    func configure(view with: ViewType) {
        // configure the view
        print("Disabled button")
    }
}
```

So far, we've created two `CustomViews`; the first one represents a custom enabled button and the second one represents a disabled button.

As we have two `structs` with the type of `CustomView`, we should be able to create an array with them:

```
let customViews = [CustomEnabledButton(), CustomDisabledButton()]
```

But the compiler complains that `Heterogeneous collection literal could only be inferred to '[Any]'; add explicit type annotation if this is intentional`. This means that the compiler does not see them as the same type.

Maybe type annotation can help us:

```
let customViews: [CustomView] = [CustomSwitch(), CustomEnabledButton(),
                        CustomDisabledButton()]
```

This time, the compiler complains that `Protocol 'CustomView' can only be used as a generic constraint because it has Self or associated type requirements`.

This error message is misleading because we cannot specialize an associated type using Generic syntax and protocols cannot be Generic.

Type erasure is the solution to our problem. Let's create a type-erased `AnyCustomView`:

```
struct AnyCustomView<ViewType>: CustomView {
    private let _configure: (ViewType) -> Void
```

```
    init<Base: CustomView>(_ base: Base) where ViewType ==
    Base.ViewType {
        _configure = base.configure
    }

    func configure(view with: ViewType) {
        _configure(with)
    }
}
```

`AnyCustomView` is the type-erased version of `CustomView` and we can use it as a type when we create an array:

```
let views = [AnyCustomView(CustomEnabledButton()),
AnyCustomView(CustomDisabledButton())]

let button = Button()

for view in views {
    view.configure(view: button)
    print(view)
}
```

This time, the compiler does not complain and prints the following:

```
Enabled button
AnyCustomView<Button>(_configure: (Function))
Disabled button
AnyCustomView<Button>(_configure: (Function))
```

This is what we needed. Let's see if we can trick the compiler to add a `CustomView` with a different `ViewType` into an array:

```
struct Switch {}

struct CustomSwitch: CustomView {
    typealias ViewType = Switch
    func configure(view with: ViewType) {
        // configure the view
        print("Custom switch")
    }
}

let views = [AnyCustomView(CustomSwitch()),
AnyCustomView(CustomDisabledButton())]
```

Again, the compiler will complain that `error: heterogeneous collection literal could only be inferred to '[Any]'; add explicit type annotation if this is intentional`, and that is desirable because we tried to add a custom switch and a custom button to the same array. In Swift, array elements should have the same type, so we should not be able to do that. As seen from the preceding example, we were able to be more flexible with our type while we did not sacrifice type safety.

Type erasure empowers us to convert a protocol with associated types into a Generic type. Therefore, we will be able to use them as types when we define properties or parameters of functions, or when we return values. In fact, in any case that we cannot use protocols directly we will be able to use type-erased versions.

Extending Generic types

In Swift, it is possible to extend a Generic type. For instance, we can extend our `Queue` example `struct` and add new behaviors to it:

```
extension Queue {
    func peek() -> Element? {
        return elements.first
    }
}
```

As seen in this example, we were able to use the Generic `Element` type in the extension.

Subclassing Generic classes

In Swift, it is possible to subclass a Generic class. Suppose that we have a Generic `Container` class. There are two different ways to subclass it. In our first example, `GenericContainer` subclasses the `Container` class and stays as a Generic class. In our second example, `SpecificContainer` subclasses `Container` and becomes a `Container` of `Int`; therefore, it is not Generic anymore:

```
class Container<Item> {
}

// GenericContainer stays generic
class GenericContainer<Item>: Container<Item> {
}

// SpecificContainer becomes a container of Int type
```

```
class SpecificContainer: Container<Int> {
}
```

Generics manifesto

Even though Swift 3 provides great Generics features, it is not complete. According to the *Generics Manifesto*, there are a number of Generics features the standard library requires to fully realize its vision, including *"recursive protocol constraints, and the ability to make a constrained extension conform to a new protocol"* (that is, an `array` of `Equatable` elements is `Equatable`). Swift 3.0 should provide those Generics features needed by the standard library, because they affect the standard library's **application binary interface (ABI)**.

An ABI is the interface between two program modules, at the level of machine code. An ABI determines how functions are called and in which binary format information should be passed from one program component to the next.

The Generics Manifesto, which is accessible via `https://github.com/apple/swift/blob/master/docs/GenericsManifesto.md`, and the Swift ABI Stability Manifesto, which is accessible via `https://github.com/apple/swift/blob/master/docs/ABIStabilityManifesto.md`, are great reads for the curious.

Summary

In this chapter, we understood how to define and use Generics. We also understood the types of problem Generics solve. Then we explored type constraints, Generic data structures, associated type protocols, and type erasure with examples.

Generics are great tools that, once you are accustomed to them, make your code more flexible, useful, and robust, so we will use them a lot in the rest of the book.

In the following chapter, we will be introduced to some category theory concepts, such as Functors, Applicative Functors, and Monads. We will also explore higher-order functions such as *map*, *filter*, and *reduce*.

6
Map, Filter, and Reduce

In previous chapters, we briefly touched on the `map` function as an example of a built-in higher-order function. In this chapter, we will explore this topic further and get familiar with the `map`, `flatMap`, `filter`, and `reduce` functions in Swift, together with examples. We will also get familiar with the category/type theory concepts such as higher-kinded types (Monad, Functor, and Applicative Functor).

This chapter will cover the following topics with coding examples:

- Functors
- Applicative Functors
- Monads
- The map function
- The flatMap method
- The filter function
- The reduce function
- The apply function
- The join function
- Chaining higher-order functions
- The zip function
- Practical examples

Collections are used everywhere in our day-to-day development, and to be able to use collections declaratively, we need means such as `map`, `filter`, and `reduce`. Before going through these functions that are built into Swift, let's explore the theoretical background of these concepts.

Higher-kinded types

Higher-kinded types have the ability to reason about generic types with their type parameters as variables. Functors, Monads, and Applicative Functors are higher-kinded types and are not supported natively in the Swift 3.0 type system!

For curious readers, it is recommended to read the *Swift Evolution Proposal* (`https://lists.swift.org/pipermail/swift-evolution/Week-of-Mon-20151214/002736.html`) and the *Generic manifesto* (`https://github.com/apple/swift/blob/master/docs/GenericsManifesto.md#higher-kinded-types`).

According to the *Generic Manifesto*, higher-kinded types allow us to express the relationship between two different specializations of the same nominal type within a protocol. For example, if we think of the `Self` type in a `protocol` as really being `Self<T>`, it allows us to talk about the relationship between `Self<T>` and `Self<U>` for some other type `U`. For instance, it could allow the `map` operation on a collection to return a collection of the same kind but with a different operation, for example:

```
let intArray: Array<Int> = [1, 2, 3]
let newArray = intArray.map { String($0) } // produces Array<String>
let intSet: Set<Int> = [1, 2, 3]
let newSet = intSet.map { String($0) }   // produces Set<String>
```

This proposal suggests to use `~=` as a similarity constraint to describe a `Functor` protocol:

```
protocol Functor {
    associatedtype A
    func fmap<FB where FB ~= Self>(f: A -> FB.A) -> FB
}
```

Here, the `map` function declaration specifies a function, `fmap`, on the `Self` type (where `Self` is a `Functor` with `associatedtype A`) with the type parameter `FB`, that is the same kind of `Functor` as `Self`, with an arbitrarily different `A` type alias. We will talk about map in detail in the *The map function* section of this chapter.

As Swift 3.0 does not support higher-kinded types, we are not going to dive deeper in to these topics. We will consider `Functor`, Monad, and Applicative Functor concepts briefly in upcoming sections and outline their part in Swift functional programming. As these concepts are not very easy to grasp and may not be very practical for most readers, we will not dive deep in to these topics. For curious readers, it is highly recommended to read references such as *Swift Functors, Applicatives, and Monads in pictures*, which can be found here: `http://www.mokacoding.com/blog/functor-applicative-monads-in-pictures/`.

Functors

In Chapter 3, *Types and Type Casting*, we talked a little about category theory. Here we go a little further in category theory and talk about Functors. A Functor contains morphisms such as a map function, which transforms the Functor. We can think about a Functor as a functional design pattern.

Knowing category theory is great, but we do not have to. So simply put, a Functor is a structure or container that we can map over. In other words, a Functor is any type that implements the map function. Examples of Functors are Dictionary, Array, Set, Optional, and Closure types.

A Functor applies morphisms or functions to the values it contains, instead of itself. Suppose if we call a function such as doSomething(param: Double), then it will require a Double argument to be passed as a parameter. If we have an Optional<Double>, doSomething(param: Double) will not know how to deal with it. But as Optional<Double> is a Functor, it will understand how to take doSomething and execute it on the value inside itself, then return a new Optional.

Simply put, whenever we talk about Functors, the first thing that should come to our mind is containers that we can call the map function over them and transform them.

We will talk about the map function in more detail in the upcoming sections and explore the usage of Functors.

Applicative Functors

An Applicative Functor is a Functor equipped with a function that takes a value to an instance of a Functor containing that value. Applicative Functors provide us with the ability to operate on not just values, but values in a functorial context, such as optionals, without needing to unwrap or map over their contents.

Let's suppose that we have an *optional Functor* (an optional that has the map function), and suppose we cannot directly apply the map function on optionals as we need to unwrap them first. Applicative Functors come to the rescue. They add a new function, for instance, apply to the Functor to make it possible to apply map on the Functor.

In other words, Applicative Functors enable us to put a function inside a container or `Functor`. Remember that Functors are containers with `map` functions! Suppose we want to have a function in the `Functor` and `apply` it to values in another `Functor` of the same kind. For instance, we can extend a `Functor` by adding an `apply` function that takes a function and applies it to the `Functor`.

So, Applicative Functors are Functors with `apply` functions. We will talk about the `apply` function in an upcoming section.

Monads

A Monad is a type of `Functor`, a type that, along with `map`, implements the `flatMap` function. It is simple, right? We have a `Functor` with an extra functionality, and that's the `flatMap` implementation. So, any types that we can call `map` and `flatMap` functions over are Monads. Arrays and optionals are examples of Monads.

Monads are Functors with `flatMap` functions! In the following sections, we will talk about `map` and `flatMap` functions.

So far, we have learned that Functors are structures with `map` functions. Applicative Functors are Functors with `apply` functions and Monads are Functors with `flatMap` functions. Now, let's talk about these important functions.

The map function

Swift has a built-in higher-order function named `map` that can be used with collection types such as arrays. The `map` function solves the problem of transforming the elements of an array using a function. The following example presents two different approaches to transform a set of numbers:

```
let numbers = [10, 30, 91, 50, 100, 39, 74]
var formattedNumbers: [String] = []

for number in numbers {
    let formattedNumber = "\(number)$"
    formattedNumbers.append(formattedNumber)
}

let mappedNumbers = numbers.map { "\($0)$" }
```

The first approach to solve the problem is imperative and uses a `for-in` loop to go through the collection and transform each element in the array. This iteration technique is known as external iteration because we specify how to iterate. It requires us to explicitly access the elements sequentially from beginning to end. Also, it is required to create a variable that is mutated repeatedly while the task is performed in the loop.

This process is error-prone as we could initialize `formattedNumbers` incorrectly. Instead of the external iteration technique, we can use the internal iteration technique.

Without specifying how to iterate through the elements or declare and use any mutable variables, Swift can determine how to access all the elements to perform the task and hide the details from us. This technique is known as internal iteration.

One of the internal iteration methods is the `map` method. The `map` method elegantly simplifies our code and makes it declarative. Let's examine the second approach using the `map` function this time:

```
let mappedNumbers = numbers.map { "\($0)$" }
```

As seen in the preceding example, we could achieve the same result in one line of code. One of the benefits of using `map` is that we can clearly declare the transformation that we are trying to apply to the list of elements. The `map` function allows us to declare what we want to achieve rather than how it is implemented. This makes reading and reasoning about our code simpler.

The `map` function can be applied to any container type that wraps a value or multiple values inside itself. Any container that provides the `map` function becomes the `Functor`, as we have seen previously.

We know what the benefits of the `map` function/method usage are and how it is used. Let's explore the dynamics of it and create a `map` function.

In Chapter 5, *Generics and Associated Type Protocols,* we had the following example:

```
func calculate<T>(a: T,
                  b: T,
                  funcA: (T, T) -> T,
                  funcB: (T) -> T) -> T {
    return funcA(funcB(a), funcB(b))
}
```

The `calculate` function could take a, b, `funcA`, and `funcB` as parameters. Let's simplify this function with only two parameters and change the return type:

```
func calculate<T, U>(a: T, funcA: (T) -> U) -> U  {
    return funcA(a)
}
```

Now, the `calculate` function takes a of type T and `funcA` that transforms T into U. The `calculate` function returns U. Even though this function does not work on arrays, it would be easy to add the array transformation:

```
func calculate<T, U>(a: [T], funcA: ([T]) -> [U]) -> [U] {
    return funcA(a)
}
```

So far, we have a `calculate` function that takes an array of the generic type T and a function that transforms an array of T into an array of U and finally returns the transformed array of U.

By just changing the name of the function and parameters, we can make this even more generic. So let's change the function and parameter names:

```
func map<T, U>(a: [T], transform: ([T]) -> [U]) -> [U] {
    return transform(a)
}
```

At this point, we have a half-baked `map` function that takes an array of T and applies the `transform` function to it to return a transformed array of U.

In fact, this function does nothing and mapping happens in the `transform`. Let's make this function usable and more understandable:

```
func map<ElementInput, ElementResult>(elements: [ElementInput], transform:
(ElementInput) -> ElementResult) -> [ElementResult] {

    var result: [ElementResult] = []
    for element in elements {
        result.append(transform(element))
    }
    return result
}
```

Now, our `map` function takes an array of elements (*domain* in the *category theory*), iterates through each element in array, transforms it, and appends it to a new array (*codomain* in *category theory*).

The result will be another array of the `ElementResult` type, which has in fact transformed elements of the input array. Let's test this function:

```
let numbers = [10, 30, 91, 50, 100, 39, 74]
let result = map(elements: numbers, transform: { $0 + 2 })
```

The result will be `[12, 32, 93, 52, 102, 41, 76]`.

This example shows us that with higher-order functions and generics, we are able to define functions such as `map` that are already a part of the Swift language.

Now, let's examine the `map` method provided in Swift:

```
func map<T>(_ transform: (Element) throws -> T) rethrows -> [T]
```

This definition is very similar to our implementation, with some differences that we will cover here.

First of all, this is a method that can be called on collections such as an array, so we do not need any input type such as `[ElementInput]`.

Secondly, this method accepts a transform closure that can `throw`, and the method itself can rethrow.

Finally, `transform` accepts an element of this sequence as its parameter and returns a transformed value of the same or of a different type.

The `Element` type is the same type of object as the type contained in the collection. In our implementation, it is generic.

The flatMap method

`flatMap` is a generic instance method for any type that conforms to `Sequence` protocol. It can be used to flatten one level of a dimension of a sequence or to remove nil values in the sequence. The following example presents a two-dimensional array, in other words, nested arrays.

Calling `flatMap` on this array reduces one dimension and flattens it so the resulting array becomes `[1, 3, 5, 2, 4, 6]`:

```
let twoDimArray = [[1, 3, 5], [2, 4, 6]]
let oneDimArray = twoDimArray.flatMap { $0 }
```

In this example, `flatMap` returns an array containing the concatenated results of the mapping transform over itself. We can achieve the same result by calling `joined` on our array and then `map`, as follows:

```
let oneDimArray = twoDimArray.joined().map { $0 }
```

To be able to transform each element in an array, we will need to provide a `map` method as the closure to the `flatMap` method as follows:

```
let transofrmedOneDimArray = twoDimArray.flatMap { $0.map { $0 + 2 } }
```

The result will be `[3, 5, 7, 4, 6, 8]`.

The same result can be achieved with the following:

```
let oneDimArray = twoDimArray.joined().map { $0 + 2 }
```

Let's examine another example with an array of three dimensions:

```
let threeDimArray = [[1, [3, 5]], [2, [4, 6]]]
let twoDimArray = threeDimArray.flatMap { $0 }
```

The resulting array will be `[1, [3, 5], 2, [4, 6]]`.

Therefore, `flatMap` only flattens one dimension, and to handle more dimensions and transformations, we need to call the `flatMap` and `map` methods multiple times accordingly.

We also know that `twoDimArray` and `threeDimArray` are Monads, as we could call `map` and `flatMap` on them.

The filter function

The `filter` function takes a function that, given an element in array, returns `Bool`, indicating whether the element should be included in the resulting array. The `filter` method is declared as follows in Swift standard library:

```
public func filter(_ isIncluded: (Element) throws -> Bool) rethrows ->
[Element]
```

The definition is similar to the map method with the following differences:

- The filter function takes a closure that receives elements of itself and returns a Bool value
- The result of the filter method will be an array of its own type

Let's examine the following code to understand how it works:

```
let numbers = [10, 30, 91, 50, 100, 39, 74]
let evenNumbers = numbers.filter { $0 % 2 == 0 }
```

The resulting evenNumbers array will be [10, 30, 50, 100, 74].

Let's implement the filter function ourselves. In fact, its implementation is going to be similar to the implementation of map, except that it does not require a second generic specifying the codomain. Instead, it conditionally adds the original elements to the new array:

```
func filter<Element>(elements: [Element],
                     predicate: ((Element) -> Bool)) -> [Element] {
    var result = [Element]()
    for element in elements {
        if predicate(element) {
            result.append(element)
        }
    }
    return result
}
```

The filter function iterates through each element in our array and applies the predicate function to it. If the result of the predicate function becomes true, then the element is added to our new array. We can test our filter function as follows:

```
let filteredArray = filter(elements: numbers) { $0 % 2 == 0 }
```

The resulting array will be [10, 30, 50, 100, 74], which is identical to the Swift standard library-provided filter method.

The reduce function

The reduce function reduces a list into a single value. Often referred to as fold or aggregate, it takes two parameters: a starting value and a function.

A function takes a running total and an element of the list as parameters and returns a value that is created by combining the elements in the list.

Unlike `map`, `filter`, and `flatMap`, which would return the same type, reduce changes the type. In other words, `map`, `filter`, and `flatMap` would take an array and provide a changed array. This is not the case with `reduce` as it can change an array to, for instance, a `tuple` or single value.

Swift provides the `reduce` method on sequences and has the following definition:

```
public func reduce<Result>(_ initialResult: Result, _ nextPartialResult:
(Result, Element) throws -> Result) rethrows -> Result
```

If we use the `reduce` method on our `numbers` array, the result of this call becomes 394:

```
let total = numbers.reduce(0) { $0 + $1 }
```

We could also call `reduce`, as follows, as the + operator is a function in Swift:

```
let total = numbers.reduce(0, +)
```

Like the `map` and `filter` methods, developing a `reduce` function is also simple:

```
func reduce<Element, Value>(elements: [Element],
                            initial: Value,
                            combine: (Value, Element) -> Value) -> Value {

    var result = initial
    for element in elements {
        result = combine(result, element)
    }

    return result
}
```

We can achieve the same result (394) with the following call:

```
let total = reduce(elements: numbers, initial: 0) { $0 + $1 }
```

The `reduce` method can be used with other types, such as arrays of `Strings`.

The map function in terms of reduce

The reduction pattern is so powerful that every other function that traverses a list can be specified in terms of it. Let's develop a map function in terms of reduce:

```
func mapIntermsOfReduce<Element, ElementResult>(elements: [Element],
transform: (Element) -> ElementResult) -> [ElementResult] {

    return reduce(elements: elements, initial: [ElementResult]()) {
        $0 + [transform( $1 )]
    }
}

let result = mapIntermsOfReduce(elements: numbers, transform: { $0 + 2 })
```

The result is identical to our map function's result that we developed earlier in this chapter. This is a good example to understand the basics of reduce.

In the function body, we provide elements and an initial empty array of ElementResult, and finally, we provide a closure to combine the elements.

The filter function in terms of reduce

It is also possible to develop a filter function in terms of reduce:

```
func filterIntermsOfReduce<Element>(elements: [Element], predicate:
(Element) -> Bool) -> [Element] {

    return reduce(elements: elements, initial: []) {
        predicate($1) ? $0 + [ $1 ] : $0
    }
}

let result = filterIntermsOfReduce(elements: numbers) { $0 % 2 == 0 }
```

Again, the result is identical to our previously developed filter function.

In the function body, we provide elements, an empty initial array, and finally, predicate as a combinator.

The flatMap function in terms of reduce

To understand the power of `reduce`, we can implement the `flatMap` function in terms of `reduce` as well:

```
func flatMapIntermsOfReduce<Element>(elements: [Element], transform:
(Element) -> Element?) -> [Element] {

    return reduce(elements: elements, initial: []) {
        guard let transformationResult = transform($1) else {
            return $0
        }
        return $0 + [transformationResult]
    }
}

let anArrayOfNumbers = [1, 3, 5]
let oneDimensionalArray = flatMapIntermsOfReduce(elements:
anArrayOfNumbers) { $0 + 5 }
```

Also, we can flatten a two-dimensional array using the `reduce` method as follows:

```
func flatMapIntermsOfReduce<Element>(elements: [[Element]], transform:
(Element) -> Element) -> [Element] {

    return elements.reduce([]) { $0 + $1 }
}

let aTwoDimArrayOfNumbers = [[1, 3, 5],[2, 4, 6]]
let flatMappedArray = flatMapIntermsOfReduce(elements:
aTwoDimArrayOfNumbers) { $0 }
```

The `flatMappedArray` will be `[1, 3, 5, 2, 4, 6]`.

The flatten function in terms of reduce

And finally, let's implement the `flatten` function in terms of `reduce`:

```
func flattenIntermsOfReduce<Element>(elements: [[Element]]) -> [Element] {
    return elements.reduce([]) { $0 + $1 }
}

let flattened = flattenIntermsOfReduce(elements: aTwoDimArrayOfNumbers)
```

`flattened` will be `[1, 3, 5, 2, 4, 6]`.

The apply function

`apply` is a function that applies a function to a list of arguments.

Unfortunately, Swift does not provide any `apply` method on arrays. To be able to implement Applicative Functors, we need to develop the `apply` function. The following code presents a simple version of the `apply` function with only one argument:

```
func apply<T, V>(fn: ([T]) -> V, args: [T]) -> V {
    return fn(args)
}
```

The `apply` function takes a function and an array of any type and applies the function to the first element of the array. Let's test this function as follows:

```
let numbers = [1, 3, 5]

func incrementValues(a: [Int]) -> [Int] {
    return a.map { $0 + 1 }
}

let applied = apply(fn: incrementValues, args: numbers)
```

The join function

The `join` function takes an array of objects and joins them with a provided `separator`. The following example presents a simple version of `join`:

```
func join<Element: Equatable>(elements: [Element], separator: String) ->
String {

    return elements.reduce("") {
        initial, element in
        let aSeparator = (element == elements.last) ? "" : separator
        return "\(initial)\(element)\(aSeparator)"
    }
}
```

This function takes an array with a `separator`, joins elements in an array, and provides a single `String`. We can test it as follows:

```
let items = ["First", "Second", "Third"]
let commaSeparatedItems = join(elements: items, separator: ", ")
```

The result will be `"First, Second, Third"`.

Chaining higher-order functions

So far, we have learned about different functions and seen some examples of them. Let's see if we can combine them to solve problems that we may encounter in our day-to-day application development.

Let's assume that we need to receive an object from a backend system as follows:

```
struct User {
    let name: String
    let age: Int
}

let users = [
    User(name: "Fehiman",  age: 60),
    User(name: "Neco",  age: 29),
    User(name: "Grace",  age: 1),
    User(name: "Tamina",  age: 6),
    User(name: "Negar", age: 27)
]
```

Then we need to calculate the total of ages by using `totalAge` in the `users` array. We can use a combination of the `map` and `reduce` functions to calculate `totalAge` as follows:

```
let totalAge = users.map { $0.age }.reduce(0) { $0 + $1 }
```

We were able to chain the `map` and `reduce` methods to achieve this.

The zip function

The `zip` function is provided by the Swift standard library and creates a sequence of pairs built out of two underlying sequences, where the elements of the ith pair are the ith elements of each underlying sequence.

For instance, in the following example, `zip` takes two arrays and creates a pair of these two arrays:

```
let numbers = [3, 5, 9, 10]
let alphabeticNumbers = ["Three", "Five", "Nine", "Ten"]

let zipped = zip(alphabeticNumbers, numbers).map { $0 }
```

The value for `zipped` will be `[("Three", 3), ("Five", 5), ("Nine", 9), ("Ten", 10)]`.

Practical examples

Let's explore some practical examples of higher-order functions.

Sum and product of an array

We can use our `reduce` function to calculate the sum of a list of numbers as follows:

```
let listOfNumbers = [1, 2, 3, 4, 5, 6, 7, 8, 9, 10]
let sumOfNumbers = reduce(elements: listOfNumbers, initial: 0, combine: +)
print(sumOfNumbers)
```

The result will be `55`, as expected.

We can use our `reduce` function to calculate the product of array values as follows:

```
let productOfNumbers = reduce(elements: listOfNumbers, initial: 1,
combine: *)
print(productOfNumbers)
```

The result is going to be `3628800`, as expected.

Removing nil values from an array

We can use `flatMap` to get values out of `optionalArray` and remove `nil` values:

```
let optionalArray: [String?] = ["First", "Second", nil, "Fourth"]
let nonOptionalArray = optionalArray.flatMap { $0 }
print(nonOptionalArray)
```

The result will be `["First", "Second", "Fourth"]`, as expected.

Removing duplicates in an array

We can use `reduce` to remove duplicate elements in an array as follows:

```
let arrWithDuplicates = [1, 1, 2, 3, 3, 4, 4, 5, 6, 7]

let arrWithoutDuplicates = arrWithDuplicates.reduce([]) {
    (a: [Int], b: Int) -> [Int] in
    if a.contains(b) {
        return a
    } else {
        return a + [b]
    }
}
print(arrWithoutDuplicates)
```

The result will be `[1, 2, 3, 4, 5, 6, 7]`, as expected.

Partitioning an array

We can use `reduce` to partition an array with a specific criterion. For instance, in the following example, we partition `numbersToPartitionArray` into two partitions, keeping all even numbers in the left partition:

```
func partition<T>(list: [T], criteria: (T) -> Bool) -> (lPartition: [T],
rPartition: [T]) {

    return list.reduce((lPartition: [T](), rPartition: [T]())) {
        (accumlator: (lPartition: [T], rPartition: [T]), pivot: T) ->
        (lPartition: [T], rPartition: [T]) in
        if criteria(pivot) {
            return (lPartition: accumlator.lPartition + [pivot],
            rPartition: accumlator.rPartition)
        } else {
```

```
            return (rPartition: accumlator.rPartition + [pivot],
            lPartition: accumlator.lPartition)
        }
    }
}

let doublesToPartition = [3.0, 4.0, 5.0, 6.0, 7.0, 8.0, 9.0]
let partitioned = partition(list: doublesToPartition) {
    $0.truncatingRemainder(dividingBy: 2.0) == 0
}
print(partitioned)
```

The result will be ([4.0, 6.0, 8.0], [3.0, 5.0, 7.0, 9.0]), as expected.

Summary

In this chapter, we started with the category theory concepts such as Functor, Applicative Functor, and Monad, and explored higher-order functions such as map, filter, flatMap, joined, and reduce. Then, we examined Swift-provided versions of higher-order functions and implemented a simple version ourselves. Also, we developed map, filter, flatMap, and flatten functions in terms of the reduce function.

Then, we continued with the apply, join, and zip functions and were introduced to chaining higher-order functions.

Finally, we explored some practical examples of higher-order functions such as removing nil values from an array, removing duplicates, and partitioning arrays.

These functions are going to be great tools in our day-to-day development toolkit to use and solve a lot of different kinds of problem.

In the following chapter, we will get familiar with optional types and discuss non-functional and functional ways to deal with them.

7
Dealing with Optionals

In Chapter 6, *Map, Filter, and Reduce* we talked about `map` and `flatMap` functions, and we said that optionals are *Monads*. In this chapter, we will look at optionals. We need to deal with optionals as some of the functions/methods that we need to call or provide may return some values or none. This chapter explores the concept of optionals and provides different techniques to deal with them.

This chapter will cover the following topics with coding examples:

- Optional types
- Unwrapping optionals
- Optional binding
- Guard
- Coalescing
- Optional chaining
- Optional mapping
- Dealing with optionals functionally
- Using `fmap` and `apply` for multiple functional mapping
- Error handling

Optional types

In our day-to-day application development, we encounter situations where we expect to receive a value but we do not receive it. For instance, suppose that we have a list of items and we need to search for a particular value in the list. The particular value that we are looking for might not be on the list. Other examples can be calling a web service and receiving a JSON payload without the fields that we are looking for, or querying a database and not receiving the expected values.

What are we going to receive when the value is not there, and how will we handle this absence?

In programming languages such as C, it is possible to create a variable without giving it a value. If we try to use the variable before assigning a value, we would get an undefined value.

In Swift, we can define a variable without giving it a value, but we cannot use it without assigning some value to it. In other words, we need to initialize it before being able to use it. This feature of Swift ensures that we will not receive undefined values.

What about the scenarios where we need to define a variable and we do not know what the value is going to be?

To overcome these kinds of scenario, Swift provides optional types that can have `some` or `none` values and can be used in situations where a value may be absent.

A question mark (?) is used to define a variable as optional. The following example presents an example of optional definition:

```
// Optional value either contains a value or contains nil
var optionalString: String? = "A String literal"
optionalString = nil
```

In this example, we have defined a variable that is of an optional type. The `String?` type is an optional type that may wrap a `String` value in it.

We were able to assign `nil` to `optionalString`. If we try to assign `nil` to any non-optional type in Swift, the compiler will complain about it, unlike some other languages such as Objective-C.

For instance, in the following example, the compiler will complain that `Nil cannot be assigned to type 'String'`:

```
var aString: String = "A String literal"
aString = nil // Compile error                          🛇 Nil cannot be assigned to type 'String'
```

The compile time checking of non-existent values in Swift to prevent runtime errors is one of the features of type safety in Swift. Type safety makes it easier to catch problems in the earlier stages of development. Let's examine an example in Objective-C to see the real value of `Optionals`:

```
NSString *searchedItem = [self searchItem: @"an item"];
NSString *text = @"Found item: ";
NSString *message = [text stringByAppendingString: searchedItem];
```

Suppose that we have a list for which we initiate a search by calling `searchItem`. In this case, our `searchItem` method takes `NSString` and returns `NSString`. The result of this call can be `nil`. If we use the returned `NSString` and try to append it to another `NSString`, it will compile but may crash the application if `searchItem` is `nil`.

We could remedy this problem by checking whether `searchedItem` is not `nil` before using it. However, there might be some cases where other developers forgot to do it or did not see the necessity of it.

For sure, it is safer to receive compile time complaints about these kinds of usage. As Swift is type-safe, we will not encounter any such surprises during runtime.

So, we have understood why we need an optional type, but what is it and how is it defined? Under the hood, `Optional` is an `enum` with two cases in it--one is `none` and the other one is `some` with its associated generic value, as follows:

```
enum Optional<T> {
    case None
    case Some(T)
}
```

Unwrapping optionals

So far, we know that `Optionals` wrap values in themselves. Wrapping means that the actual data is stored within an outer structure or container (See *Higher-kinded types* in the previous chapter).

For instance, we print `optionalString` as follows:

```
print(optionalString)
```

The result will be `Optional("A String literal")`.

How will we unwrap `Optionals` and use the values that we need? There are different methods to unwrap `Optionals` that we will go through in the following sections.

Force unwrapping

To unwrap `Optionals`, the easiest and most dangerous method that we can use is force unwrapping. In short, `!` can be used to force unwrap the value from `Optional`.

The following example forcefully unwraps `optionalString`:

```
optionalString = "An optional String"
print(optionalString!)
```

Force unwrapping the `Optionals` may cause errors if the optional does not have a value, so it is not recommended to use this approach as it is very hard to be sure if we are going to have values in `Optionals` in different circumstances.

In fact, force unwrapping eliminates the benefits of type safety and may cause our applications to crash during runtime.

nil checking

Force unwrapping an `optional` could crash our applications. To eliminate the crashing problem, we can check whether the variable is not `nil` before unwrapping it.

The following example presents a simple `nil` checking approach:

```
if optionalString != nil {
    print(optionalString!)
}
```

This approach is safe in compile and runtime but may cause problems during editing. For instance, if we accidentally move the `print` line outside the `if` block, the compiler is not going to complain and it may crash our application during runtime.

Optional binding

The better approach would be to use the optional binding technique to find out whether an optional contains a value or not. If it contains a value, we will be able to unwrap it and put it into a temporary constant or variable.

The following example presents optional binding:

```
let nilName: String? = nil
if let familyName = nilName {
    let greetingfamilyName = "Hello, Mr. \(familyName)"
} else {
    // Optional does not have a value
}
```

The `if let familyName = nilName` statement will assign the optional value to a new variable named `familyName`. The right-hand side of the assignment has to be an `optional`, otherwise, the compiler will issue an error. Also, this approach ensures that we are using the unwrapped temporary version so it is safe.

This approach is also called *if-let binding,* and is useful to unwrap `Optionals` and access the underlying values, but if we get into a complex structure of nested objects such as a JSON payload, the syntax becomes cumbersome.

We will need to have lots of nested `if-let` expressions in these cases:

```
let dict = ["One": 1, "Two": 2, "Three": 3]

if let firstValue = dict["One"] {
    if let secondValue = dict["Two"] {
        if let thirdValue = dict["Three"] {
            // Do something with three values
        }
    }
}
```

To overcome this issue, we can use multiple optional bindings as follows:

```
if let firstValue = dict["One"],
    let secondValue = dict["Two"],
    let thirdValue = dict["Three"] {
        print("\(firstValue) \(secondValue) \(thirdValue)")
        // prints 1 2 3
}
```

This syntax makes the code more readable but still is not the best approach when we need to bind multiple levels of Optionals. In the following sections, we will look at different methods to further improve the readability and maintainability of our optional handlings.

Guard

The guard is another method provided in the Swift library to handle Optionals. The guard method differs from the Optionalif-let binding in that the guard statement can be used for early exits. We can use a guard statement to require that a condition must be true in order for the code after the guard statement to be executed.

The following example presents the guard statement usage:

```
func greet(person: [String: String]) {
    guard let name = person["name"] else {
        return
    }
    print("Hello Ms \(name)!")
}
greet(person: ["name": "Neco"]) // prints "Hello Ms Neco!"
```

In this example, the greet function requires a value for a person's name; therefore, it checks whether it is present with the guard statement. Otherwise, it will return and not continue to execute.

Using guard statements, we can check for failure scenarios first and return if it fails. Unlike if-let statements, guard does not provide a new scope, so in the preceding example, we were able to use name in our print statement, which is not inside { }.

Similar to if-let statements, we can use multiple guard statements as follows:

```
func extractValue(dict: [String: Int]) {
    guard let firstValue = dict["One"],
        let secondValue = dict["Two"],
        let thirdValue = dict["Three"]
        else {
            return
    }
    print("\(firstValue) \(secondValue) \(thirdValue)")
}
```

Implicitly-unwrapped optionals

We can define *implicitly-unwrapped* Optionals by appending an exclamation mark (!) to the end of the type. These types of Optionals will unwrap themselves.

The following example presents two ways to get a value from a dictionary. In the first example, the resulting value will be an optional so should be unwrapped. The second example will implicitly unwrap the value:

```
let optionalDict: Dictionary<String, Int>? = ["One": 1, "Two": 2, "Three": 3]
let implicitlyUnwrappedDict: Dictionary<String, Int>! = ["One": 1, "Two": 2, "Three": 3]

let firstValue = optionalDict["One"]        🔵 Value of optional type 'Dictionary<String, Int>?' not unwrapped; did you mean to use '!' or '?'?
let implictlyUnwrappedFirstValue = implicitlyUnwrappedDict["One"]
```

Like forcefully unwrapping, implicitly-unwrapped Optionals may cause runtime crashes in our applications, so we need to be cautious when we use them.

Nil-coalescing

Swift provides the ?? operator for nil-coalescing. It unwraps Optionals and provides fallback or default values for the nil case.

For instance, a ?? b unwraps optional a if it has a value and returns a default value b if a is nil.

In this example, if optional a is not nil, the expression after the nil-coalescing operator is not going to be evaluated. Nil-coalescing is suitable for scenarios where we can provide a fallback or default value.

Optional chaining

Optional chaining is a process to query and call properties, methods, and subscripts on an optional that may currently be nil. Optional chaining in Swift is similar to messaging nil in Objective-C but in a way that works for any type and can be checked for success or failure.

The following example presents two different classes. One of the classes, `Person`, has a property of type of `Optional` (residence), which wraps the other class type `Residence`:

```
class Residence {
    var numberOfRooms = 1
}

class Person {
    var residence: Residence?
}
```

We will create an instance of the `Person` class, `sangeeth`:

```
let residence = Residence()
residence.numberOfRooms = 5

let sangeeth = Person()
sangeeth.residence = residence
```

To check for `numberOfRooms`, we need to use the `residence` property of the `Person` class, which is an `optional`. Optional chaining enables us to go through `Optionals` as follows:

```
if let roomCount = sangeeth.residence?.numberOfRooms {
    // Use the roomCount
    print(roomCount)
}
```

The `roomCount` variable will be 5, as expected. Optional chaining can be used to call methods and subscripts that reside in optional types or return `Optionals`.

We can add force unwrapping to any chain items by replacing the question mark with an exclamation mark as follows:

```
let roomCount = sangeeth.residence!.numberOfRooms
```

Again, we need to be cautious when we use force unwrapping in optional chains.

Dealing with Optionals' functionally

We have covered different approaches and tools to deal with `Optionals` so far. Let's examine if we can use functional programming paradigms to simplify the process.

Optional mapping

Mapping over an `array` would generate one element for each element in the array. Can we `map` over an optional to generate non-optional values? If we have `some`, `map` it; otherwise, return `none`. Let's examine the following code:

```
func mapOptionals<T, V>(transform: (T) -> V, input: T?) -> V? {
    switch input {
    case .some(let value): return transform(value)
    case .none: return .none
    }
}
```

Our `input` variable is a `generic` optional and we have a `transform` function that takes `input` and transforms it into a generic type. The result will be a `generic` optional type. In the `function` body, we use pattern matching to return the respective values. Let's test this `function`:

```
class User {
    var name: String?
}
```

We create a class named `User` with an optional variable. We use the variable as follows:

```
func extractUserName(name: String) -> String {
    return "\(name)"
}

var nonOptionalUserName: String {
    let user = User()
    user.name = "John Doe"
    let someUserName = mapOptionals(transform: extractUserName,
                                    input: user.name)
    return someUserName ?? ""
}

print(nonOptionalUserName)
```

The result will be a non-optional `String`. Our `mapOptionals` function is similar to the `fmap` function in Haskell, which is defined as the `<^>` operator.

Let's convert this function to the operator:

```
precedencegroup AssociativityLeft {
    associativity: left
}
```

```
infix operator <^> : AssociativityLeft

func <^><T, V>(transform: (T) -> V, input: T?) -> V? {
    switch input {
    case .some(let value): return transform(value)
    case .none: return .none
    }
}
```

Here, we've just defined an `infix` operator and defined the respective function. Let's try this function to see if it provides the same result:

```
var nonOptionalUserName2: String {
    let user = User()
    user.name = "John Doe"
    let someUserName = extractUserName <^> user.name
    return someUserName ?? ""
}

print(nonOptionalUserName2)
```

The result is identical to our previous example, but the code is more readable, so we may prefer to use it instead.

Multiple optional value mapping

Our previous example demonstrated single optional value mapping using FP techniques. What if we need to `map` multiple optional values together? In the optional binding section, we covered a non-functional way to handle multiple optional value binding, and in this section, we will look at multiple optional value mapping. As `Optionals` are *high-kinded* types, we will develop an `apply` function to use over `Optionals`:

```
func apply<T, V>(transform: ((T) -> V)?, input: T?) -> V? {
    switch transform {
    case .some(let fx): return fx <^> input
    case .none: return .none
    }
}
```

The `apply` function is very similar to the `fmap` function. The `transform` function is optional, and we use pattern matching to return `none` or `some` over it.

In Haskell, the `apply` function is represented as the `<*>` operator. This operator has been adopted by the Swift functional programming community as well, so we use it as the `apply` function:

```
infix operator <*> : AssociativityLeft

func <*><T, V>(transform: ((T) -> V)?, input: T?) -> V? {
    switch transform {
    case .some(let fx): return fx <^> input
    case .none: return .none
    }
}
```

We can test our `apply` function as follows:

```
func extractFullUserName(firstName: String) -> (String) -> String {
    return {
        (lastName: String) -> String in
        return "\(firstName) \(lastName)"
    }
}
```

Now we can use this function to extract the full username:

```
class User2 {
    var firstName: String?
    var lastName: String?
}

var fullName: String {
    let user = User2()
    user.firstName = "John"
    user.lastName = "Doe"
    let fullUserName = extractFullUserName <^>
                        user.firstName <*>
                        user.lastName

    return fullUserName ?? ""
}
print(fullName)
```

Combining `fmap` and apply functions, we were able to `map` two `Optionals`.

In fact, the `optional` type is a Monad, so it implements the `map` and `flatMap` methods and we do not need to develop it ourselves.

The following example presents calling the `map` method on an optional type:

```
let optionalString: String? = "A String literal"
let result = optionalString.map { "\($0) is mapped" }
```

The result will be an optional string with the following value:

```
"A String literal is mapped".
```

Also, we can use `flatMap` to filter `nil` values and convert an `array` of `Optionals` to an `array` of unwrapped values.

In the following example, calling `flatMap` on our `optionalArray` will eliminate the third element (`index: 2`) of our `Array`:

```
let optionalArray: [String?] = ["First", "Second", nil, "Fourth"]
let nonOptionalArray = optionalArray.flatMap { $0 }
print(nonOptionalArray)
```

The result is going to be `["First", "Second", "Fourth"]`.

Error handling

`Optionals` are used to represent the existence/absence of a value. A result of an operation can be optional, so when that operation fails we will receive `nil`. The optional itself will not provide any information about how our operation failed and what the cause of the failure, and in most of cases it is useful to know the context and cause of the failure to be able to respond accordingly in our code.

Error handling is the process of responding to and recovering from error conditions in our applications. The Swift standard library provides first-class support for *throwing, catching, propagating,* and *manipulating* recoverable *errors* at runtime.

Let's go through an example to explore the error handling concept. Suppose that we need to read a file and return the content of that file. Using `Optionals`, we can develop it as follows:

```
func checkForPath(path: String) -> String? {
    // check for the path
    return "path"
}

func readFile(path: String) -> String? {
    if let restult = checkForPath(path: path) {
```

```
        return restult
    } else {
        return nil
    }
}
```

Here, `checkForPath` is an incomplete function that checks for file existence.

When we call the `readFile` function, we will need to check for the resulting `optional`:

```
if let result = readFile(path: "path/to") {
    // Do something with result
}
```

Instead of using `Optionals` in this scenario, we can use error handling to redirect the flow of control to eliminate errors and provide recoveries:

```
enum Result: Error {
    case failure
    case success
}

func readFile(path: String) throws -> String {
    if let restult = checkForPath(path: path) {
        return restult
    } else {
        throw Result.failure
    }
}
```

When we call this function, we will need to wrap it inside a `do` block, `try` the operation, and `catch` the exception:

```
do {
    let result = try readFile(path: "path/to")
} catch {
    print(error)
}
```

In this example, we used the default `try` but there are other flavours of `try` that we are going to explore in upcoming sections.

try!

We can use `try!` if we know that there is no way a method call will fail, or if it fails then our code will be broken and we should crash the application.

When we use the `try!` keyword, it disables *error propagation* and we do not need to have `do` and `catch` around our code block because we promise it will never fail! It is a big promise that we should avoid.

In case we have to bypass error handling such as checking whether a database file exists, we can do the following:

```
let result = try! readFile(path: "path/to")
```

try?

We can use `try?` to handle an `error` by converting it to an optional value.

If an error is thrown while evaluating the `try?` expression, the value of the expression is going to be `nil`. For instance, in the following example, the result is going to be `nil` if we cannot read the file:

```
let result = try? readFile(path: "path/to")
```

Summary

In this chapter, we got familiar with optional types. We talked about built-in techniques to deal with `Optionals` such as optional binding, guard, coalescing, and optional chaining. Then we explored functional programming techniques to deal with `Optionals`. We created `fmap` and `apply` functions and related operators to tackle multiple optional binding problems. Even though some developers may prefer to use built-in multiple optional binding, exploring functional programming techniques practically provides a better understanding of concepts that we will be able to apply to other problems.

Finally, we briefly looked into error handling concepts and how to convert `errors` to optional values.

In the next chapter, we will explore some examples of functional data structures such as `Semigroup`, `Monoid`, `Binary Search Tree`, `Linked List`, `Stack`, and `Lazy List`.

8

Functional Data Structures

We are familiar with imperative data structures. In fact, there are lots of references to imperative data structures in different programming languages. In contrast, there aren't many references to declarative data structures or functional data structures. This is because FP languages are not as mainstream as imperative programming languages. Additionally, designing and implementing functional data structures is more difficult in comparison to imperative counterparts because of the following reasons:

- Mutability is not recommended in FP
- Functional data structures are expected to be more flexible than their imperative counterparts

Imperative data structures rely heavily on mutability and assignments and making them immutable needs extra development effort. Whenever we change an imperative data structure, we basically override the previous version; however, this is not the case with declarative programming as we expect that both the previous and new versions of the functional data structure will continue to survive and be utilized.

We might think: why bother with functional data structures as they are more difficult to design and implement? There are two answers to this question: first of all, functional data structures are efficient and immutable data structures. Secondly, they support FP paradigms. We have already seen an example of these when we were introduced to algebraic data types in Chapter 4, *Enumerations and Pattern Matching*.

In this chapter, we will further explore functional data structures with coding examples. The content of this chapter is heavily inspired by *Purely Functional Data Structures, Chris Okasaki, Cambridge University Press*, which is a great reference on this topic to date and has various examples with ML and *Haskell* programming languages. Reading *Okasaki's* book is highly recommended for functional programmers. In this chapter, we will cover the topic and explore some of the examples in *Okasaki's* book in Swift.

Particularly, we will utilize `structs` and `enums` to implement the following functional data structures:

- Semigroups
- Monoids
- Binary Search Trees
- Linked lists
- Stacks
- Lazy lists

Coding examples for these data structures serve as a presentation of FP paradigms and techniques and they are not going to be complete.

We know that immutability is the most important property of functional data structures. To design and implement immutable data structures, we will not change a functional data structure and instead create a new version that lives along with the previous version. In fact, we will copy the parts that need to be changed without touching the original version of the data structure. So we will use value types such as `structs` and `enumerations` to be able to achieve this. In addition, as we will not change the original data structure directly, we will be able to share the original data structure parts with the new structure without being worried about how changing one version would affect the other version. Let's examine how we will achieve this by implementing different functional data structures.

Semigroups

In computer science, a *Semigroup* is an algebraic structure that has a set and a binary operation that takes two elements in the set and returns a Semigroup that has an associative operation. An associative operation is a binary operation that has a valid rule of replacement or transformation for expressions.

To start, we need to have a set and a specific binary operation, or we can make this behavior generic and define a `protocol` as follows:

```
protocol Semigroup {
    func operation(_ element: Self) -> Self
}
```

Any type that conforms to this protocol requires us to implement the `operation` method. Here, `self` presents the type that is conforming to this protocol. For instance, we can extend `Int` to conform to the `Semigroup protocol` and provide a summation on itself:

```
extension Int: Semigroup {
    func operation(_ element: Int) -> Int {
        return self + element
    }
}
```

We can test this as follows:

```
let number: Int = 5
number.operation(3)
```

This test does not ensure the associativity of the binary operations. Let's try this:

```
let numberA: Int = 3
let numberB: Int = 5
let numberC: Int = 7

if numberA.operation(numberB.operation(numberC)) ==
(numberA.operation(numberB)).operation(numberC) {
    print("Operation is associative")
}
```

The preceding code ensures that our binary operator is associative; therefore, our Semigroup is verified. It does not look very nice though; let's implement an operator for our `operation` to make it look better and more math friendly:

```
precedencegroup AssociativityLeft {
    associativity: left
}

infix operator <> : AssociativityLeft

func <> <S: Semigroup> (x: S, y: S) -> S {
    return x.operation(y)
}
```

Let's re-write our test with the `<>` operator:

```
if (numberA <> (numberB <> numberC)) == ((numberA <> numberB) <> numberC) {
    print("Operation is associative")
}
```

So far, we extended only `Int` but we can extend any type. Let's extend `arrays` as an example:

```
extension Array: Semigroup {
    func operation(_ element: Array) -> Array {
        return self + element
    }
}
```

The operation method is very similar to what we have for `Int`. The only difference is in the type, which is an `array` in this case:

```
print([1, 2, 3, 4] <> [5, 6, 7]) // prints "[1, 2, 3, 4, 5, 6, 7]"
```

Furthermore, we can extend `String` as follows:

```
extension String: Semigroup {
    func operation(_ element: String) -> String {
        return "\(self)\(element)"
    }
}
```

We have established a general principle of composition (two objects combining into one) using a `protocol`. This pattern can be used for different purposes. For instance, we can implement a shorter version of `reduce` for `arrays` over `Semigroups`:

```
func sconcat <S: Semigroup> (initial: S, elements: [S]) -> S {
    return elements.reduce(initial, <>)
}
```

The `sconcat` function name stands for `Semigroup sconcat`; we can test it as follows:

```
print(sconcat(initial: 0, elements:[1, 2, 3])) // 6
print(sconcat(initial: "", elements: ["A", "B", "C"])) // ABC
print(sconcat(initial: [], elements: [[1, 2], [3, 4, 5]])) // [1, 2, 3, 4, 5]
```

Our last `sconcat` example works like `flatMap` and flattens elements.

Finally, our `Semigroup` becomes the following:

```
precedencegroup AssociativityLeft {
    associativity: left
}

infix operator <> : AssociativityLeft

func <> <S: Semigroup> (x: S, y: S) -> S {
```

```
        return x.operation(y)
    }

protocol Semigroup {
    func operation(_ element: Self) -> Self
}

extension Int: Semigroup {
    func operation(_ element: Int) -> Int {
        return self + element
    }
}

extension String : Semigroup {
    func operation(_ element: String) -> String {
        return self + element
    }
}

extension Array : Semigroup {
    func operation(_ element: Array) -> Array {
        return self + element
    }
}

func sconcat <S: Semigroup> (initial: S, elements: [S]) -> S {
    return elements.reduce(initial, <>)
}
```

A Semigroup is a great example of a simple data structure, but it is not as popular as a Monoid, which we will examine in the next section.

Monoids

In mathematics, Monoids can be considered as categories with a single object. They capture the idea of function composition within a set. In fact, all functions from a set into itself naturally form a Monoid with respect to function composition.

In computer science, there are different types of Monoid, such as free, transition, syntactic, trace, and history. A set of strings built from a given set of characters is a free Monoid. The transition Monoid and syntactic Monoid are used to describe finite state machines, whereas trace Monoids and history Monoids provide a foundation for process calculi and concurrent computing.

Simply put, in computer science, a Monoid is a set, a binary operation, and an element of the set with the following rules:

- Associativity of binary operations
- The element is the identity

Simply put, a structure is a `Monoid` if the structure is a `Semigroup` with an element that is the `identity`. So let's define a new `protocol` that extends our `Semigroupprotocol`:

```
protocol Monoid: Semigroup {
    static func identity() -> Self
}

extension Int: Monoid {
    static func identity() -> Int {
        return 0
    }
}

extension String: Monoid {
    static func identity() -> String {
        return ""
    }
}

extension Array: Monoid {
    static func identity() -> Array {
        return []
    }
}
```

We can test our structure as follows:

```
numberA <> Int.identity() // 3
"A" <> String.identity() // A
```

As a `Monoid` has an element, we can use this as an initial and simplify our `reduce` method as follows:

```
func mconcat <M: Monoid> (_ elements: [M]) -> M {
    return elements.reduce(M.identity(), <>)
}
```

Let's test this:

```
print(mconcat([1, 2, 3])) // 6
print(mconcat(["A", "B", "C"])) // ABC
print(mconcat([[1, 2], [3, 4, 5]])) // [1, 2, 3, 4, 5]
```

For curious readers, the following references are great reads:

- `http://www.fewbutripe.com/swift/math/algebra/2015/02/17/algebraic-structure-and-protocols.html`
- `http://www.fewbutripe.com/swift/math/algebra/monoid/2017/04/18/algebra-of-predicates-and-sorting-functions.html`

Also, Kickstarter OSS code at `https://github.com/kickstarter/ios-oss` and `https://github.com/kickstarter/Kickstarter-Prelude` are great examples of real world, in production usages of FP paradigms.

Trees

In computer science, a Tree is a very popular **abstract data type** (**ADT**) or a data structure implementing this ADT that simulates a hierarchical Tree structure with a root value and subtrees of the children with a parent node, represented as a set of linked nodes.

A Tree data structure can be defined recursively (locally) as a collection of nodes (starting at a root node), where each node is a data structure consisting of a value, together with a list of references to nodes (the children) with the constraints that no reference is duplicated and none point to the root.

Alternatively, a Tree can be defined abstractly as a whole (globally) as an ordered Tree, with a value assigned to each node. Both these perspectives are useful: while a Tree can be analyzed mathematically as a whole, when actually represented as a data structure, it is usually represented and worked separately by a node (rather than as a list of nodes and an adjacency list of edges between nodes, as one may represent a digraph, for instance). For example, looking at a Tree as a whole, one can talk about the parent node of a given node, but in general as a data structure, a given node only contains the list of its children, but not a reference to its parent (if any).

The following figure presents an example Tree:

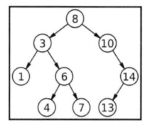

In Chapter 5, *Generics and Associated Type Protocols, in the Generic Data Structures* section, we implemented a generic binary Tree in Swift. The following is an improved version of that:

```
enum Tree<Element: Comparable> {
    case leaf(Element)
    indirect case node(lhs: Tree, rhs: Tree)
}
```

We define the Tree as an enum with two different cases:

- **Leaf**: If we are at the end of a branch of the Tree; simply put, if a node does not have any children, then it is a leaf.
- **Node**: A structure that has a left-hand side and right-hand side to it

This Tree is generic and the elements in it are comparable.

Using this Tree is as simple as follows:

```
let functionalTree = Tree.node(lhs: Tree.leaf("First"),
                               rhs: Tree.node(lhs: Tree.leaf("Second"),
                               rhs: Tree.leaf("Third")))
print(functionalTree)
```

Our functionalTree is immutable or, in other words, it is persistent. It has a leaf as lhs and a node with two leaves as rhs. As this structure is immutable, we will not be worried whether it is going to change or not and we will be able to share this Tree with other Trees:

```
let secondFT = Tree.node(lhs: functionalTree,
                    rhs: Tree.node(lhs: Tree.leaf("Fourth"),
                    rhs: Tree.leaf("Fifth")))

let thirdFT = Tree.node(lhs: Tree.node(lhs: Tree.leaf("Fourth"),
                    rhs: Tree.leaf("Fifth")),
                    rhs: functionalTree)
```

In the preceding examples, we used our first `Tree` called `functionalTree` as a part of `secondFT` and `thirdFT`.

The contains method

This `Tree` is far from complete and needs lots of functionality. For instance, we may need to check whether the `Tree` contains a specific value. To be able to do this, we need to add the following method to our `Tree`:

```
static func contains(_ key: Element, tree: Tree<Element>) -> Bool {
    switch tree {
    case .leaf(let element):
        return key == element
    case node(let lhs, let rhs):
        return contains(key, tree: lhs) || contains(key, tree: rhs)
    }
}
```

We can test the `contains` method as follows:

```
let isFound = Tree.contains("First", tree: functionalTree)
print(isFound) // prints true
```

Binary Search Trees

Our assumption in our simple `Tree` was that only leaves contain a value. This is not always true. In fact, there are different types of Tree with different utilities, and Binary Search Tree (BST) is one of them.

In computer science, BSTs, sometimes called *ordered* or *sorted binary trees*, are a particular type of container: data structures that store items (such as numbers, names, and so on) in memory. They allow fast lookup, the addition and removal of items, and implementation of either dynamic sets of items or lookup tables that allow finding an item by its key (for example, finding the phone number of a person by name).

BSTs keep their keys in sorted order so that lookup and other operations can use the principle of binary search: when looking for a key in a Tree (or a place to insert a new key), they traverse the Tree from root to leaf, making comparisons to keys stored in the nodes of the Tree and deciding, based on the comparison, whether to continue searching in the left or right subtrees. On average, this means that each comparison allows the operations to skip about half of the Tree so that each lookup, insertion, or deletion takes time proportional to the logarithm of the number of items stored in the Tree. This is much better than the linear time required to find items by key in an (unsorted) array, but slower than the corresponding operations on hash tables.

Let's improve our simple `Tree` and convert it to a BST:

```
enum BST<Element: Comparable> {
    case leaf
    indirect case node(lhs: BST,
                        element: Element,
                        rhs: BST)
}
```

The `BST` is very similar to the previous `Tree` and the only difference is that `node` contains the element and not the `leaf`. Using it is as simple as follows:

```
let functionalBST = BST.node(lhs: BST.node(lhs: BST.leaf,
                                            element: 1,
                                            rhs: BST.leaf),
                             element: 5,
                             rhs: BST.node(lhs: BST.leaf,
                                           element: 9,
                                           rhs: BST.leaf))
```

Here, we create a BST as values stored in `lhs` are smaller than the root and values stored in `rhs` are larger than the root. In this example, `lhs` is a BST with 1 as value. The root has a value of 5 and `rhs` is a BST with a value of 9, which is larger than the root value.

The contains method

Additionally, our `contains` method requires to be modified as it will search only in leaves. Let's improve this, assuming that our `Tree` is a `BST`:

```
static func contains(_ item: Element, tree: BST<Element>) -> Bool {
    switch tree {
    case .leaf:
        return false
    case .node(let lhs, let element, let rhs):
        if item < element {
            return contains(item, tree: lhs)
        } else if item > element {
            return contains(item, tree: rhs)
        }
        return true
    }
}
```

This method searches for a specific element and returns `true` if it finds it in `node`.

The following presents an example usage of this method:

```
let isFound = BST.contains(9, tree: functionalBST)
```

The `isFound` variable is going to be `true` in this case.

Size

To make this `BST` a little more complete, let's implement a property to check for its `size`:

```
var size: Int {
    switch self {
    case .leaf:
        return 0
    case .node(let lhs, _, let rhs):
        return 1 + lhs.size + rhs.size
    }
}
```

This computed property is going to provide the `size` of the `BST`, and we can use it as follows:

```
print(functionalBST.size) // prints "3"
```

Elements

It would be great to be able to generate an `array` from `BSTelements`. This can be done as follows:

```
var elements: [Element] {
    switch self {
    case .leaf:
        return []
    case .node(let lhs, let element, let rhs):
        return lhs.elements + [element] + rhs.elements
    }
}
```

Empty

We can implement a helper method to generate empty BSTs as follows:

```
static func empty() -> BST { return .leaf}
```

The following is a computed property to check whether the BST is `empty`:

```
var isEmpty: Bool {
    switch self{
    case .leaf:
        return true
    case .node(_, _, _):
        return false
    }
}
```

Let's test these functions and computed properties:

```
let emptyBST = BST<Int>.empty()
print(emptyBST.isEmpty)
```

In the preceding code, we created an empty BST and checked whether it is `empty` using the `isEmpty` property. Obviously, the result is going to be `true`.

This BST implementation is far from complete and needs to be improved by implementing methods to check whether it is a BST.

At the end, our BST becomes the following:

```
enum BST<Element: Comparable> {
    case leaf
    indirect case node(lhs: BST,
                        element: Element,
                        rhs: BST)

    var size: Int {
        switch self {
        case .leaf:
            return 0
        case .node(let lhs, _, let rhs):
            return 1 + lhs.size + rhs.size
        }
    }

    var elements: [Element] {
        switch self {
        case .leaf:
            return []
        case .node(let lhs, let element, let rhs):
            return lhs.elements + [element] + rhs.elements
        }
    }

    var isEmpty: Bool {
        switch self {
        case .leaf:
            return true
        case .node(_, _, _):
            return false
        }
    }

    init() {
        self = .leaf
    }

    static func empty() -> BST {
        return .leaf
    }

    init(element: Element) {
        self = .node(lhs: .leaf, element: element, rhs: .leaf)
    }

    static func contains(_ item: Element, tree: BST<Element>) -> Bool {
```

```
        switch tree {
        case .leaf:
            return false
        case .node(let lhs, let element, let rhs):
            if item < element {
                return contains(item, tree: lhs)
            } else if item > element {
                return contains(item, tree: rhs)
            }
            return true
        }
    }
}
```

Even though it does not represent a full implementation of a BST, we were able to develop it in a functional style, and we will be able to share and reuse the tree among other Trees because they are immutable.

Lists

There are multiple types of lists including linked lists, doubly linked lists, multiple linked lists, circular linked lists, queues, and stacks.

In this section, we will present a simple linked list that is one of the simplest and most popular data structures in imperative programming languages.

A linked list is a linear collection of data elements called nodes pointing to the next node using pointers. Linked lists contain their data in a linear and sequential manner. Simply put, each node is composed of data and a reference to the next node in the sequence, as shown in the following figure:

Let's start with a simple version:

```
enum LinkedList<Element: Equatable> {
    case end
    indirect case node(data: Element, next: LinkedList<Element>)
}
```

Our approach is similar to our BST implementation approach. The difference resides in the node case that has a data element and a pointer to its next element, which is also a LinkedList.

Empty LinkedList

Our `LinkedList` needs a method to create it as `empty`:

```
static func empty() -> LinkedList {
    return .end
}
```

This is as simple as returning `.end`.

Cons

We need to have a way to append items to `LinkedList`; we name it `cons`.

`cons` refers to a fundamental function in most dialects of the Lisp programming language that constructs memory objects that hold two values or pointers to values.

It is loosely related to the object-oriented notion of a constructor/initializer, and more closely related to the constructor function of an algebraic data type system.

In FP jargon, operators that have a similar purpose, especially in the context of list or collection processing, are pronounced `cons`.

We implement `cons` as follows:

```
func cons(_ element: Element) -> LinkedList {
    return .node(data: element, next: self)
}
```

This simple method appends the data to the front of `LinkedList`; in other words, it is like a push operation to a stack.

We can test it as follows:

```
let functionalLinkedList = LinkedList<Int>.end.cons(1).cons(2).cons(3)
```

The result of this operation should be the following:

```
node(3, LinkedList<Swift.Int>.node(2, LinkedList<Swift.Int>.node(1,
LinkedList<Swift.Int>.end)))
```

FP languages such as Haskell and Scala have operators for `cons`. It is : in Haskell and : : in Scala. As we cannot use : in Swift to define an `infix operator`, we are going to use `<|` instead:

```
precedencegroup AssociativityRight {
    associativity: right
}

infix operator <| : AssociativityRight

func <| <T>(lhs: T, rhs: LinkedList<T>) -> LinkedList<T> {
    return .node(data: lhs, next: rhs)
}
```

We will be able to test it as follows:

```
let functionalLLWithCons = 3 <| 2 <| 1 <| .end
```

This statement produces the exact same result.

Again, this `LinkedList` is far from complete but we already achieved great reusability as it is functional. We can use/share our `functionalLinkedList` with other linked lists without worrying about changes and inconsistencies. Let's examine the following:

```
let secondLL = functionalLinkedList.cons(4)
let thirdLL = functionalLinkedList.cons(5)
let fourthLL = LinkedList<Int>.node(data: 1, next: secondLL)
```

In the preceding examples, we use `functionalLinkedList` and add a new item 4 to it to obtain `secondLL` and 5 to obtain `thirdLL`. Also, we use `secondLL` to create `fourthLL`.

Contains

To make this `LinkedList` a little more interesting, we will develop a `contains` method similar to the one that we developed for the BST:

```
static func contains(_ key: Element, list: LinkedList<Element>) -> Bool {
    switch list {
    case .end:
        return false
    case .node(let data, let next):
        if key == data {
            return true
        } else {
            return contains(key, list: next)
```

```
        }
      }
  }
```

This method recursively checks for a specific element in `LinkedList` and returns `true` if it finds the element:

```
print(LinkedList.contains(1, list: functionalLinkedList))
```

The result of this expression is going to be `true`.

Size

We can implement a computed `size` property to calculate the size of a linked list as follows:

```
var size: Int {
    switch self {
    case .node(_, let next):
        return 1 + next.size
    case .end:
        return 0
    }
}
```

This method recursively goes through `LinkedList` and counts the number of `nodes`:

```
print(functionalLinkedList.size)
```

The result is going to be 3 in this example.

Elements

We can implement a computed property to provide an `array` of `elements` as follows:

```
var elements: [Element] {
    switch self {
    case .node(let data, let next):
        return [data] + next.elements
    case .end:
        return []
    }
}
```

Here, we recur through `LinkedList` and return an `array` of `data`. We will be able to use this property as follows:

```
print(functionalLinkedList.elements)
```

This statement prints `[3, 2, 1]`.

isEmpty

Another common operation that `LinkedList` requires is a way to check whether it is empty. We can easily implement it in the following way:

```
var isEmpty: Bool {
    switch self {
    case .node(_ , _):
        return false
    case .end:
        return true
    }
}
```

To test this computed property, we will create an `emptyLinkedList` as follows:

```
let emptyLL = LinkedList<Int>.end
print(emptyLL.isEmpty)

print(functionalLinkedList.isEmpty)
```

In the preceding example, the first `print` statement results in `true` and the second results in `false`.

map, filter, and reduce

You may have wondered if we are going to be able to apply higher-order functions such as `map`, `filter`, and `reduce` to our linked list. We have implemented our linked list with a recursive `enum` and the recursive pattern is well suited to higher-order functions.

Let's start with `map`:

```
func map<T>(_ transform: (Element) -> T) -> LinkedList<T> {
    switch self {
    case .end:
        return .end
    case .node(let data, let next):
        return transform(data) <| next.map(transform)
    }
}
```

Using this method, we will be able to transform elements in our linked list. Nothing fancy here; we use the same `cons operator` that we defined before. The following statement will test our method:

```
let mappedFunctionalLL = functionalLinkedList.map { $0 * 2 }
print(mappedFunctionalLL)
```

The result should be the following:

```
node(6, LinkedList<Swift.Int>.node(4, LinkedList<Swift.Int>.node(2,
LinkedList<Swift.Int>.end)))
```

So we can easily multiply elements in our linked list by 2.

Let's continue with the `filter` method:

```
func filter(_ predicate: ((Element) -> Bool)) -> LinkedList<Element> {
    switch self {
    case .end:
        return .end
    case .node(let data, let next):
        return predicate(data) ? data <| next.filter(predicate) :
                next.filter(predicate)
    }
}
```

Here, we check whether the `predicate` yields a result first. If it does, then we apply our `consoperator` to the `data` and recursively `filter` the `next` element. Otherwise, we just recursively apply `filter` to the `next` element. We can test this method as follows:

```
let filteredFunctionalLL = functionalLinkedList.filter { $0 % 2 == 0 }
print(filteredFunctionalLL)
```

In the preceding code example, we `filter` our linked list to the ones that are even. This statement results in the following:

```
node(2, LinkedList<Swift.Int>.end)
```

It is great to be able to `map` and `filter` our linked list, but we need to have a `reduce` method as well. Let's implement this:

```
func reduce<Value>(_ initial: Value,
                   combine: (Value, Element) -> Value) -> Value {
    switch self {
    case .end:
        return initial
    case .node(let data, let next):
        return next.reduce(combine(initial, data), combine: combine)
    }
}
```

In the preceding code example, we go through the linked list's `elements` recursively and `reduce` the values to a single value. The following code presents a usage example:

```
let reducedFunctionalLL = functionalLinkedList.reduce(0) { $0 + $1 }
print(reducedFunctionalLL)
```

The result of this expression is going to be 6.

At the end, our `LinkedList` becomes the following:

```
/// Operator
precedencegroup AssociativityRight {
    associativity: right
}

infix operator <| : AssociativityRight

func <| <T>(lhs: T, rhs: LinkedList<T>) -> LinkedList<T> {
    return .node(data: lhs, next: rhs)
}

/// LinkedList
```

```
enum LinkedList<Element: Equatable> {
    case end
    indirect case node(data: Element, next: LinkedList<Element>)

    var size: Int {
        switch self {
        case .node(_, let next):
            return 1 + next.size
        case .end:
            return 0
        }
    }

    var elements: [Element] {
        switch self {
        case .node(let data, let next):
            return [data] + next.elements
        case .end:
            return []
        }
    }

    var isEmpty: Bool {
        switch self {
        case .node(_ , _):
            return false
        case .end:
            return true
        }
    }

    static func empty() -> LinkedList {
        return .end
    }

    func cons(_ element: Element) -> LinkedList {
        return .node(data: element, next: self)
    }

    func map<T>(_ transform: (Element) -> T) -> LinkedList<T> {
        switch self {
        case .end:
            return .end
        case .node(let data, let next):
            return transform(data) <| next.map(transform)
        }
    }
```

```
func filter(_ predicate: ((Element) -> Bool)) -> LinkedList<Element> {
    switch self {
    case .end:
        return .end
    case .node(let data, let next):
        return predicate(data) ? data <| next.filter(predicate) :
                next.filter(predicate)
    }
}

func reduce<Value>(_ initial: Value,
                   combine: (Value, Element) -> Value) -> Value {
    switch self {
    case .end:
        return initial
    case .node(let data, let next):
        return next.reduce(combine(initial, data),
                           combine: combine)
    }
}

static func contains(_ key: Element,
                     list: LinkedList<Element>) -> Bool {
    switch list {
    case .end:
        return false
    case .node(let data, let next):
        if key == data {
            return true
        } else {
            return contains(key, list: next)
        }
    }
}
}
```

Stacks

A stack is a collection that is based on the **Last In First Out (LIFO)** policy.

The following figure presents a sample stack:

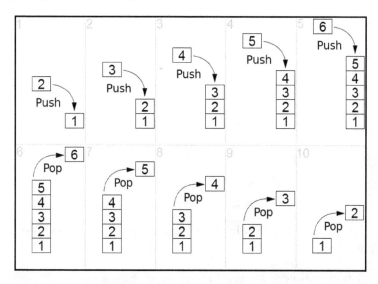

To implement a simple functional stack, we need to provide push, pop, isEmpty, and size operations. We implemented a functional LinkedList in the previous section, which can be used to implement a simple functional stack with the following operations:

- **push**: The cons operation in LinkedList
- **pop**:
- **isEmpty**: The isEmpty operation in LinkedList
- **size**: The size method in LinkedList

As seen here, the only operation that is missing is pop. Let's implement that:

```
func pop() -> (element: Element, list: Stack)? {
    switch self {
    case .node(let data, let next):
        return (data, next)
    case .end:
        return nil
    }
}
```

To test this, we can execute the following:

```
let stack = Stack<Int>.end.cons(1).cons(2).cons(3)

if let (elment, stack) = stack.pop() {
    print(elment)
    if let newStack = stack.pop() {
        print(newStack)
    } else {
        print("Stack is empty")
    }
}
```

The result of the first `print` will be 3 and the result of the second `print` will be the following:

```
Optional((2, LinkedList<Swift.Int>.Node(1, LinkedList<Swift.Int>.End)))
```

This is just an example implementation, and we utilize `Optional Tuple` as a return to obtain the popped element as well as the resulting new linked list.

One more thing that we need to do is to change the name of our `enum` to something more generic, such as list.

Finally, our `stack` becomes very similar to the list.

Lazy lists

So far, we have implemented a linked list and a stack as a list. One of the key concepts in FP is the concept of lazy evaluation. We can make our list lazy so that the elements will be evaluated once we access them. We need to change `node` in such a way that it will return a function containing list as `next`, instead of the list itself. The function will be evaluated when it is called; therefore, our list will be lazy.

We start with modifying our `node` case. In our `LinkedList` example, next was of the `LinkedList<Element>` type. To make our list lazy, we will modify `next` to be a function that returns our list:

```
enum LazyList<Element: Equatable> {
    case end
    case node(data: Element, next: () -> LazyList<Element>)
}
```

As we can see in the preceding code, our `node` case is not defined as `indirect` because `next` is not of the `LazyList` type and is a reference to a function that returns `LazyList`.

We need to accommodate this change into our properties and methods. It is going to be as easy as changing any `next` to `next()`. For example, our `size` property becomes the following:

```
var size: Int {
    switch self {
    case .node(_, let next):
        return 1 + next().size
    case .end:
        return 0
    }
}
```

If we followed the code and changed it properly, we would see that our `map` and `filter` do not compile. We need to change the `operator` as follows:

```
precedencegroup AssociativityRight {
    associativity: right
}

infix operator <|| : AssociativityRight

func <|| <T>(lhs: T, rhs: @escaping () -> LazyList<T>) -> LazyList<T> {
    return .node(data: lhs, next: rhs)
}
```

Here, we change our `rhs` to a function type that matches our `LazyList`'s next. This change did not fix our `map` and `filter` problems. It seems that the right-hand side of the `infix` `operator` is evaluated before being passed to it, and we do not want this.

This is because we do not pass a closure to our operator in the `map` and `filter` methods:

```
func map<T>(_ transform: @escaping (Element) -> T) -> LazyList<T> {
    switch self {
    case .end:
        return .end
    case .node(let data, let next):
        return transform(data) <|| next().map(transform)
    }
}
```

In our `map` method example, `next().map(transform)` is not a closure. If we wrap it in `{ }`, then it becomes a closure. We can modify our `infix operator` as follows:

```
func <|| <T>(lhs: T, rhs: @autoclosure @escaping () -> LazyList<T>) ->
LazyList<T> {

    return .node(data: lhs, next: rhs)
}
```

The `@autoclosure` attribute creates an automatic closure around the expression. So when we write an expression such as `next().map(transform)`, it is automatically wrapped in a closure to become `{ next().map(transform) }` before it is passed to our `infix operator`.

Starting in Swift 1.2, `autoclosure` defaults to `noescape`. This attribute ensures that parameters are not stored for later execution and will not outlive the lifetime of the call. The `noescape` implementation adds minor performance optimizations and bypasses the need to annotate properties and methods with `self`.

The `escaping` annotation is necessary in order to signify that the closure will last longer than the lifetime of the scope that it is declared in.

Finally, we need to change our `cons` method by wrapping `self` in `{ }` as follows:

```
func cons(_ element: Element) -> LazyList {
    return .node(data: element, next: { self })
}
```

Let's test our `LazyList` and see if it works properly:

```
let ourLazyList = 3 <|| 2 <|| 1 <||  LazyList.end // node(3, (Function))
print(ourLazyList.size) // prints 3
```

Our lazy list now becomes as follows:

```
/// Operator
precedencegroup AssociativityRight {
    associativity: right
}

infix operator <|| : AssociativityRight

func <|| <T>(lhs: T, rhs: @autoclosure @escaping () -> LazyList<T>) ->
LazyList<T> {

    return .node(data: lhs, next: rhs)
```

```
}

/// Lazy List
enum LazyList<Element: Equatable> {
    case end
    case node(data: Element, next: () -> LazyList<Element>)

    var size: Int {
        switch self {
        case .node(_, let next):
            return 1 + next().size
        case .end:
            return 0
        }
    }

    var elements: [Element] {
        switch self {
        case .node(let data, let next):
            return [data] + next().elements
        case .end:
            return []
        }
    }

    var isEmpty: Bool {
        switch self {
        case .node(_ , _):
            return false
        case .end:
            return true
        }
    }

    static func empty() -> LazyList {
        return .end
    }

    func cons(_ element: Element) -> LazyList {
        return .node(data: element, next: { self })
    }

    func removeLast() -> (element: Element, linkedList: LazyList)? {
        switch self {
        case .node(let data, let next):
            return (data, next())
        case .end:
            return nil
```

```
        }
    }

    func map<T>(_ transform: @escaping (Element) -> T) -> LazyList<T> {
        switch self {
        case .end:
            return .end
        case .node(let data, let next):
            return transform(data) <|| next().map(transform)
        }
    }

    func filter(_ predicate: @escaping ((Element) -> Bool)) ->
    LazyList<Element> {
        switch self {
        case .end:
            return .end
        case .node(let data, let next):
            return predicate(data) ? data <|| next().filter(predicate):
                next().filter(predicate)
        }
    }

    func reduce<Value>(_ initial: Value,
                        combine: (Value, Element) -> Value) -> Value {
        switch self {
        case .end:
            return initial
        case .node(let data, let next):
            return next().reduce(combine(initial, data),
                                 combine: combine)
        }
    }

    static func contains(_ key: Element, list: LazyList<Element>) -> Bool {
        switch list {
        case .end:
            return false
        case .node(let data, let next):
            if key == data {
                return true
            } else {
                return contains(key, list: next())
            }
        }
    }
}
```

Summary

In this chapter, we covered the concept of functional data structures and explored examples of data structures implemented in a functional way, such as Semigroups, Monoids, BST, linked lists, stacks, and lazy lists.

Even though none of the data structures are complete, they serve as structures that present FP paradigms and techniques. It would also be beneficial to examine the performance of any of these data structures.

In the following chapter, we will cover the importance of immutability by examining its benefits. We will also examine an example of a mutable versus an immutable implementation, as well as the means to get and set immutable objects in a functional way, such as copy constructors and lenses.

9
Importance of Immutability

In object-oriented and functional programming, immutable objects are objects whose state cannot be changed or altered after they are initiated. Therefore, a mutable object stays the same until the end of its life cycle, when it is de-initialized. In contrast, a mutable object can be altered countless times by other objects after it is initiated.

Immutable objects improve readability and runtime efficiency, and using them simplifies our applications.

This chapter will cover the concept of immutability by discussing the following topics with coding examples:

- Immutability
- Benefits of immutability
- Cases for mutability
- An example with approach comparisons
    - Side-effects and unintended consequences
    - Testability
- Copy constructors
- Lenses

Immutability

An immutable object is an object whose state cannot be modified after it is initiated. This quality of immutable objects is essential in multi-threaded applications because it allows a thread to act on the data represented by immutable objects without worrying about changes from other threads. In addition, immutability provides lots of benefits, such as referential transparency and low coupling, which we will talk about in upcoming sections.

An object is considered immutable if the object itself, and in fact all of its properties, are immutable. In some cases, an object is considered immutable even if some of its internal properties change but the object's state appears to be immutable from an external point of view. For instance, an object that uses the memoization technique to cache the results of resource-greedy calculations can be considered as an immutable object.

Immutable objects have the following features:

- They are simple to construct, test, and use
- They are simple to understand and reason about
- They are inherently thread-safe and have no synchronization issues
- They do not require a copy constructor
- They always have failure atomicity so if an immutable object throws an exception, it will not be stuck in an undesirable/indeterminate state
- They offer higher security

Immutable variables

In the imperative programming style, values held in application variables whose contents never change are known as constants to differentiate them from variables that could be altered during execution. Examples might include a view's height and width or the value of π to several decimal places.

Unlike programming languages such as Objective-C in which some types are mutable and some are not, Swift provides a way to create an immutable or mutable version of the same type. In Swift, we use the `let` and `var` keywords to create and store values:

- The `var` keyword is used to create a variable that can be altered later, in other words, to create mutable variables
- The `let` keyword is used to create a constant that cannot be altered later, in other words, immutable variables or constants

Therefore, in Swift, we do not need to have types such as NSMutableArray as opposed to NSArraym, or NSMutableDictionary as opposed to NSDictionary to differentiate between mutability and immutability. We can simply define Dictionary with var or let to make it mutable or immutable.

In addition, the Swift compiler always suggests and warns us about variables that are not changed and will be converted to constants later.

Weak versus strong immutability

Sometimes, certain properties of an object can be immutable while the others may be mutable. These types of objects are called *weakly immutable*. Weak immutability means that we cannot change the immutable parts of the object state even though other parts of the object may be mutable. If all properties are immutable, then the object is immutable. If the whole object cannot be mutated after its creation, the object is called strongly immutable.

Reference types versus value types

We covered this topic in Chapter 3, *Types and Type Casting*, but it is important to emphasize that in most OOP languages, instances can be shared and objects can be passed around with their references. This is true for Swift classes and closures as well. In those cases, it is important to understand that the state of an object can be altered when objects are shared via references. In other words, if any user of a reference to a mutable object changes the object, all other users of that object will be affected by the change.

Benefits of immutability

We already know that immutability helps safety and performance, but in a real-world application development, immutability can provide us with more benefits, which will be explained in the following sections.

Thread safety

Immutable objects are useful in multi-threaded applications because multiple threads can act on the data of immutable objects without worrying about changes to the data by other threads.

As immutable objects are closed to change, it is safe to assume that they will stay unchanged while we access the object from different threads. This assumption simplifies most of the multithreading problems that are complex to solve and maintain. For instance, we do not need to think about synchronization/locking mechanisms at all.

Suppose that we have a mutable object that includes a mutable `array` of a type, for example, a `Product` class that has four properties:

```
struct Producer {
    let name: String
    let address: String
}

class Product {
    var name: String = ""
    var price: Double = 0.0
    var quantity: Int = 0
    var producer: Producer

    init(name: String,
         price: Double,
         quantity: Int,
         producer: Producer) {

        self.name = name
        self.price = price
        self.quantity = quantity
        self.producer = producer
    }
}
```

As seen from the preceding example, all properties are defined as mutable. Now let's create an `array` of `Product`:

```
let producer = Producer(name: "ABC",
                        address: "Toronto, Ontario, Canada")
var bananas = Product(name: "Banana",
                      price: 0.79,
                      quantity: 2,
                      producer: producer)
var oranges = Product(name: "Orange",
                      price: 2.99,
                      quantity: 1,
                      producer: producer)
var apples = Product(name: "Apple",
                     price: 3.99,
                     quantity: 3,
```

```
                    producer: producer)

    var products = [bananas, oranges, apples]
```

Suppose that we need the products `array` to be shared between different threads. Different threads may change the `array` in different ways. Some may change the `price` , while others may change the `quantity`. Some may add or remove items from the `array`.

The first issues to solve are keeping track of changes and knowing who changes the `array` and when. This is already complex, so let's simplify the issue and only add an item to the `array`. Also, let's assume that we are only interested in the latest change.

To be able to track the latest change, let's create another object:

```
class ProductTracker {
    private var products: [Product] = []
    private var lastModified: Date?

    func addNewProduct(item: Product) -> (date: Date,
                                          productCount: Int) {
        products.append(item)
        lastModified = Date()
        return(date: lastModified!, productCount: products.count)
    }

    func lastModifiedDate() -> Date? {
        return lastModified
    }

    func productList() -> [Product] {
        return products
    }
}
```

The `ProductTracker` class has an `array` of `products` and a `lastModified` variable to track the latest change. In addition, it has three methods: one to add a new `product` to the `array`, another to retrieve the last modification date, and the last one to retrieve the `product` list.

Suppose that we want to make our `ProductTracker` class thread-safe and allow multiple objects to access our `ProductTracker` object. We cannot allow multiple threads to execute `addNewProduct` while multiple others list `products`. First of all, we will need a locking mechanism to lock the class during the modifications, second, we need to protect `lastModified` against modification without locking, and finally, an unlocking mechanism.

Apple provides multiple multi-threading mechanisms such as `NSThread`, **Grand Central Dispatch (GCD)**, and operation queues to overcome these types of issues but still multi-threading remains complex.

Referential transparency

Referential transparency generally means that we can always replace a function with its return value without an effect on the application's behavior.

Referential transparency is a guarantee of code reusability. Also, it denies the mutable state of data. In the case of a mutable state, two calls of the same function can potentially produce two different results, which is very difficult to test and maintain.

Low coupling

Coupling is the measure of code dependency. We always want to reduce coupling and make our code components as independent of each other as possible. Low coupling allows us to change a component without affecting other code components. Low-coupled code is easier to read because each component has its own relatively small area of responsibility, though we need to understand only this code without spending time on figuring out how the entire system works.

Immutability helps in achieving low coupling. Immutable data can be safely passed through different code blocks without worrying about it being transformed and affecting other parts of the code. Pure functions transform the data and return the result without affecting the input data. So, if the function contains errors, we can easily find it. Also, using value types and immutable data structures means that we can significantly reduce object referencing.

The following shows the data transformation idea. We have immutable `array numbers`, and we need the `sum` of all the even numbers that it contains:

```
let numbers: [Int] = [1, 2, 3, 4, 5]
let sumOfEvens = numbers.reduce(0) {
    $0 + (($1 % 2 == 0) ? $1 : 0)
}
```

The `numbers` array is not changed and can be passed to any other function without any side-effects:

```
print(numbers) // [1, 2, 3, 4, 5]
print(sumOfEvens) // 6
```

Using in-place transformation of the immutable data will help us reduce coupling.

Avoiding temporal coupling

Suppose that we have a code statement that is dependent on another code statement, as shown in the following code:

```
func sendRequest() {
    let sessionConfig = URLSessionConfiguration.default
    let session = URLSession(configuration: sessionConfig,
                             delegate: nil,
                             delegateQueue: nil)
    var url: URL?
    var request: URLRequest

    /* First request block starts: */
    url = URL(string: "https://httpbin.org/get")
    request = URLRequest(url: url! as URL)
    request.httpMethod = "GET"

    let task = session.dataTask(with: request) {
        (data: Data?, response: URLResponse?, error: Error?) -> Void in

        if (error == nil) {
            let statusCode = (response as! HTTPURLResponse).statusCode
            print("URL Session Task Succeeded: HTTP \(statusCode)")
        } else {
            print("URL Session Task Failed: %@",
            error!.localizedDescription);
        }
    }
    task.resume()
    /* First request block ends */

    /* Second request block starts */
    url = URL(string: "http://requestb.in/1g4pzn21")
    // replace with a new requestb.in
    request = URLRequest(url: url! as URL)

    let secondTask = session.dataTask(with: request) {
```

```
        (data: Data?, response: URLResponse?, error: Error?) -> Void in

        if (error == nil) {
            let statusCode = (response as! HTTPURLResponse).statusCode
            print("URL Session Task Succeeded: HTTP \(statusCode)")
        } else {
            print("URL Session Task Failed: %@",
            error!.localizedDescription);
        }
    }
    secondTask.resume()
}
```

In the preceding code example, we set two different HTTP requests. Suppose that we do not need our first request anymore and we delete the following code block:

```
url = URL(string: "https://httpbin.org/get")
request = URLRequest(url: url! as URL)
request.httpMethod = "GET"
```

The compiler will not complain but as we deleted request.httpMethod = "GET", our second request is not going to work. This situation is called temporal coupling. If we had immutable definitions with let, we would avoid *temporal coupling*.

Avoiding identity mutability

We may need objects to be identical if their internal states are the same. When modifying the state of an object, we are not expecting it to change its identity. Immutable objects avoid this completely.

Failure atomicity

A class can be left in a broken state if it throws a runtime exception. Immutability prevents this problem. An object will never be left in a broken state because its state is modified only during its initialization. The initialization will either fail, rejecting object initialization, or succeed, making a valid solid object, which never changes its encapsulated state.

Parallelization

Immutability makes it easier to parallelize code execution as there are no conflicts among objects and instances.

Exception handling and error management

If we use immutable types only, the internal state of our application will be consistent even if we have exceptions because our immutable objects do not maintain different states.

Caching

References to immutable objects can be cached as they are not going to change; therefore, the same immutable object will be retrieved quickly the next time we try to access it. An example technique is memoization, which we explained in Chapter 2, *Functions and Closures*.

State comparison

The state of an application is the state of all its objects at a given time. The state changes rapidly over time, and an application needs to change state in order to continue running.

Immutable objects, however, have a fixed state over time. Once created, the state of an immutable object does not change, although the state of the application as a whole might change. This makes it easy to keep track of what is happening and simplify state comparison.

Compiler optimization

The compiler optimizes let statements better for items whose values will not change during their lifetime. For example, Apple writes, *It is good practice to create immutable collections in all cases where the collection does not need to change. Doing so enables the Swift compiler to optimize the performance of the collections you create.* (Prefer using let over var where appropriate.)

Cases for mutability

Whenever we require to change an immutable object, we will need to create a new, modified copy of it. This might not be costly and tedious for small and simple objects, but will be in cases where we have large or complex objects with lots of properties and operations.

Also, changing an existing object is simpler and much more intuitive than creating a new, modified copy of it for objects with a distinct identity, for instance, a profile of a user. We may want to maintain a single object of a user's profile and modify it when necessary. This might not be a great example as it is hard to see the performance penalty for this case, but the speed of execution can be a very important differentiator for some types of application, such as games. As an example, representing our game characters with mutable objects may make our game run faster than an alternative implementation where we will need to create a new, modified copy of the game character whenever we need to change it.

Furthermore, our real-world perception is inevitably based on the concept of mutable objects. We deal with all objects around us in our real life. These objects are identical most of the time, and we change some of their characteristics if required.

For instance, we paint a wall in our home instead of replacing the whole wall. We perceive the wall as the same object with a modified property: in this case, color. The wall's identity is maintained while its state changes when we paint it.

Therefore, whenever we model a real-world domain to represent real-world objects in our applications, it is inevitably easier to perceive and implement the domain model using mutable objects.

An example

We understand that there are cases where immutability makes our life harder. We barely touched the surface of these problems in a previous section. We will examine issues in more detail in the following chapters.

Let's redevelop our `Product` example with a FP style and compare the outcome to its OOP counterpart.

Let's use `struct` and make all properties in our `Product` example immutable and examine the outcome:

```
struct FunctionalProduct {
    let name: String
    let price: Double
    let quantity: Int
    let producer: Producer
}
```

Now we have `struct` instead of `class` and all properties are immutable. Also, we do not need an `init` method as `struct` provides it automatically.

We also need to modify our `ProductTracker` class:

```
struct FunctionalProductTracker {
    let products: [FunctionalProduct]
    let lastModified: Date

    func addNewProduct(item: FunctionalProduct) -> (date: Date,
    products: [FunctionalProduct]) {
        let newProducts = self.products + [item]
        return (date: Date(), products: newProducts)
    }
}
```

Our `FunctionalProductTracker` is simplified: it is `struct` with an immutable array of `products` and our `addNewProduct` does not modify the state of our object but provides a new `array` of `products` each time. In fact, we can remove the `addNewProduct` method from this `struct` and handle it in a client object.

Side-effects and unintended consequences

Our mutable example's design can produce unpredictable side-effects. If multiple clients hold a reference to the `ProductTracker` instance, there are two ways for the products to change from underneath any of these clients:

- We could simply reassign a value to the `products` directly. This is fixable by making it `private` for client calls but it is not fixable for in-class modifications.
- We could call `addNewProduct()` from any client and modify the `products`.

Either way, there are going to be side-effects and unintended consequences because of the mutation.

In our immutable example, it is impossible to cause those unintended consequences because our `FunctionalProductTracker` is a value type and all the properties are immutable. The products cannot be changed directly (it is a constant), and `addNewProduct()` returns a whole new instance, so all clients will be dealing with the instance that they expect to deal with.

Testability

Our mutable example's `addNewProduct()` method has no return values. While it is possible to write a unit test for it, it is not obvious how we should implement asserting because the method causes a side-effect in our existing instance that we need to know about.

Our immutable example's `addNewProduct()` method returns a new `array` of product. We simply inspect the value of `products` and assert. We still have both the old and new instances, so we have everything we need to ensure that our code works as intended.

Although we do not cover unit-testing in this book, it is highly recommended that you explore QuickCheck-based libraries such as Quick (`https://github.com/Quick/Quick`) and SwiftCheck (`https://github.com/typelift/SwiftCheck`) as they employ FP techniques to ease the unit testing process of our applications.

Copy constructors and lenses

After examining our immutable example implementation, we are not able to say that it covers all the functionalities of the imperative approach. For instance, it does not provide us with a way to change the producer of a product. After all, we cannot change it.

Whenever we need to change any property of the `product`, we need to go through the following process:

```
let mexBananas = FunctionalProduct(name: bananas.name,
                                   price: bananas.price,
                                   quantity: bananas.quantity,
                                   producer: Producer(name: "XYZ",
                                                      address: "New
                                                      Mexico, Mexico"))
```

This solution is verbose and does not look nice. Let's examine how we can improve this process.

Copy constructors

The first solution is to provide a new init method that copies the current instance. This approach is called a *copy constructor*. Let's add our new init method and leverage it:

```
init(products: [FunctionalProduct], lastModified: Date) {

    self.products = products
    self.lastModified = lastModified
}

init(productTracker: FunctionalProductTracker,
     products: [FunctionalProduct]? = nil,
     lastModified: Date? = nil) {

    self.products = products ?? productTracker.products
    self.lastModified = lastModified ?? productTracker.lastModified
}
```

We added the default init as well because by adding a new init method to our struct, we lost the benefit of automatic init generation. We also need to change our addNewProduct to accommodate these following changes:

```
func addNewProduct(item: FunctionalProduct) -> FunctionalProductTracker {

    return FunctionalProductTracker(productTracker: self,
                                    products: self.products + [item])
}
```

Whenever we need to modify our object partially, we will be able to do so easily using this technique.

Lenses

In the previous section, we covered copy constructors. Here, we will examine a functional structure called a **lens**. Simply put, lenses are functional getters and setters that are implemented for a whole object and its parts:

- **Getters**: We can look through the lens at an immutable object to get its parts
- **Setters**: We can use the lens to change a part of an immutable object

Let's implement a `lens`:

```
struct Lens<Whole, Part> {
    let get: (Whole) -> Part
    let set: (Part, Whole) -> Whole
}
```

Let's use it to change our `FunctionalProduct` object to `get` and `set` the `producer` property:

```
let prodProducerLens: Lens<FunctionalProduct, Producer> =
    Lens(get: { $0.producer },
        set: {
            FunctionalProduct(name: $1.name,
                              price: $1.price,
                              quantity: $1.quantity,
                              producer: $0) })
```

Let's change the `producer` for `mexBananas`:

```
let mexBananas2 = prodProducerLens.set(Producer(name: "QAZ",
                                        address: "Yucatan,
                                        Mexico"), mexBananas)
```

Through our `lens`, we can change it as shown in the preceding code.

Let's examine another example. Suppose that we have a `Producer` object as follows:

```
let chineeseProducer = Producer(name: "KGJ",
                            address: "Beijing, China")
```

We want to change the `address`:

```
let producerAddressLens: Lens<Producer, String> =
    Lens(get: {
            $0.address },
        set: {
            Producer(name: $1.name,
                address: $0) })
```

```
let chineeseProducer2 = producerAddressLens.set("Shanghai, China",
chineeseProducer)
```

Suppose that we had `mexBananas2` and needed to have a Chinese banana producer, then we could use:

```
let chineeseBananaProducer =
prodProducerLens.set(producerAddressLens.set("Shanghai, China",
chineeseProducer), mexBananas2)
```

This syntax does not look very simple, and it seems that we did not gain much after all. In the next section, we will simplify it.

Lens composition

Lens composition will help to simplify our lens; let's examine how:

```
infix operator >>> : AssociativityRight

func >>><A, B, C>(l: Lens<A,B>, r: Lens<B, C>) -> Lens<A, C> {
    return Lens(get: {
                    r.get(l.get($0))
            },
            set: {
                (c, a) in
                l.set(r.set(c, l.get(a)), a)
        })
}
```

Let's test this:

```
let prodProducerAddress = prodProducerLens >>> producerAddressLens
let mexBananaProducerAddress = prodProducerAddress.get(mexBananas3)

let newProducer = prodProducerAddress.set("Acupulco, Mexico", mexBananas2)
print(newProducer)
```

The result is going to be as follows:

```
FunctionalProduct(name: "Banana",
                  price: 0.79,
                  quantity: 2,
                  producer: Producer(name: "QAZ",
                                     address: "Acupulco, Mexico"))
```

Using lenses and composition, we were able to `get` and `set` a product's producer address.

For more curious readers, following Kickstarter GitHub repositories provide real life working examples of lenses:

- `https://github.com/kickstarter/ios-oss`
- `https://github.com/kickstarter/Kickstarter-Prelude`

Summary

In this chapter, we started by exploring the concept of immutability. We looked into its importance and benefits with examples. Then we looked at cases for mutability and went through an example to compare mutability and immutability effects on our code.

Finally, we explored the means to get and set immutable objects in a functional way, such as copy constructors and lenses.

In the following chapter, we will be introduced to OOP, **protocol-oriented programming (POP)**, and **Functional Reactive Programming (FRP)**. Then, we will explore the concept of mixing OOP and FP paradigms, in other words, object functional programming.

10

Best of Both Worlds and Combining FP Paradigms with OOP

"Objects are closures with multiple methods, closures are objects with a single method. So yes [OOP and FP can be used together]."

- Erik Meijer

In previous chapters, we talked mostly about **Functional Programming** (**FP**). We learned various techniques and paradigms of FP. In contrast, we barely touched on **object-oriented programming** (**OOP**). Mostly, we talked about the disadvantages of imperative programming. In practice, most of us have to work on applications that are designed by OOP principles. The reality is that even if we do not like OOP, we are stuck with it. For instance, in iOS and Mac OS development, we have to deal with Cocoa and Cocoa Touch frameworks that are designed by OOP principles.

On the other hand, we are familiar with OOP because most of us learned it at some point and some of us find it natural to model real-world problems with it.

There is a huge discussion about the benefits of one paradigm over the other. Some claim that they can be unified; some claim that they are exclusive and we should choose one paradigm over the other. Also, different programming languages and their communities follow different approaches.

For instance, Haskell is a purely FP language, and it is almost impossible to do OOP with it. In fact, it is absurd to do OOP with it. On the other hand, languages such as Java, Ruby, Python, and C# are OOP languages with limited FP capabilities. There are also languages such as Scala that mix OOP with FP and embrace both worlds.

How would we picture Swift in these settings? We know that Swift is not a pure FP language and has FP capabilities, but we need to further evaluate it in this regard.

In addition to these, the Swift programming community has been introduced to another paradigm: **protocol-oriented programming (POP)**. Furthermore, **Functional Reactive Programming (FRP)** became very popular and is loved by lots of developers.

What are the advantages and disadvantages of one paradigm over the others? How would we design our applications to benefit from all these paradigms? These are the questions that we will try to answer in this chapter. Hence, we will start by introducing OOP, POP, and FRP, and then we will mix OOP paradigms with FP.

This chapter will cover the following topics by coding examples:

- A brief introduction to OOP paradigms
- OOP design patterns/principles
- A brief introduction to POP
- Functional reactive programming (FRP)
- Mixing OOP and FP

OOP paradigms

In this section, we will examine general paradigms in OOP. We start with objects because they are the most fundamental artifacts in OOP. Next, we will look into classes that are blueprints to create objects. Then we will continue with paradigms such as inheritance, polymorphism, and dynamic binding.

Objects

In an OOP application, objects are the runtime entities or instances that take space in memory, and more specifically, in the heap. Objects have an associated/allocated memory address to store their state and a set of functions or methods that define the suitable operations on the object state. In short, in OOP, an object encapsulates state and behavior.

To create an object, a blueprint or recipe is required, which is called a class in OOP.

The following section will explore the class concept in more detail. For now, we will define a very simple class in order to be able to talk about objects:

```
class User {
    let name = "Constant name"
    var age: Int = 0

    func incrementUserAgeByOne() {
        self.age += 1
    }
}
```

In this example, name and age are constants and variables that can be used to store the state of the object. The incrementUserAgeByOne method is a behavior definition that changes the state of the object. We have to create an instance/object of this class to be able to use it:

```
let object1 = User()
object1.age = 2
object1.incrementUserAgeByOne()
```

In the first line of the preceding example, we created an object with our User recipe. At the same time, we allocated a memory address to our object and initialized it. The object, which is an instance of User, can be used; we can use its methods to do operations or to change its state.

From a design perspective, objects model the entities in the application domain. In our example, object represents User.

It is important to understand the following about classes:

- Classes are reference types
- Classes encapsulate states that are mutable

Suppose that we create a new instance of class as follows:

```
let object2 = object1
```

This assignment is not going to copy object1, and will make object2 refer to the same instance.

Let's examine the following:

```
print(object2.age)
object2.incrementUserAgeByOne()
print(object1.age)
```

Here, when we print `object2.age`, it will produce the same result with `object1.age`, and when we call `incrementUserAgeByOne`, it will change the instance's `age`; therefore, it will be changed for `object1` as well as `object2`.

This behavior can be helpful in some circumstances, for instance, if we need to share an instance between different objects.

Examples are database or file management system operations and `AppDelegate` in iOS and Mac OS applications.

On the other hand, it can complicate the reasoning about the code. For instance, if we had lots of references to the same instance, and changing one of them would change all the instances, we would need to react to those changes for all the instances.

If we do not need to share instances, then we can create a new object and use it:

```
let object3 = User()
object3.age = 5

object3.incrementUserAgeByOne()
print(object3.age)
print(object1.age)
```

In the preceding example, as we allocate and initialize a new memory space for our `object3`, it does not refer to the same instance with `object1` and `object2`. Any changes on `object3` are not going to affect `object1` and `object2`.

Classes

A class defines a set of properties and suitable operations. From a type-safe programming language point of view, a class is a structure to implement a user-defined type, such as our `User` class in the preceding example.

Preferably, a class should be an implementation of an **Abstract Data Type** (**ADT**) that hides the implementation details.

An implementation of an ADT as a class can be composed of two kinds of method:

- Methods that return meaningful abstractions about the state of an instance
- Transformational methods to move from a valid instance state to another valid state

To be able to hide implementation details and for the sake of abstraction, all the data within a class should be private to the class.

Let's improve the abstraction in our `User` class example:

```
class User {
    fileprivate let name: String
    fileprivate let age: Int

    init(name: String, age: Int) {
        self.name = name
        self.age = age
    }

    func incrementUserAgeByOne() {
        self.age + 1
    }
}
```

We made our properties `fileprivate` so that no other object can access/change them unless it is inside the same Swift file. Also, we added an `init` method to initialize the object from our `User` class. Class clients will use the `init` method to initialize the object with the initial `name` and `age` information:

```
let object1 = User(name: "Grace", age: 1)
```

Finally, we left the access level of `incrementUserAgeByOne` as `internal` (by default it is `internal`); therefore, any other object in the same module will be able to use it.

The `incrementUserAgeByOne` method changes the state of our object, and this change will affect all objects that refer to the same instance. We can change it as follows:

```
func incrementUserAge(n: Int) -> Int {
    return self.age + n
}
```

Our `incrementUserAge` method returns the new `age` and does not modify the state of the object. We will need to initialize a new object and use this `age` instead.

Finally, as we do not need to modify `age`, we can make it immutable. Our `User` class has two immutable properties with a method that does not modify its properties. Therefore, despite the fact that it is a very simple class, it is functional.

Inheritance

Inheritance is a relation between classes that makes it possible to define and implement a class based on other existing classes.

Also, inheritance helps code reusability and allows independent extensions of the original class (the `super` class) through public classes and interfaces. The relationship between classes through inheritance causes a hierarchy.

Inheritance inevitably minimizes the amount of rework when we need to add additional information and functionalities to an existing class, as we can use the class as the `super` class and subclass it to add new state information and behavior.

Moreover, when it is coupled with polymorphisms and dynamic binding, inheritance minimizes the amount of existing code that should be changed when extending a class.

In programming languages such as C++, it is possible to inherit from more than one class, but in Swift, a class can only subclass one other class.

The following example presents a `UIViewController` subclassing:

```
class BaseViewController: UIViewController { }
```

Our `BaseViewController` will inherit all behaviors and properties of the `UIViewController` class, and we will be able to add new properties and behaviors to it. This way, we do not need to rewrite everything from scratch, and can reuse properties and behaviors in `UIViewController`.

Overriding

Swift permits a class or object to replace the implementation of a behavior/property that it has inherited. This process is called overriding. The `override` keyword is used to specify overridden methods in subclasses.

We can override an inherited instance or class property to provide our own custom/computed getters and setters or add property observers to enable the overriding property to observe when the underlying property value changes.

We can mark a property or behavior as `final` to prevent overriding it in subclasses.

Overriding brings a complication that needs to be handled. We need to ensure which version of the behavior/property an instance of the subclass should use: the one that is part of its own class (`self`) or the one from the parent (`super`) class.

In Swift, the `self` and `super` keywords can be used as prefixes to specify the version of the required behavior/property.

Design constraints

Using inheritance extensively in designing applications imposes certain constraints.

For instance, suppose we define a subclass of `User` called `WebAppUser` that contains the extra acceptable behaviors, and another subclass of `User` called `MobileAppUser` that contains the mobile app modules of `User`.

In defining this inheritance hierarchy, we have already defined certain restrictions, not all of them desirable.

Singleness

In Swift, a subclass can inherit from only one superclass. From the preceding example, `User` can be either `WebAppUser` or `MobileAppUser`, but not both.

Static

The inheritance hierarchy of an object is fixed at initiation, while the object's type is selected and does not change with time.

For example, the inheritance graph does not allow a `MobileAppUser` object to become a `WebAppUser` object while retaining the state of its `User` superclass (this can be achieved with the decorator pattern).

Visibility

Whenever client code has access to an object, it generally has access to all the object's superclass data. Even if the superclass has not been declared `public`, the client can still cast the object to its superclass type.

Composite reuse

The composite reuse principle is an alternative to inheritance. This technique supports polymorphism and code reuse by separating behaviors from the primary class hierarchy and including specific behavior classes, as required in any class. This approach avoids the static nature of a class hierarchy by allowing behavior changes at runtime and permitting a subclass to implement behaviors selectively, instead of being restricted to the behaviors of its super classes.

Issues and alternatives

Implementation inheritance is controversial among OOP programmers and theoreticians. For instance, the authors *Erich Gamma, John Vlissides, Ralph Johnson*, and *Richard Helm*, of the book *Design Patterns: Elements of Reusable Object-Oriented Software*, advocate interface inheritance instead of implementation inheritance and recommend preferring composition over inheritance.

For example, the decorator pattern (as stated previously) has been proposed to overcome the static nature of inheritance between classes.

Furthermore, the OOP community agrees that inheritance introduces unnecessary coupling and breaks encapsulation, so modifications to the super classes can cause undesirable behavioral changes in subclasses.

In Swift, the usage of protocols and extensions is encouraged. Using protocols avoids the coupling problem because no implementation is shared. We will talk more about protocols and protocol extensions in the POP section of this chapter.

When to inherit

There are circumstances where we do not have any other choice but subclassing. Here are some of examples of where subclassing is required:

- **When it is required by the APIs**: For instance, many Cocoa APIs require the use of classes and being controversial is not recommended. For instance, `UIViewController` has to be subclassed.
- **When we need to manage and communicate our value types between instances of other classes**: For example, when we need to draw a custom view in a Cocoa class provided by another drawing class, we will need to communicate it between them. Using a value type in this case is not beneficial.
- **When we need to share an instance between multiple owners**: Core data persistence is an example. It can be very useful to have a synchronization mechanism across multiple owners while using core data. This will cause concurrency issues, but we have to deal with them as we require mutable data.
- **When the lifetime of an instance is connected to external effects or we require a stable identity**: Singletons and `AppDelegate` are two examples.

Polymorphism

Polymorphism means many forms. In general, the ability to take more than one form is called polymorphism. In an OOP language such as Swift, a polymorphic reference is one that can, over time, refer to instances of more than one class. Let's examine an example of the iOS SDK, `UIView`.

There are lots of `UIView` subclasses, including the following:

- `UILabel`
- `UITextField`
- `UIButton`

We can declare a view that can take many forms, such as the following:

```
var view: UIView
view = UIButton()
view = UILabel()
view = UITextField()
```

Polymorphism allows us to write a more generic code that works with families of objects rather than writing code for a specific class.

In this example, regardless of which class we initiate, we can access all the properties and methods declared in the `UIView` class that are inherited by all the subclasses.

For instance, we will be able to check the `bounds` and `origins` of any of them as follows:

```
view.bounds
view.frame.origin
```

We are able to refer to more than one type of object; therefore, a polymorphic reference has both a static and dynamic type associated with it.

The static type is determined from the declaration of the object in the code. It is known at compile time and determines the set of valid types that the object can accept at runtime. This determination is made from an analysis of the inheritance graphs in the system.

The dynamic type of the reference may change over time during the application execution. In Swift, the runtime system keeps all polymorphic references automatically tagged with their dynamic type.

Dynamic binding

Associating a method call to the code to be executed is called binding. As opposed to static binding, where the code associated with the method call is bound during the compile time, dynamic binding means that the code associated with a given method call is not known and will be determined during runtime.

Dynamic binding is associated with polymorphism and inheritance because a method call associated with a polymorphic reference may depend on the dynamic type of that reference.

For instance, our view's static type is `UIView`, and its dynamic type may be `UILabel`, `UITextField`, or `UIButton`. Let's suppose that some of the methods in `UIView` are overridden for `UIButton`. When we call those methods, runtime will dynamically bind the method that needs to be called.

OOP design principles

In this section, we will look at some of the problems with the OOP approach, and OOP and FP solutions to these problems.

In general, OOP is being criticized in the following manner:

- Binding a data structure to behavior is a mechanism of state encapsulation that hides the underlying problem instead of solving it.
- A great deal of effort goes into making inheritance possible. Ironically, object-orientated patterns themselves favor composition over inheritance. Ultimately, in handling two responsibilities--subtyping and reusing-inheritance is not good with either subtyping or reusing.

OOP solutions to these problems include **SOLID** and **Domain-driven Design (DDD)** principles. The following are the SOLID principles:

- The **Single Responsibility principle (SRP)**
- The **Open/Closed principle (OCP)**
- The **Liskov Substitution principle (LSP)**
- The **Interface Segregation Principle (ISP)**
- The **Dependency Inversion principle (DIP)**

DDD principles are proposed to solve OOP problems. Also, FP addresses these problems by the following distinguishing characteristics:

- Explicit management of state is avoided through immutability
- Explicit return values are favored over implicit side-effects
- Powerful composition facilities promote reuse without compromising encapsulation
- The culmination of these characteristics is a more declarative paradigm

SRP

The SRP states that every class should have a single responsibility, where a responsibility is defined as a reason to change.

This principle supports the anti-pattern where large classes play multiple roles. Classes can be large for a few reasons. A core principle of OOP is the binding of the data structure to behavior. The problem is that optimizing for data--structure encapsulation not only weakens composition characteristics, but also hides the underlying problem of explicit state. As a result, OOP code typically contains many data structures, with relatively few functions per data structure. Adding methods to a class brings pressure on the SRP, and reducing the number of methods can either make the data structure difficult to compose or altogether useless. Furthermore, the simple syntactical cost of declaring a class often compels programmers to marginalize.

The FP counterpart

In FP, the fundamental unit of abstraction is the function. Given that a function has a single output, functions naturally have a single responsibility. One could certainly define an arbitrarily generic function, though this would not be intuitive. Moreover, functions are syntactically less resource-hungry.

OCP

The OCP states that software entities should be open for extension but closed for modification.

The ambiguity of this statement can be resolved through two variations of the principle:

- Existing classes should be modified only in order to correct bugs. This restriction delivers the closed aspect of the principle. The open aspect is delivered through implementation inheritance or, in other words, inheritance with the goal of reusing rather than subtyping.
- Openness through polymorphism by definition also provides for closure, as extensibility is supported through substitution rather than modification. Unfortunately, substitution often leads to accidental complexity, which must be addressed by yet another principle--the LSP.

The primary utility of the OCP is the confinement of cascading changes while providing extensibility. This is achieved by designing for extensibility and prohibiting changes to existing entities. Extensibility is attained by fancy tricks with abstract classes and virtual functions. Closure is achieved by encapsulation, or rather by the hiding of moving parts.

The FP counterpart

In FP, functions can be substituted at will and, as such, there is no need to design for extensibility. Functionality requiring parameterization is naturally declared as such. Instead of inventing a concept of a virtual method and inheritance, one can rely on an existing, elementary concept--the higher-order function.

LSP

The LSP states that objects in a program should be replaceable with instances of their subtypes without altering the correctness of that program.

The LSP is essentially a restricted instance of subtyping, which aims to guarantee semantic portability across class hierarchies. Portability is achieved by ensuring that whatever is true of a base type is also true of all subtypes. Subclasses must not strengthen preconditions. They must accept all input and initial states that the base class accepts, and subclasses must not weaken post-conditions. Behavioral expectations declared by the super class must be met by the subclass. These characteristics cannot be enforced by the type system alone.

The LSP as a relation of inheritance is thus deceptive, hence the need for a compensating principle. As such, the need for this principle demonstrates a pitfall in subtype (inclusion-based) polymorphism. Implicit factoring by class hierarchy imposes the needless inclusion of restrictions and requires complex principles to place a boundary on accidental complexity.

The FP counterpart

Functional languages favor parametric polymorphism with bounded quantification, thereby avoiding some of the pitfalls of inheritance. Informally, functional languages emphasize substitutability and de-emphasize implementation reuse, as reuse is better achieved through composition. Most ambitions of the LSP are effectively trivial in FP languages.

ISP

The ISP states that many client-specific interfaces are better than one general-purpose interface. In other words, no client should be forced to depend on methods that it does not use.

In essence, ISP is a restatement of the SRP for interfaces and reflects the same underlying problem--the difficulty of balancing responsibility assignment, composition, and encapsulation in object-oriented design. On the one hand, it is desirable to encapsulate; on the other hand, it is desirable to compose. Furthermore, the problem with employing the ISP alone is that it doesn't directly protect against large classes and in some ways hides the problem.

The FP counterpart

FP reduces the need for encapsulation by avoiding state and breeds composition at the core. There is no augmented concept of role-based interfaces because function roles are explicit at inception. Functions are segregated by default.

DIP

The DIP states that one should depend upon abstractions. Do not depend upon concretions. In other words, high-level modules should be decoupled from low-level modules through abstractions. This principle states that code should be structured around the problem domain, and the domain should declare dependencies on required infrastructure as protocols. Dependencies thus point inward to the domain model.

The reason that this principle is an inversion is because typical architectures promoted by OOP (via layer architecture) exhibit dependency graphs, where high-level modules consume low-level modules directly.

Initially, this dependency graph seems natural as, in expressing domain models in code, one inevitably depends upon the constructs of the language. Procedural programming allows dependencies to be encapsulated by procedures.

Subtype polymorphism defers procedure implementation. Unfortunately, the use of protocols is often overlooked to express domain dependencies in OOP implementations. Given that infrastructure code is typically more voluminous, the focus of the code drifts away from the domain. DDD was devised in part to balance this drift.

The FP counterpart

The declarative and side-effect-free nature of FP provides dependency inversion. In OOP, high-level modules depend on infrastructure modules primarily to invoke side-effects. In FP, side-effects are more naturally triggered in response to domain behavior, as opposed to being directly invoked by domain behavior. Thus, dependencies become not merely inverted, but pushed to outer layers altogether.

DDD

DDD is an approach to software development for complex needs by connecting the implementation to an evolving model.

Concepts

Concepts of the model include the following:

- **Context**: The setting in which a word or statement appears that determines its meaning.
- **Domain**: An ontology, influence, or activity. The subject area to which the user applies a program is the domain of the software.
- **Model:** A system of abstractions that describes selected aspects of a domain and can be used to solve problems related to that domain.
- **Ubiquitous language**: A language structured around the domain model and used by all team members to connect all the activities of the team with the software.

Premise

The premise of DDD is as follows:

- Placing the project's primary focus on the core domain and domain logic
- Basing complex designs on a model of the domain
- Initiating a creative collaboration between technical and domain experts to iteratively refine a conceptual model that addresses particular domain problems.

Building blocks

In DDD, there are artifacts to express, create, and retrieve domain models that are explored from an FP perspective in the following sections.

Aggregate

This is a collection of objects that are bound together by a root entity, otherwise known as an aggregate root. The aggregate root guarantees the consistency of changes being made within the aggregate by forbidding external objects from holding references to its members.

The concept of the aggregate remains in FP; however, it is not represented in terms of a class. Instead, it can be expressed as a structure, including a set of aggregate states, initial state, set of commands, set of events, and function-mapping the set of commands to the set of events given a state. Cohesion is provided by a module mechanism.

Immutable value objects

Immutable value objects are objects that contain attributes but have no conceptual identity. They should be treated as immutable.

In a previous chapter, we saw that Swift provides immutable product and sum types with auto-implemented structural equality, which addresses this pattern trivially. Heavy reliance on state in OOP makes references first-class citizens rather than the structure of the data itself.

Domain events

A domain event is a domain object that defines an event.

Domain events are powerful mechanisms to keep domain models encapsulated. This can be accomplished by allowing various observers from outer layers to register for a domain event (signal).

The problem with domain events in OOP is that the typical implementation is complex and relies on side-effects. Event observations are typically declared in the composition root and thus, it is not immediately obvious from the perspective of the producer which observers will be invoked. In FP, a domain event is simply a value returned by a function in an aggregate. Observers can be explicitly registered as filters.

Furthermore, FRP can handle domain events very effectively. On the other hand, returning domain events from aggregate methods in OOP is prohibitive due to the lack of union types and pattern matching.

Intention-revealing interface

In imperative OOP code, intent leaks through side-effects and focuses on the how rather than the what. Always having to bind behavior to the data structure can also be problematic.

As FP is more declarative, function names and interfaces tend to be more focused on intent rather than the underlying mechanics. In addition, the interfaces of side-effect-free functions are by nature more revealing because behavior is made explicit through the return value. As a result, in addition to the purely linguistic benefit of naming with intent, intent is also encoded by the type system. This is not to say that expressing intent is effortless in FP--only that it is better supported by the FP paradigm.

Side-effect-free functions

Side-effects are in direct opposition to encapsulation, yet all too often they are the most useful tools.

Unlike imperative programming, FP avoids side-effects. This pattern is yet another example of how a well-crafted object-oriented design converges upon a functional style.

Assertions

Like many patterns rooted in imperative object-oriented design, assertions claim to use implicit side-effects.

As with intention-revealing interfaces, assertions in FP languages are automatically encoded in the return type of a function in addition to the function name.

Conceptual contours

Conceptual contours emerge when domain knowledge is spread throughout the code to a sufficient degree. In OOP, this can be achieved by carefully following the principles of DDD.

In FP, conceptual contours emerge more readily, once again due to the declarative and side-effect-free nature of the paradigm. Specifically, clients of the domain model can rely on cohesive functionality attained with composition and yet still have access to constituents without breaking encapsulation.

Closure of operations

Closure of operations illustrates yet another example of coercing composition and structure upon object-oriented designs.

Essentially, closure simplifies reasoning about a problem by restricting the domain of the discourse. The example of a functional implementation of a domain exhibits this characteristic at a fundamental level. The operation of applying a domain event is closed under the set of domain states. In terms of persistence, this naturally translates to event-sourcing, but also supports persistence in a key-value store or ORM with no required modification.

Declarative design

The overall intent of the aforementioned patterns is to cultivate a declarative design. As witnessed, FP is inherently more declarative, and therefore more accommodating in this regard. Through declarative design, we can distill the distinguishing characteristics of the domain better and reduce or eliminate coupling to orthogonal concerns of infrastructure. Consequently, re-usability, testability, correctness, maintainability, and productivity are tremendously enhanced.

POP

POP encourages us to develop protocols and extend them instead of classes and inheritance. POP is new in the Objective-C and Swift development community, but what it provides is not very different from the concept of `Abstract` classes in languages such as Java and C#, and `pure-virtual` functions in C++.

In Swift, classes, structs, and enumerations can conform to protocols. This makes protocols more usable because inheritance does not work for structs and enumerations.

POP paradigms

In this section, we will explore POP paradigms. To start with, we will look at an example:

```
protocol UserProtocol {
    func greet(name: String) -> String
    func login(username: String, password: String) -> Bool
}
```

This protocol defines two functions to be implemented by the struct, enumeration, or classes that need to conform to this protocol.

Protocol composition

Protocol composition allows types to conform to more than one protocol. This is one of the many advantages that POP has over OOP. With OOP, a class can have only one superclass, which can lead to very monolithic super classes. With POP, we are encouraged to create multiple smaller protocols with very specific requirements.

Protocol extensions

Protocol extensions are among the most important parts of the POP paradigm. They allow us to add functionality to all types that conform to a given protocol. Without protocol extensions, if we had common functionality that was necessary for all types that conformed to a particular protocol, then we would need to add that functionality to each type. This would lead to large amounts of duplicated code.

The following example extends our protocol by adding a `logout` method and its implementation; thus, any `struct`, `enum`, or `class` that conforms to `UserProtocol` will have the logout functionality:

```
extension UserProtocol {
    func logout(userName: String) -> Bool {
        return true
    }
}
```

Protocol inheritance

Protocol inheritance is where one protocol can inherit the requirements from one or more other protocols, as shown in the following code:

```
protocol MobileAppUserProtocol: UserProtocol { }
```

`MobileAppUserProtocol` inherits from `UserProtocol` so it will have all the defined and extended methods.

Associated types

Associated types can be used to make our protocols work with generic types:

```
protocol MobileAppUserProtocol: UserProtocol {
    associatedtype applicationModuleList
    func listSelectedModules() -> [applicationModuleList]
}
```

Conforming to a protocol

The following code presents an example of protocol conformance with associated type usage:

```
enum MobileAppUserType: MobileAppUserProtocol {
    case admin
    case endUser

    func greet(name: String) -> String {
        switch self {
        case .admin:
            return "Welcome \(name) - You are Admin"
        case .endUser:
            return "Welcome \(name)!"
        }
    }
    func login(username: String, password: String) -> Bool {
        return true
    }
    func listSelectedModules() -> [String] {
        return ["Accounting", "CRM"]
    }
}
```

Then we can create a new mobile user as follows:

```
let mobileUser: MobileAppUserType = MobileAppUserType.admin
mobileUser.logout(userName: "Su Tamina")

mobileUser.listSelectedModules()
```

POP minimizes the inheritance and subclassing necessities by enabling us to conform to protocols and extend them with default implementations.

Functional reactive programming

FP avoids immutability and side-effects. In some circumstances, the application should react to dynamic value/data changes. For instance, we may need to change the user interface of an iOS application to reflect received data from a backend or database system. How would we do this without states and mutable values?

Imperative programming captures these dynamic values only indirectly, through state and mutations. The complete history (past, present, and future) has no first-class representation. Moreover, only discretely evolving values can be (indirectly) captured, as the imperative paradigm is temporally discrete.

FRP provides a way to handle dynamic value changes while still retaining the FP style. FRP, as its name suggests, is a combination of FP and reactive programming. Reactive programming makes it possible to deal with certain data types that represent values over time. These data types are called time flow or event streams in different FP languages. Computations that involve these changing-over-time/evolving values will themselves have values that change over time. FRP captures these evolving values directly and has no difficulty with continuously evolving values.

In addition, FRP can be presented as the following set of principles/rules:

- Data types or dynamic/evolving over time values should be first-class citizens. We should be able to define, combine, and pass them to functions and return them from functions.
- Data types should be built from a few primitives such as constant/static values and time with sequential and parallel combinations. The n behaviors are combined by applying an n-ary function to static values continuously over time.
- To account for discrete phenomena, we should have additional event types, each of which has a stream (finite or infinite) of occurrences. Each occurrence has an associated time and value.
- To come up with the compositional vocabulary out of which all behaviors and events can be built, play with some examples. Keep deconstructing into pieces that are more general/simple.
- We should be able to compose the whole model, using the technique of denotational semantics:
    - Each type has a corresponding simple and precise mathematical type of meaning
    - Each primitive and operator has a simple and precise meaning as a function of the meanings of the constituents

Building blocks of FRP

It is important to understand FRP building blocks to be able to understand FRP. The following sections explain these building blocks with one of the great FRP libraries for the Cocoa framework, called *ReactiveCocoa* and its related library, *ReactiveSwift*, developed by GitHub. *ReactiveCocoa* was developed for Objective-C and, as of version 3.0, all major feature development is concentrated on the Swift API and all primitives are now a part of *ReactiveSwift*.

ReactiveSwift offers composable, declarative and flexible primitives that are built around the concept of streams of values over time. These primitives can be used to uniformly represent observation patterns. *ReactiveCocoa* wraps various aspects of Cocoa frameworks with the declarative *ReactiveSwift* primitives.

Events

An event represents the fact that something has happened. An event might represent the press of a button, data received from an API, the occurrence of an error, or the completion of an async operation. In short, a source generates the events and sends them over a signal to any number of observers.

Event is an enumeration type representing either a value or one of three events (failed, completed, and interrupted).

Signals

Signals are event streams that send values over time that are already in progress. We can imagine them as pipes that send values without knowing about the previous values they have sent or future values they are going to send. Signals can be composed, combined, and chained declaratively.

Signals can unify all Cocoa common patterns for asynchrony and event handling:

- Delegate methods
- Callback blocks
- Notifications
- Control actions and responder chain events
- Future and promises
- Key-value observing

As all of these mechanisms can be represented in the same way, it is easy to declaratively chain and combine them together.

ReactiveSwift represents signals as `Signal`. Signals can be used to represent notifications, user input, and so on. As work is performed or data is received, events are sent on the signal, which pushes them out to any observers. All observers see the events at the same time.

Users must observe a signal in order to access its events. Observing a signal does not trigger any side-effects. In other words, signals are entirely producer-driven and push-based, and observers cannot have any effect on the signal's lifetime. While observing a signal, the user can only evaluate the events in the same order as they are sent on the signal. There is no random access to values of a signal.

Signals can be manipulated by applying the following operations:

- `map`, `filter`, and `reduce` to manipulate a single `signal`
- `zip` to manipulate multiple signals at once

These operations can be applied only on the next events of a signal.

The lifetime of a signal may consist of various numbers of next events, followed by one terminating event, which may be any one of the following:

- Failed
- Completed
- Interrupted

Terminating events are not included in the signal's values and they should be specially handled.

Pipes

A `signal` that can be manually controlled is called `pipe`. In *ReactiveSwift*, we can create a pipe by calling `Signal.pipe()`.

The `pipe` method returns `signal` and `observer`. The signal can be controlled by sending events to the `observer`.

Signal producers

A signal producer creates signals and performs side-effects. `SignalProducer` can be used to represent operations, or tasks such as network requests, where each invocation of `start()` will create a new underlying operation and allow the caller to observe the result. Unlike a signal, no work is started (and thus no events are generated) until an `observer` is attached, and the work is restarted for each additional observer.

Starting a signal producer returns a `disposable` that can be used to `interrupt` / `cancel` the work associated with the produced `signal`.

Signal producers can also be manipulated via operations such as `map`, `filter`, and `reduce`. Every signal operation can be `lifted` to operate upon signal producers instead, using the `lift` method.

Observers

An `observer` is anything that observes or is capable of observing events from a `signal`. Observers can be implicitly created using the callback-based versions of the `Signal.observe()` or `SignalProducer.start()` methods.

Lifetimes

When observing a signal or starting a signal producer, it is important to consider how long the observation should last. The concept is represented as `Lifetime` and is useful any time an observation might outlive the observer.

Actions

An action will do some work when executed with an input. Actions are useful in performing side-effecting work upon user interaction, such as when a button is clicked. Actions can also be automatically disabled based on a property, and this disabled state can be represented in a user interface by disabling any controls associated with the action.

Properties

A property stores a value and notifies observers about future changes to that value. The current value of a property can be obtained from the value getter. The producer getter returns a signal producer that will send the property's current value, followed by all changes over time.

Disposables

A disposable is a mechanism for memory management and cancellation. When starting a signal producer, a disposable will be returned. This disposable can be used by the caller to cancel the work that has been started, clean up all temporary resources, and then send a final interrupted event with regard to the particular signal that was created.

Schedulers

A scheduler is a serial execution `queue` to perform work or deliver results upon. `Signals` and `signal producers` can be ordered to deliver events on a specific scheduler. `Signal producers` can additionally be ordered to start their work on a specific scheduler.

Schedulers are similar to the **Grand Central Dispatch** (GCD) queues, but schedulers support cancellation via `disposables` and always execute serially. With the exception of `ImmediateScheduler`, schedulers do not offer synchronous execution. This helps avoid deadlocks and encourages the use of `signal` and `signal producer` operations instead of blocking work.

`Schedulers` are also somewhat similar to `NSOperationQueue`, but schedulers do not allow tasks to be reordered or depend on one another.

An example

Let's suppose that we have an outlet and we want to observe its changes:

```
@IBOutlet weak var textFieldUserName: UITextField!
```

We can create a `SignalProducer` as follows:

```
let userNameSignalProducer =
textFieldUserName.rac_textSignal().toSignalProducer.map {
    text in
    text as! String
}
```

The `rac_textSignal` method is a ReactiveCocoa extension for `UITextField` that can be used to create the `signal producer`.

Then, we can start our `SignalProducer` as follows:

```
userNameSignalProducer.startWithNext {
    results in
    print("User name:\(results)")
}
```

This will print any changes in our `textField` to the console.

Also, we can execute operations such as `map`, `flatMap`, `filter`, and `reduce` on this `signal producer`, which we covered in `Chapter 6`, *Map, Filter, and Reduce*.

Mixing OOP and FP

So far, we have seen that adding FP capabilities to an OOP language leads to benefits in the OOP design.

In summary, OOP fits perfectly with FP when our objects are as immutable as possible. To make our objects as immutable as possible, we can consider the following principles:

- Objects should be types that encapsulate related pieces of data.
- Objects can have methods; however, these methods shouldn't change the object and should instead return a new one of the appropriate type.
- All the required state data should be injected into the class's initialization so that it will be ready to use immediately.
- Static methods can be used freely and static variables should be avoided. Protocols and generics should be used to avoid code duplicates.

These principles not only empower us to employ functional design patterns, but also enrich our object-oriented code.

Problems

There are a few problems in unifying and mixing OOP with FP, which we will cover in the following sections.

Granularity mismatch

FP and OOP operate on different design-granularity levels. While in FP, functions/methods are the most important building blocks and programming is done at a low level, in OOP, classes/objects/modules are the most important building blocks and programing is done at a high level.

To overcome this granularity mismatch, we need to find answers for the following questions:

- Where do we locate the source of individual functions in an OOP architecture?
- Where do we relate such individual functions to an OOP architecture?

In Swift, we can place functions inside source files and outside of classes, or we can place them as static or class methods.

FP paradigm availability

So far, we have explored a lot of different FP paradigms in Swift. Here, we check conceptually whether Swift is a suitable language for FP. We will explore the paradigms in the following sections.

First-class values

In an FP language, functions/methods should be first-class citizens.

First-class-citizen functions will enable us to use most FP paradigms if they satisfy the following rules:

- Functions/methods should be usable as function/method parameters and arguments
- Functions/methods can be returned as a result of a function/method
- Functions can take place in data structures

So far, we have seen an example implementation of all these rules.

Closures

First-class functions/methods should be implemented as closures. For instance, they should be associated with specific private environments.

As we already know, Swift functions are implemented as closures.

FP-OOP interrelation tools

Standalone functions/methods should be explicitly relatable to the class/object level.

Swift extensions enable us to add methods to existing classes without creating new derived classes.

FP support

FP paradigms should be reinforced by related constructs, predefined definitions, occurrences in standard libraries, and so on.

They should satisfy the following rules:

- Overloading for generic function types
- First-class multiple invocation and multicasting
- Function marshalling and serialization (closures as data structures)

Swift supports the preceding FP paradigms.

Effects of having FP capabilities in OOP

Having FP capabilities in the OOP language causes idiomatic and architectural effects, which are explored in the following sections.

Idiomatic effects

Having FP capabilities in OOP makes it possible to abstract our code in a function level and program in small.

The following subsections explain these effects.

Code abstraction at a function/method level

First-class functions/methods make it possible to separate the concerns at the function/method level in our code. We can define generic functions that can act as pattern templates at the function/method level, as we have seen in Chapter 2, *Functions and Closures*, in the *First-class functions* section.

Generic iterator operations

Higher-order functions/methods such as map, filter, and reduce make it possible to declaratively operate through collections and transform them, as we have seen in Chapter 6, *Map, Filter, and Reduce*.

Operation compositions and sequence comprehensions

First-class functions/methods can provide convenient means of expressing a sequence of operations as a composition of higher-order functions, as we have seen in Chapter 2, *Functions and Closures*, in the *Function composition* section.

Function partial applications and currying

Using higher-order functions, every n-ary function can be transformed into a composition of n-unary functions, that is, into a curried function, as we have seen in Chapter 2, *Functions and Closures*, in the *Function composition* and *Function currying* sections.

Architectural effects

Using FP capabilities affects our approach in OOP architectural design, which is explained in the following subsections.

Reduction of the number of object/class definitions

Using first-class and higher-order functions/methods makes it possible to avoid cluttering the OOP architecture with new classes/objects.

Name abstraction at a function/method level

Using first-class functions/methods allows parameters to be initialized by any method/function satisfying their declared type.

OOP design patterns - a FP perspective

Design patterns describe recurring solutions to common problems in object-oriented software design. Patterns are categorized into three types:

- Creational: design patterns that deal with object-creation mechanisms, trying to create objects in a manner suitable to the situation.
- Structural: design patterns that ease the design by identifying a simple way to realize relationships between entities.
- Behavioral: design patterns that identify common communication patterns between objects and realize these patterns. By doing so, these patterns increase flexibility in carrying out this communication.

This section introduces some OOP design patterns on a very high level, as well as the FP counterparts:

- Strategy
- Command
- Observer
- Proxy
- Visitor

Strategy pattern

The strategy pattern is a behavioral pattern that lets an algorithm vary independently of the clients that use it. In other words, it allows one of a family of algorithms to be selected on-the-fly at runtime.

From an FP perspective, a strategy is just a case of abstracting code at a method level.

Command pattern

The command pattern is a behavioral pattern that encapsulates requests (method calls) as objects so that they can be transmitted, stored, and applied easily.

FP provides closures and first-class functions.

Observer pattern

The observer pattern is a behavioral pattern that allows a one-to-many dependency between objects so that when one object changes state, all its dependents are notified and updated.

FRP handles this pattern very effectively and declaratively.

Virtual proxy pattern

The virtual proxy pattern is a structural pattern that provides placeholders for other objects in such a way that their data is created/computed only when needed.

FP provides lazy instantiation and evaluation.

Visitor pattern

The visitor pattern is a behavioral pattern that allows us to define new operations without changing the classes of the elements on which they operate.

FP makes functions independent of object changes.

Summary

In this chapter, we covered OOP principles and paradigms. Then we discussed POP. Next, we introduced FRP. Finally, we explored how to mix FP with OOP paradigms.

In the following chapter, we will develop a Todo backend and an iOS application, employing the concepts that we have covered so far.

We will use FP techniques to parse and map the data, and we will use FRP to reactively manage the events in the applications. Additionally, we will employ POP and OOP techniques.

11
Case Study - Developing an iOS Application with FP and OOP Paradigms

In the previous chapters, we covered a variety of concepts and techniques. We started with FP paradigms and explored related topics in detail. Also, in the previous chapter, we covered other paradigms such as OOP, FRP, and POP, and mixed them together. In this chapter, we will create a simple application using those paradigms.

Most iOS applications need a backend to be able to provide advanced functionalities such as integration with other systems. In this chapter, we will create a simple backend with Swift that is going to be used as a `Todo` application API. Then, we will develop an iOS application that will leverage our backend and provide some essential functionality such as listing and updating `Todo` items coming from the backend. Also, our iOS application will be able to create new `Todo` items. Our iOS application development will include the FP, OOP, POP, and FRP paradigms.

This chapter will cover the following topics:

- Requirements
- High-level design
- Backend development
    - Environment configuration
    - Swift Package Manager
    - Vapor
    - Application development

- Frontend development
    - `CocoaPods` dependency management configuration
    - Third-party libraries
    - Backend communication
    - JSON parsing and model mapping
    - State management
    - Listing items with a `UITableView`
    - Updating and creating items
    - Filtering items

Requirements

This section presents the requirements for our case study. Since the focus of this book is not on requirement engineering, we will define very simple requirements. This section does not present best practices for requirement engineering.

The requirements for the iOS application user are as follows:

- Users should be able to list `Todo` items
- Users should be able to see the details of each item
- Users should be able to modify items
- Users should be able to create a new item
- Users should be able to filter items by their status

High-level design

This section explains the high-level design of the frontend and backend.

Frontend

Application design follows a slightly different version of the **Model-View-Controller (MVC)** pattern, with the addition of the `Actions`, `Store`, `State`, and `Communication` layers to simplify the controller layer of the traditional iOS application MVC pattern. All application layers are explained in the following sections.

Models

Plain old model structures. These models do not have any logic and only consist of properties. There are four types of model:

- `TodoRequest`: This is a `struct` that is used in backend request calls and conforms to `RequestProtocol`
- `Todo`: This is a `struct` that represents `Todo` data, and uses the `Argo` and `Curry` libraries to decode the object from JSON
- `TodoViewModel` and `TodosViewModel`: These structs represent data and are used in views and shown to the user
- `TodoLens`: These lenses modify the `Todo` model

All the aforementioned models are immutable value types.

Views

We have two View subclasses: one to provide a custom `UITableViewCell` called `TodoTableViewCell`, and a subclass of `UIView` named `FooterView`.

Both of these Views are subclasses of iOS SDK-provided classes. Besides these classes, we will have our `UIViewController` scenes in the storyboard.

ViewController

`ViewController` is a subclass of `UIViewController` or `UITableViewController`, and it connects views to logic:

- `MasterViewController`: This is a subclass of `UITableViewController` to present `Todo` items
- `DetailsViewController`: This is a subclass of `UIViewController` to present details of each `Todo` item to the user

To develop iOS applications, we have to rely on iOS SDK-provided classes such as `UIViewController` and `UITableViewController`. The `ViewController` and `UIView` subclasses are the only classes that will be used in this case study.

State

In iOS application development, we need to handle states. We use the `Delta`, `ReactiveCocoa`, and `ReactiveSwift` libraries to manage our Todo app's `State`.

`Delta` takes an App that has custom `State` management spread throughout all the `ViewControllers` and simplifies it by providing a simple interface to change `State` and subscribe to its changes.

`ReactiveSwift` offers composable, declarative, and flexible primitives that are built around the concept of streams of values over time. These primitives can be used to uniformly represent observation patterns. `ReactiveCocoa` wraps various aspects of Cocoa frameworks with the declarative `ReactiveSwift` primitives.

We will implement a `State struct` to `observable` properties.

Store

Our `Store struct` will wrap `State struct` and provide properties to observe its changes. `Store struct` conforms to the `Delta` library's `StoreType protocol`, which defines the storage of an `observable` state and dispatch methods to modify it. Also, `Store struct` uses the `ReactiveSwift` library's `MutableProperty` value and allows observation of its changes in a thread-safe manner.

Actions

`Actions` are structs that conform to the `ActionType protocol` from the `Delta` library. `ActionType` is used when we want to make modifications to the `Store` struct's `State`. All changes to the `Store struct` go through this type.

We will develop the following `Actions` in the application:

- `ClearCompletedTodosAction`: This is used to delete completed `Todo` items from the list
- `CreateTodoAction`: This is used to create a new `Todo` item
- `DeleteTodoAction`: This is used to delete a `Todo` item
- `DetailsTodoAction`: This is used to present the details of an item
- `LoadTodosAction`: This is used to list all `Todo` items

- `SetFilterAction`: This is used to filter `Todo` items
- `ToggleCompletedAction`: This is used to mark a `Todo` item as completed
- `UpdateTodoAction`: This is used to update a `Todo` item

Manager

`TodoManager` provides global functions to handle backend API calls and JSON payload mapping. `TodoManager` uses `WebServiceManager` for backend calls and the `Argo` library to map JSON payloads to the `Todo` model. Also, `TodoManager` will update the `State` in the `Store` through `Lenses` and `Action`.

Communication

The `Communication` layer is responsible for backend communication. It includes the following components:

- `WebServiceManager`: This provides a global function named `sendRequest` that is used by `TodoManager` to call the backend API. Also, it uses `configureHeaders` to perform a reflection on request to get its properties and respective values.
- `Urls`: This `enum` provides a proper HTTP request method and a full URL address by pattern-matching and extensions.
- `Alamofire`: This is a library that is used by `WebServiceManager` for HTTP request handling.
- `Argo`: This library maps model objects from and to JSON functionally.

Communication between layers

The application uses `closures` and `ReactiveCocoa` signals for communication between layers.

Third-party libraries/frameworks

The following third-party libraries/frameworks are used in our iOS application:

- `Alamofire`: This is a web service calling and management framework
- `Argo`: This is a functional JSON parsing library
- `CocoaPods`: This is responsible for dependency management
- `Delta`: This is the state management library
- `ReactiveCocoa`: This is a **Functional Reactive Programming (FRP)** library to handle signals and streams

Cross-cutting concerns

This section explains cross-cutting concerns such as error management, exception handling, and so on.

Error management and exception handling

We discussed these in previous chapters of this book.

Tools

We will use Xcode to develop our application. AppCode by JetBrains is another IDE for iOS application development that can be used for this case study.

Backend

There are various web frameworks and HTTP servers for Swift, that are works-in- progress. **Kitura**, **Perfect**, and **Vapor** are three of the most popular ones. None of them are designed and developed in the FP style. We will use Vapor in our example to provide a backend that can be leveraged by our frontend application.

Vapor

Vapor (`https://github.com/qutheory/vapor`) is a popular Laravel/Lumen-inspired web framework that is MIT-licensed. It is purely written in Swift and is modular.

Vapor provides CLI tools to simplify building and running Vapor applications.

`vapor new <project-name>` can be used to create a new project, `vapor build` can be used to build the project and download dependencies, `vapor xcode` can be used to create the Xcode project, and `vapor run` can be used to run the project.

Vapor uses **Swift Package Manager (SPM)** as the dependency manager: starting an application with Vapor is as easy as importing Vapor and adding the following lines to the main file:

```
let drop = Droplet()
drop.run()
```

Routing

Routing in Vapor is simple as the following:

```
drop.get("welcome") { request in
    return "Hello, World"
}
```

Adding the preceding code to the main file will make our web application respond to all GET requests to `localhost:8080/welcome` with the string, `Hello, World`.

JSON

It is easy to respond with JSON:

```
drop.get("version") { request in
    return try JSON(node: ["version": "0.1"])
}
```

The preceding code responds to all GET requests to `localhost:8080/version` with the JSON dictionary `{"version": "0.1"}` and `Content-Type: application/json`.

Request data

Every route call gets passed a `request` object that can be used to grab `query` and `path` parameters.

The following example shows how to access JSON, Query, and form-encoded data from the request:

```
drop.post("hello") { request in
    guard let name = request.data["name"]?.string else {
```

```
        return "Please include a name"
    }

    return "Hello, \(name)!"
}
```

In this example, we read the request data and return a string.

Vapor also provides the means for session management, database connection, and view responses with HTML or Stencil template-included HTML pages. There is an example Vapor project (`https://github.com/qutheory/vapor-example`) that can be used and modified for our purposes. We are not going to explore Vapor in depth since it is still a work-in-progress and the Vapor documentation (`https://vapor.github.io/documentation`) already provides information required to get familiar with it.

SPM

SPM is an open source build and dependency management tool provided for Swift 3.0. It is integrated with the Swift build system to automate the process of downloading, compiling, and linking dependencies.

Vapor uses SPM; to create a Vapor project we need to add the following dependency to the `Packages.swift` file:

```
Package(url: "https://github.com/qutheory/vapor.git", majorVersion: xx,
minor: x)
```

As stated in the *Vapor* section, we can use Vapor CLI tools to build and run the application with SPM.

We recommend you to read more about Vapor and SPM since we do not cover most related topics in this book. In the following section, we will develop a very simple backend with Vapor.

Backend development

We want to develop a very simple backend for a `Todo` application. Please note that Vapor is in active development and our backend application will need regular updates to keep up. Therefore, our GitHub (`https://github.com/PacktPublishing/Swift-Functional-Programming`) repository will be updated frequently.

Model

We will start by creating our model. The code is as follows:

```
import Vapor
import Fluent

final class Todo: Model {
    var id: Node?
    var todoId: Int
    var name: String
    var description: String
    var notes: String
    var completed: Bool
    var synced: Bool

    var exists: Bool = false

    init(node: Node, in context: Context) throws {
        id = try node.extract("id")
        todoId = try node.extract("todoId")
        name = try node.extract("name")
        description = try node.extract("description")
        notes = try node.extract("notes")
        completed = try node.extract("completed")
        synced = try node.extract("synced")

    }

    init(todoId: Int, name: String, description: String, notes: String,
    completed: Bool, synced: Bool) {
        self.todoId = todoId
        self.name = name
        self.description = description
        self.notes = notes
        self.completed = completed
        self.synced = synced
    }

    func makeNode(context: Context) throws -> Node {
        return try Node(node: [
            "id": id,
            "todoId": todoId,
            "name": "\(name)",
            "description": "\(description)",
            "notes": "\(notes)",
            "completed": completed,
            "synced": synced
```

```
                        ])

            }
        }
```

This class imports Vapor and Fluent and includes some `Todo`-related properties as well as an `init` method.

To be able to pass this model into JSON arrays and dictionaries, we provided a `makeNode(context: Context) throws -> Node` implementation.

Store

Then we want to store the list of `Todo` items in memory. To be able to achieve this, we will create a new class called `TodoStore`. The code is as follows:

```
import Vapor

final class TodoStore {

    static let sharedInstance = TodoStore()
    fileprivate var list: [Todo] = Array<Todo>()
    private init() {
    }
}
```

For the sake of simplicity, we make this class a singleton that stores a list of `Todo` items. Also, we make the `init` method `private` to avoid non-shared instance initiation.

Next, we add the following methods:

```
func addOrUpdateItem(item: Todo) {
    if self.find(id: item.todoId) != nil {
        _ = update(item: item)
    } else {
        self.list.append(item)
    }
}

func listItems() -> [Todo] {
    return self.list
}
```

As the names suggest, these methods will be used for adding or updating and listing items. We will need a very simple find method, so let's develop it:

```
func find(id: Int) -> Todo? {
    return self.list.index { $0.todoId == id }.map { self.list[$0] }
}
```

Here, we use the `index` and `map` higher-order functions to find the `index` and return the respective array element.

Then, we will need to develop `update` and `delete` methods:

```
func delete(id: Int) -> String {
    if self.find(id: id) != nil {
        self.list = self.list.filter { $0.todoId != id }
        return "Item is deleted"
    }
    return "Item not found"
}

func deleteAll() -> String {
    if self.list.count > 0 {
        self.list.removeAll()
        return "All items were deleted"
    }
    return "List was empty"

}

func update(item: Todo) -> String {
    if let index = (self.list.index { $0.todoId == item.todoId }) {
        self.list[index] = item
        return "item is up to date"
    }
    return "item not found"
}
```

At this point our `TodoStore` is capable of all **Create, Read, Update, and Delete (CRUD)** operations.

Controller

The next step will be to develop routing, request, and response handling. For the sake of simplicity, we will modify `main.swift` in the Vapor example.

We will need to make our changes after the following definition because we are going to use `drop`:

```
let drop = Droplet()
```

Posting a new Todo item

The first step will be to develop a post method to create a `Todo` item as follows:

```
/// Post a todo item
drop.post("postTodo") { request in
    guard let id = request.headers["id"]?.int,
        let name = request.headers["name"],
        let description = request.headers["description"],
        let notes = request.headers["notes"],
        let completed = request.headers["completed"],
        let synced = request.headers["synced"]
        else {
            return try JSON(node: ["message": "Please include mandatory
            parameters"])
    }

    let todoItem = Todo(todoId: id,
                        name: name,
                        description: description,
                        notes: notes,
                        completed: completed.toBool()!,
                        synced: synced.toBool()!)

    let todos = TodoStore.sharedInstance
    todos.addOrUpdateItem(item: todoItem)

    let json: [Todo] = todos.listItems()
    return try JSON(node: json)
}
```

The preceding example is going to create a `Todo` item. First, we check if the API user is provided with all the necessary `HTTP` headers with a `guard` expression and then we use our `addOrUpdateItem()` method in the `TodoStore` class to add / update that specific item. In the preceding code example, we needed to convert `completed` from `Bool` to `String`, so we extended the String function as follows and we called `toBool()` on `completed`:

```
extension String {
    func toBool() -> Bool? {
        switch self {
        case "True", "true", "yes", "1":
```

```
            return true
        case "False", "false", "no", "0":
            return false
        default:
            return nil
        }
    }
}
```

We will need to build and run our backend app with the `vapor build` and `vapor run` directives in the terminal application. At this point, we should get the following prompt:

```
● ● ●      vapor-example — App ‹ swift -frontend -interpret /u...
Last login: Sun Apr 24 20:04:28 on ttys001
[fnayebi:vapor-example fatih$ vapor build
Compiling Swift Module 'App' (6 sources)
Linking .build/debug/App
[fnayebi:vapor-example fatih$ vapor run
Running...
Visit http://localhost:8080
[1461544239] [INFO] Server starting on 0.0.0.0:8080
```

If we point to `localhost:8080` in a web browser, we should see Vapor up-and-running. Also, we can use the `curl` tool to test our `POST` method in the terminal by copying and pasting the following command:

```
curl -X "POST" "http://localhost:8080/postTodo/" \
    -H "Cookie: test=123" \
    -H "id: 3" \
    -H "notes: do not forget to buy potato chips" \
    -H "Content-Type: application/json" \
    -H "description: Our first todo item" \
    -H "completed: false" \
    -H "name: todo 1" \
    -d "{}"
```

The result will resemble the following screenshot:

```
● ● ●                          vapor-example — -bash — 80×24
Last login: Mon Apr 25 22:12:54 on ttys001
fnayebi:vapor-example fatih$ curl -X "POST" "http://localhost:8080/postTodo/" \
> -H "Cookie: test=123" \
> -H "id: 3" \
> -H "notes: do not forget to buy potato chips" \
> -H "Content-Type: application/json" \
> -H "description: Our first todo item" \
> -H "completed: false" \
> -H "name: todo 1" \
> -d "{}"
[{"description":"Our first todo item","name":"todo 1","id":3,"completed":false,"
notes":"do not forget to buy potato chips"}]fnayebi:vapor-example fatih$ ▎
```

As we can see from the screenshot, we received a JSON response that includes our added `Todo` item.

Getting a list of Todo items

Our post call returns a list of items. Also, we can get items with this:

```
/// List todo items
drop.get("todos") { request in
    let todos = TodoStore.sharedInstance
    let json: [Todo] = todos.listItems()
    return try JSON(node: json)
}
```

We will build and run our application with Vapor CLI again and we can test this get request as follows:

```
curl -X "GET" "http://localhost:8080/todos" \
    -H "Cookie: test=123"
```

Getting a specific Todo item

The preceding call retrieves all the items. If we want to get a specific item, we can do that too as follows:

```
/// Get a specific todo item
drop.get("todo") { in
    guard let id = request.headers["id"]?.int else {
        return try JSON(node: ["message": "Please provide the id of
        todo item"])
    }

    let todos: [Todo] = TodoStore.sharedInstance.listItems()
    var json = [Todo]()

    let item = todos.filter { $0.todoId == id }
    if item.count > 0 {
        json.append(item[0])
    }

    return try JSON(node: json)
}
```

Here, we check for the existence of headers and use the `listItems()` method in our `TodoStore` class to retrieve that specific item. We can test it in `curl` by executing the following commands in the terminal:

```
curl -X "GET" "http://localhost:8080/todo/" \
  -H "id: 1" \
  -H "Cookie: test=123"
```

Deleting an item and deleting all Todo items

The next operation that we need to implement is deleting items from our `TodoStore`. Let's implement the `delete` and `deleteAll` methods:

```
/// Delete a specific todo item
drop.delete("deleteTodo") { request in
    guard let id = request.headers["id"]?.int else {
        return try JSON(node: ["message": "Please provide the id of
        todo item"])
    }

    let todos = TodoStore.sharedInstance
    let message = todos.delete(id: id)
```

```
        return try JSON(node: ["message": message])
    }

    /// Delete all items
    drop.delete("deleteAll") { request in
        let message = TodoStore.sharedInstance.deleteAll()

        return try JSON(node: ["message": message])
    }
```

To test the delete functionality, we can execute the following commands in the terminal:

```
curl -X "DELETE" "http://localhost:8080/deleteTodo/" \
  -H "id: 1" \
  -H "Cookie: test=123"
```

To test the deleteAll functionality, we can execute the following commands in the terminal:

```
curl -X "DELETE" "http://localhost:8080/deleteAll" \
  -H "Cookie: test=123"
```

Updating a Todo item

Finally, we want to be able to update an item in our Todo list to complete it or take some notes:

```
    /// Update a specific todo item
    drop.post("updateTodo") { request in
        guard let id = request.headers["id"]?.int,
            let name = request.headers["name"],
            let description = request.headers["description"],
            let notes = request.headers["notes"],
            let completed = request.headers["completed"],
            let synced = request.headers["synced"]
            else {
                return try JSON(node: ["message":
                                       "Please include mandatory parameters"])
            }

        let todoItem = Todo(todoId: id,
                            name: name,
                            description: description,
                            notes: notes,
                            completed: completed.toBool()!,
                            synced: synced.toBool()!)
```

```
        let todos = TodoStore.sharedInstance
        let message = todos.update(item: todoItem)
        return try JSON(node: ["message": message])
    }
```

Here, we check for the headers first and, if they are present, we use the `update` method in `TodoStore` to update a specific item in our `Store`. We can test it like this:

```
curl -X "POST" "http://localhost:8080/updateTodo" \
    -H "Cookie: test=123" \
    -H "id: 3" \
    -H "notes: new note" \
    -H "name: updated name" \
    -H "description: updated description" \
    -H "completed: yes"
```

At this point, we should have a simple backend API to create, list, update, and delete `Todo` items in memory. In the next section, we will develop an iOS application to leverage this API.

iOS application development

So far, we have looked into requirements, discussed a high-level design, and developed a simple backend API. Now, we are going to develop an iOS application that will leverage the latter.

Configuration

We will start our application development using `CocoaPods` (https://cocoapods.org/). We can install it by executing the following command in the terminal:

```
sudo gem install cocoapods
```

Then, we will create a folder using **Finder** or simply execute the following command in the terminal:

```
mkdir Frontend
```

Next, we will create a **Single View Application** project in Xcode as shown in the following screenshot:

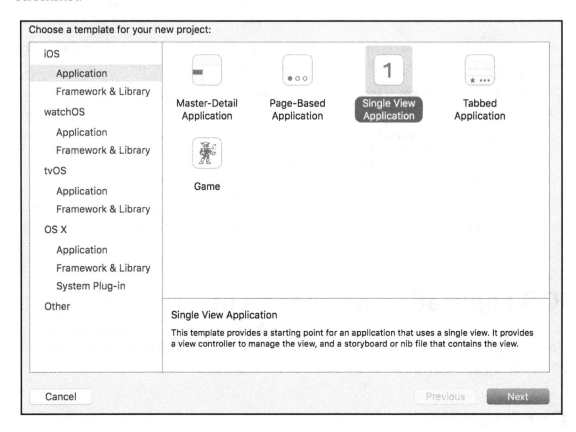

We are going to name it TodoApp and provide an organization name and identifier. The programming language is going to be **Swift**, and devices will be **Universal**. Now, we can close the project and go back to the terminal.

In the terminal, we will execute the following command:

```
cd Frontend/TodoApp
pod init
```

This will create a file named Podfile. This is where we define our dependencies.

Uncomment the first and third line so it becomes as follows:

```
platform :ios, '9.0'
use_frameworks!

target 'TodoApp' do
end

target 'TodoAppTests' do

end
```

Now, we need to define dependencies for our target. We can go to
`https://cocoapods.org/` and search for any dependency, copy the definition, and paste it
into our `Podfile`:

```
platform :ios, '9.0'
use_frameworks!

target 'TodoApp' do
    pod 'Alamofire', '~> 4.0'
    pod 'Argo'
    pod 'Curry'
    pod 'ReactiveCocoa', '~> 5.0.0'
    pod 'Delta', :git => "https://github.com/conqueror/Delta.git"
end

target 'TodoAppTests' do

end
```

Now, we can save and close our `Podfile` and move on to the terminal application. In the
terminal application, we will execute the following command:

pod install

This directive will create a workspace, download all dependencies, and link them as
frameworks into our project. Now, we can open `TodoApp.xcworkspace` with Xcode.

In the workspace, we will see two projects: `TodoApp` and `Pods`. `Pods` will contain all the
dependencies.

Next, let's create a folder hierarchy to organize our workspace. In the workspace, right-click on a folder and select **Show In Finder**. Here, we will create the following folders and files:

- Actions
- Communication
- Controllers
- Extensions
- Managers
- Models
- Resources
- State
- Views

Next, we will add these folders to our project by right-clicking on the TodoApp folder and selecting **Add Files to "TodoApp"**, as shown in the following screenshot:

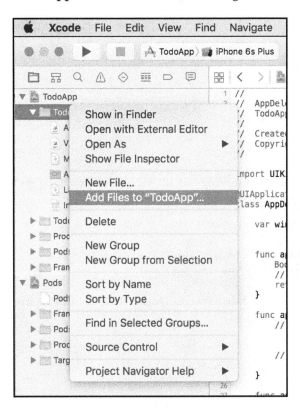

At this point we can move `ViewController` to the `Controllers` folder and any images to the `Resources` folder.

When we are done with our application, the folder and file hierarchy will be as follows:

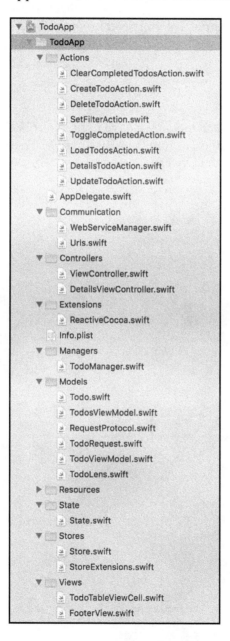

As an alternative, instead of manually creating folders, we can create our groups in Xcode and use SYNX (`https://github.com/venmo/synx`) to create folders that match our Xcode groups.

Since our backend does not comply with security policies (for example, cleartext HTTP resource load) enforced by Apple, we will need to set the `NSAllowsArbitraryLoads` key to `YES` under the `NSAppTransportSecurity` dictionary in our `.plist` file.

Models

Obviously, we can use the `Todo` model we have used in our backend example, but we want to make our frontend application as functional as possible. There is a functional JSON parsing library named `Argo` that we can leverage. Let's define our `Todo` model with `Argo`:

```
import Argo
import Curry
import Runes

enum TodoFilter: Int {
    case all
    case active
    case completed
    case notSyncedWithBackend
    case selected
}

struct Todo {
    let todoId: Int
    let name: String
    let description: String
    let notes: String?
    let completed: Bool
    let synced: Bool
    let selected: Bool?
}

extension Todo: Decodable {
    static func decode(_ json: JSON) -> Decoded<Todo> {
        return curry(Todo.init)
            <^> json <| "todoId"
            <*> json <| "name"
            <*> json <| "description"
            <*> json <|? "notes"
            <*> json <| "completed"
            <*> json <| "synced"
```

```
            <*> json <|? "selected"
    }
}

extension Todo: Equatable {}

func == (lhs: Todo, rhs: Todo) -> Bool {
    return lhs.todoId == rhs.todoId
}
```

First of all, we import three libraries: `Argo`, `Curry`, and `Runes`. `Curry` provides convenient currying functionalities. Although currying is removed from Swift 3.0 and returning closures are the norm, it will be safe to use the `Curry` library.

Our `Todo` model becomes a `struct`, and then we extend our `struct` by conforming to a `protocol` named `Decodable`. To conform to this `protocol`, we need to implement the `decode` function. This function takes a JSON payload and returns a decoded `Todo` object.

In the body of the function, we will use the currying and custom operators. According to the `Argo` documentation, currying allows us to partially apply the `init` function over the course of the decoding process. This basically means that we can build up the `init` function call bit by bit, adding one parameter at a time, if (and only if) `Argo` can successfully decode them. If any of the parameters do not meet our expectations, `Argo` will skip the `init` call and return a special failure `State`. Let's check the syntax of `Curry`:

```
public func curry<A, B, C, D, E, F>(function: (A, B, C, D, E) -> F) -> A ->
B -> C -> D -> E -> F {
    return { (`a`: A) -> B -> C -> D -> E -> F in { (`b`: B) -> C -> D
    -> E -> F in { (`c`: C) -> D -> E -> F in { (`d`: D) -> E -> F in {
    (`e`: E) -> F in function(`a`, `b`, `c`, `d`, `e`) } } } } }
}
```

The `curry` function takes a function that has five parameters A to E and returns F, that is, `curry` returns `A -> B -> C -> D -> E -> F`.

This enables us to partially apply our `init` method.

Operators

We will discuss the following different custom `infix` operators now:

- `<^>`: To map a function over a value conditionally
- `<*>`: To apply a function with context to a value with context
- `<|`: To decode a value at the specific key into the requested type
- `<|?`: To decode an optional value at the specific key into the requested type
- `<||`: to decode an array of values at the specific key into the requested type

`<^>` operator

Our first operator in the decoding process, `<^>`, is used to map our curried `init` method over a value. The definition is as follows:

```
public func <^> <T, U>(f: (T) -> U, x: Decoded<T>) -> Decoded<U> {
    return x.map(f)
}

func map<U>(_ f: (T) -> U) -> Decoded<U> {
    switch self {
    case let .success(value): return .success(f(value))
    case let .failure(error): return .failure(error)
    }
}
```

`<*>` operator

The `<*>` operator is used to conditionally apply the other parameters to our curried `init` method. The definition is as follows:

```
public func <*> <T, U>(f: Decoded<(T) -> U>, x: Decoded<T>) -> Decoded<U> {
    return x.apply(f)
}

func apply<U>(_ f: Decoded<(T) -> U>) -> Decoded<U> {
    switch (f, self) {
    case let (.success(function), _): return self.map(function)
    case let (.failure(le), .failure(re)): return .failure(le + re)
    case let (.failure(f), _): return .failure(f)
    }
}
```

<| operator

The `<|` operator is used to decode a value at the specified key path into the requested type. This operator uses a function named `flatReduce` that reduces and flattens the sequence:

```
public func <| <A: Decodable>(json: JSON, keys: [String]) -> Decoded<A>
where A == A.DecodedType {
    return flatReduce(keys, initial: json, combine: decodedJSON) >>-
    A.decode
}
```

<|? operator

The `<|?` operator is used to decode an optional value at the specified key path into the requested type:

```
public func <|? <A: Decodable>(json: JSON, keys: [String]) -> Decoded<A?>
where A == A.DecodedType {
    switch flatReduce(keys, initial: json, combine: decodedJSON) {
    case .failure: return .success(.none)
    case .success(let x): return A.decode(x) >>- {
        .success(.some($0)) }
    }
}
```

<|| operator

The `<||` operator is used to decode an array of values at a specific key into the requested type:

```
public func <|| <A: Decodable>(json: JSON, keys: [String]) -> Decoded<[A]>
where A == A.DecodedType {
    return flatReduce(keys, initial: json, combine: decodedJSON) >>-
    Array<A>.decode
}
```

Using Argo models

Whenever we receive a JSON payload from the backend, we will be able to use the `decode` function to decode our JSON payload to our model:

```
let data: Data? = nil

let json: Any? = try? JSONSerialization.jsonObject(with: data!,
                                                   options: [])
```

```
if let j: Any = json {
    let todo: Todo? = decode(j)
}
```

We can see that `Argo` can be leveraged as an example to master lots of FP paradigms. Using `Argo`, `Curry`, and custom operators, we are able to parse and decode JSON payloads to our model objects declaratively. Also, our models become immutable value types that we can use in our applications without being concerned about mutability.

Also, we defined an `enum` called `TodoFilter`. We will use this `enum` to `filter` items.

viewModel

We will have two `viewModel`, one for each `ViewController`:

```
import ReactiveCocoa

struct TodosViewModel {
    let todos: [Todo]

    func todoForIndexPath(_ indexPath: IndexPath) -> Todo {
        return todos[indexPath.row]
    }
}
```

We will use `TodosViewModel` to list `Todo` items in our table view:

```
struct TodoViewModel {
    let todo: Todo?
}
```

We will use `TodoViewModel` to present each `Todo` item's details.

Communication

So far, we have a backend API that we can use to CRUD `Todo` items and we have models in our iOS application. Let's examine how we can communicate with our backend and populate our models with received payloads.

The request protocol

First, we need to define a `protocol` for our request models:

```
protocol RequestProtocol {
    subscript(key: String) -> (String?, String?) { get }
}

extension RequestProtocol {
    func getPropertyNames()-> [String] {
        return Mirror(reflecting: self).children.filter {
            $0.label != nil
        }.map {
            $0.label!
        }
    }
}
```

Here, we defined a `protocol` and we extended the `protocol` to be able to reflect the object and get properties and their values.

Also, we added a `subscript` to our `protocol`, which any `struct` that wants to conform to this protocol should implement.

Conforming to the request protocol

Now, let's create a request model named `TodoRequest`:

```
struct TodoRequest: RequestProtocol {

    let todoId: Int
    let name: String
    let description: String
    let notes: String
    let completed: Bool
    let synced: Bool

    subscript(key: String) -> (String?, String?) {
        get {
            switch key {
            case "todoId": return (String(todoId), "todoId")
            case "name": return (name, "name")
            case "description": return (description, "description")
            case "notes": return (notes, "notes")
            case "completed": return (String(completed), "completed")
            case "synced": return (String(synced), "synced")
```

```
            default: return ("Cookie","test=123")
            }
        }
    }
}
```

As shown in the preceding code, this `struct` conforms to `RequestProtocol`. You might wonder why we have done this. First of all, this is an example of Protocol-Oriented Programming and second, we will use this request model in our post web service call.

WebServiceManager

We will create a file named `WebServiceManager` and add a function in it:

```
import Alamofire

func sendRequest(method: Alamofire.Method, request: RequestProtocol) {

    // Add Headers
    let headers = configureHeaders(request)

    // Fetch Request
    Alamofire.request(method, "http://localhost:8080/todo/",
    headers: headers, encoding: .JSON)
        .validate()
        .responseJSON { response in
            if (response.result.error == nil) {
                debugPrint("HTTP Response Body: \(response.data)")
            } else {
                debugPrint("HTTP Request failed: \
                (response.result.error)")
            }
        }
}

func configureHeaders(request: RequestProtocol) -> [String: String] {
    let listOfProperties = request.getPropertyNames()
    var configuredRequestHeaders = Dictionary<String, String>()
    for property in listOfProperties {
        let (propertyValue, propertyName) = request[property]
        if propertyName != nil {
            configuredRequestHeaders[propertyName!] = propertyValue
        }
    }
    return configuredRequestHeaders
}
```

Our `sendRequest` function takes two parameters. The first one is the HTTP request method and the second one is the type of `RequestProtocol`. Here, using the implemented protocol function called `getPropertyNames`, we prepare the header and send a request to our backend using `Alamofire`.

So far, we have a working `Communication` layer. At this point, we need to develop `Managers` and `viewController` to handle the logic and show the results to the user.

We will start by testing our `Communication` layer in our `MasterViewController` and will move the respective code to our `Managers`.

Creating a Todo item

To create a `Todo` item, we can call `sendRequest` function in our `MasterViewController` `viewDidLoad()` method to be sure that it is working:

```
let newRequest = TodoRequest(id: 1,
                             name: "First request",
                             description: "description",
                             notes: "notes",
                             completed: false)

sendRequest(Alamofire.Method.POST, request: newRequest)
```

This should add a new `Todo` item to our backend.

Our `sendRequest` method is incomplete and it does not provide a call back to receive the data. Let's improve it:

```
func sendRequest(method: Alamofire.Method,
                 request: RequestProtocol,
                 completion: @escaping (_ responseData: AnyObject?,
                 _ error: Error?) -> Void) {

    // Add Headers
    let headers = configureHeaders(request)

    // Fetch Request
    Alamofire.request(method, "http://localhost:8080/todo/",
    headers: headers, encoding: .JSON)
        .validate()
        .responseJSON { response in
            if (response.result.error == nil) {
                debugPrint("HTTP Response Body: \(response.data)")
                completion(response.result.value, nil)
```

```
        } else {
            debugPrint("HTTP Request failed: \
            (response.result.error)")
            completion(nil, response.result.error)
        }
    }
}
```

We added a closure as the function argument and called the closure in the body of the function. To test it, we will update our call in `MasterViewController`:

```
let newRequest = TodoRequest(id: 1,
                             name: "First request",
                             description: "description",
                             notes: "notess",
                             completed: false)
sendRequest(method: Alamofire.Method.POST, request: newRequest) {
    (response, error) in
    if error == nil {
        let todos: [Todo]? = decode(response!)
        print("request was successfull: \(todos)")
    } else {
        print("Error")
    }
}
```

Here, we pass a trailing `closure` in our call; once it is called, we receive the `response` or `error`. Importing and using `Argo`, we can map the payload to our model. We called this function only for testing and we need to move this call to the proper place. After all, none of our `ViewController` classes will be able to call this function directly and they have to go through other objects. Also, we will need to improve our `sendRequest` function to take the proper `url`:

```
enum Urls {
    case postTodo
    case getTodos
    case getTodo
    case deleteTodo
    case deleteAll
    case update
}

extension Urls {
    func httpMethodUrl() -> (String, String) {
        let baseUrl = "http://localhost:8080/"
        switch self {
        case .postTodo:
```

```
            return ("POST", "\(baseUrl)postTodo")
        case .getTodos:
            return ("GET", "\(baseUrl)todos")
        case .getTodo:
            return ("GET", "\(baseUrl)todo")
        case .deleteTodo:
            return ("DELETE", "\(baseUrl)deleteTodo")
        case .deleteAll:
            return ("DELETE", "\(baseUrl)deleteAll")
        case .update:
            return ("POST", "\(baseUrl)updateTodo")
        }
    }
}
```

Here, we define an `enum` and extend it. In our `httpMethodUrl` function, we perform pattern matching to return a tuple consisting of an HTTP request method and the full `url`. We need to change our `sendRequest` function as follows:

```
import Alamofire

func sendRequest(_ url: Urls,
                 request: RequestProtocol,
                 completion: @escaping (_ responseData: AnyObject?,
                 _ error: Error?) -> Void) {
    // Add headers
    let headers = configureHeaders(request)
    // Get request method and full url
    let (method, url) = url.httpMethodUrl()
    var urlRequest = URLRequest(url: URL(string: url)!)
    urlRequest.httpMethod = method
    urlRequest.allHTTPHeaderFields = headers

    // Fetch request
    let manager = Alamofire.SessionManager.default
    manager.request(urlRequest as URLRequestConvertible)
        .validate()
        .responseJSON {
            response in
            if (response.result.error == nil) {
                debugPrint("HTTP Response Body: \(response.data)")
                completion(response.result.value as AnyObject?, nil)
            } else {
                debugPrint("HTTP Request failed: \
                (response.result.error)")
                completion(nil, response.result.error)
            }
    }
}
```

```
    }
```

And our function call should be changed as follows:

```
let newRequest = TodoRequest(id: 1,
                             name: "First request",
                             description: "description",
                             notes: "notess",
                             completed: false)

sendRequest(Urls.PostTodo, request: newRequest) { (response, error) in
    if error == nil {
        let todos: [Todo]? = decode(response!)
        print("request was successfull: \(todos)")
    } else {
        print("Error")
    }
}
```

Listing Todo items

To retrieve all `Todo` items, unlike our post call, we do not need to pass any header parameters, just cookie information. So, we add the following `struct` to handle this scenario:

```
struct RequestModel: RequestProtocol {
    subscript(key: String) -> (String?, String?) {
        get {
            switch key {
                default: return ("Cookie","test=123")
            }
        }
    }
}
```

Then, we can retrieve a list of `Todo` items using the following code:

```
sendRequest(Urls.getTodos, request: RequestModel()) {
    (response, error) in
    if error == nil {
        let todos: [Todo]? = decode(response!)
        completion(todos, nil)
        print("request was successfull: \(todos)")
    } else {
        completion(nil, error)
        print("Error: \(error?.localizedDescription)")
    }
```

}

Although we added better error printing, we need to improve it further.

Let's extract the preceding function calls, create a Swift file named `TodoManager`, and put these functions in it:

```swift
import Alamofire
import Argo

func addTodo(_ completion:@escaping (_ responseData: [Todo]?,
                _ error: Error?) -> Void) {
    let newRequest = TodoRequest(todoId: 1,
                                 name: "Saturday Grocery",
                                 description: "Bananas, Pineapple,
                                 Beer, Orange juice, ...",
                                 notes: "Check expiry date of
                                 orange juice",
                                 completed: false,
                                 synced: true)

    sendRequest(Urls.postTodo, request: newRequest) {
        (response, error) in
        if error == nil {
            let todos: [Todo]? = decode(response!)
            completion(todos, nil)
            print("request was successfull: \(todos)")
        } else {
            completion(nil, error)
            print("Error: \(error?.localizedDescription)")
        }
    }
}

func listTodos(_ completion:@escaping  (_ responseData:[Todo]?,
                _ error: Error?) -> Void) {
    sendRequest(Urls.getTodos, request: RequestModel()) {
        (response, error) in
        if error == nil {
            let todos: [Todo]? = decode(response!)
            completion(todos, nil)
            print("request was successfull: \(todos)")
        } else {
            completion(nil, error)
            print("Error: \(error?.localizedDescription)")
        }
    }
}
```

Finally, we will develop two other functions: one adds or updates a `Todo` item and the other only updates a specific `Todo` item. Deleting items will be easy to implement as well. The code is as follows:

```
func addOrUpdateTodo(_ todo: [Todo]?,
                    completion:@escaping (_ responseData:[Todo]?,
                    _ error: Error?) -> Void) {
    if let todoItem = todo?.first {
        let newRequest = TodoRequest(todoId: todoItem.todoId,
                                    name: todoItem.name,
                                    description: todoItem.description,
                                    notes: todoItem.notes!,
                                    completed: todoItem.completed,
                                    synced: true)

        sendRequest(Urls.postTodo, request: newRequest) {
            (response, error) in
            if error == nil {
                let todos: [Todo]? = decode(response!)
                let newTodo = todoSyncedLens.set(true, todoItem)
                store.dispatch(UpdateTodoAction(todo: newTodo))
                completion(todos, nil)
                print("request was successfull: \(todos)")
            } else {
                completion(nil, error)
                print("Error: \(error?.localizedDescription)")
            }
        }
    }
}

func updateTodo(_ todo: [Todo]?, completion:@escaping (
_ responseData: [Todo]?, _ error: Error?) -> Void) {
    if let todoItem = todo?.first {
        let newRequest = TodoRequest(todoId: todoItem.todoId,
                                    name: todoItem.name,
                                    description: todoItem.description,
                                    notes: todoItem.notes!,
                                    completed: todoItem.completed,
                                    synced: true)

        sendRequest(Urls.update, request: newRequest) {
            (response, error) in
            if error == nil {
                let todos: [Todo]? = decode(response!)
                let newTodo = todoSyncedLens.set(true, todoItem)
                store.dispatch(UpdateTodoAction(todo: newTodo))
                completion(todos, nil)
```

```
            print("request was successfull: \(todos)")
        } else {
            completion(nil, error)
            print("Error: \(error?.localizedDescription)")
        }
    }


    }
}
```

In these functions, we have not yet covered the following concepts in detail:

- dispatch: This function dispatches an action (here, UpdateTodoAction) by setting the State struct's value to the result of calling its reduce method.
- todoSyncedLens: This is a Lens to modify the synced property of the Todo item. We will define these lenses in an upcoming section.
- UpdateTodoAction: This is a struct that conforms to ActionType, which is used when we want to make modifications to the State of the Store. All changes to the Store go through this type. We will define our Actions in an upcoming section.
- State: This is a struct that will be used to manage the State. We will define it later.
- Store: As the name suggests, this is where we Store the State. We will define it later.

Lenses

We will use lenses to modify our Todo item. Each of the following lenses will be used to modify a part of the Todo item:

```
struct Lens<Whole, Part> {
    let get: (Whole) -> Part
    let set: (Part, Whole) -> Whole
}

let todoNameLens: Lens<Todo, String> = Lens(
    get: { $0.name},
    set: {
        Todo(todoId: $1.todoId,
            name: $0,
            description: $1.description,
            notes: $1.notes,
            completed: $1.completed,
```

```
                        synced: $1.synced,
                        selected: $1.selected)
    })

    let todoDescriptionLens: Lens<Todo, String> = Lens(
        get: { $0.description},
        set: {
            Todo(todoId: $1.todoId,
                    name: $1.name,
                    description: $0,
                    notes: $1.notes,
                    completed: $1.completed,
                    synced: $1.synced,
                    selected: $1.selected)
    })

    let todoNotesLens: Lens<Todo, String> = Lens(
        get: { $0.notes!},
        set: {
            Todo(todoId: $1.todoId,
                    name: $1.name,
                    description: $1.description,
                    notes: $0,
                    completed: $1.completed,
                    synced: $1.synced,
                    selected: $1.selected)
    })

    let todoCompletedLens: Lens<Todo, Bool> = Lens(
        get: { $0.completed},
        set: {
            Todo(todoId: $1.todoId,
                    name: $1.name,
                    description: $1.description,
                    notes: $1.notes,
                    completed: $0,
                    synced: $1.synced,
                    selected: $1.selected)
    })

    let todoSyncedLens: Lens<Todo, Bool> = Lens(
        get: { $0.synced},
        set: {
            Todo(todoId: $1.todoId,
                    name: $1.name,
                    description: $1.description,
                    notes: $1.notes,
                    completed: $1.completed,
```

```
                    synced: $0,
                    selected: $1.selected)
        })
```

States

In our application, we need to manage states to keep the `State` management code as declarative as possible. We will use a library named `Delta` (`https://github.com/conqueror/Delta/blob/master/documentation/getting-started.md`).

`Delta` will be used along with `ReactiveCocoa` and `ReactiveSwift` to manage states and `State` changes reactively. The code is as follows:

```
import ReactiveCocoa
import ReactiveSwift
import Delta

extension MutableProperty: Delta.ObservablePropertyType {
    public typealias ValueType = Value
}
```

In the preceding code, we extend the `ReactiveSwift` library's `MutableProperty` by conforming to `Delta.ObservablePropertyType`.

The `ObservablePropertyType` protocol must be implemented by the `State` that is held by `Store`. To use a custom `State` type, this `protocol` must be implemented on that object.

`MutableProperty` creates a mutable property of type value and allows observation of its changes in a thread-safe way.

Using an extended `MutableProperty`, our `State` objects become the following:

```
import ReactiveSwift

private let initialTodos: [Todo] = []

struct State {
    let todos = MutableProperty(initialTodos)
    let filter = MutableProperty(TodoFilter.all)
    let notSynced = MutableProperty(TodoFilter.notSyncedWithBackend)
    let selectedTodoItem = MutableProperty(TodoFilter.selected)
}
```

Store

We will store state in our Store object:

```
import ReactiveSwift
import ReactiveCocoa
import Delta

struct Store: StoreType {
    var state: ObservableProperty<State>

    init(state: State) {
        self.state = ObservableProperty(state)
    }
}

var store = Store(state: State())
```

Store conforms to the StoreType protocol declared in the Delta library. The StoreType protocol defines the storage of an observable state and dispatch methods to modify it.

Here, we create a MutableProperty as state and store it in Store object.

We need to define properties to access and modify our state properly, so we extend our Store object as follows:

```
import ReactiveCocoa
import ReactiveSwift
import Result

// MARK: Properties
extension Store {
    var todos: MutableProperty<[Todo]> {
        return state.value.todos
    }

    var activeFilter: MutableProperty<TodoFilter> {
        return state.value.filter
    }

    var selectedTodoItem: MutableProperty<TodoFilter> {
        return state.value.selectedTodoItem
    }

}
```

```
// MARK: SignalProducers
extension Store {
    var activeTodos: SignalProducer<[Todo], NoError> {
        return activeFilter.producer.flatMap(.latest) {
            filter -> SignalProducer<[Todo], NoError> in

            switch filter {
            case .all: return self.todos.producer
            case .active: return self.incompleteTodos
            case .completed: return self.completedTodos
            case .notSyncedWithBackend: return self.notSyncedWithBackend
            case .selected: return self.selectedTodo
            }
        }
    }

    var completedTodos: SignalProducer<[Todo], NoError> {
        return todos.producer.map {
            todos in
            return todos.filter { $0.completed }
        }
    }

    var incompleteTodos: SignalProducer<[Todo], NoError> {
        return todos.producer.map {
            todos in
            return todos.filter { !$0.completed }
        }
    }

    var incompleteTodosCount: SignalProducer<Int, NoError> {
        return incompleteTodos.map { $0.count }
    }

    var allTodosCount: SignalProducer<Int, NoError> {
        return todos.producer.map { $0.count }
    }

    var todoStats: SignalProducer<(Int, Int), NoError> {
        return allTodosCount.zip(with: incompleteTodosCount)
    }

    var notSyncedWithBackend: SignalProducer<[Todo], NoError> {
        return todos.producer.map {
            todos in
            return todos.filter { !$0.synced }
        }
    }
```

```
        var selectedTodo: SignalProducer<[Todo], NoError> {
            return todos.producer.map {
                todos in
                return todos.filter {
                    todo in
                    if let selected = todo.selected {
                        return selected
                    } else {
                        return false
                    }
                }
            }
        }

        func producerForTodo(_ todo: Todo) -> SignalProducer<Todo, NoError> {
            return store.todos.producer.map {
                todos in
                return todos.filter { $0 == todo }.first
            }.skipNil()
        }
    }
```

In our `Store` object, we use the `ReactiveSwift` library's `SignalProducer` to create `Observable Signals`. We will observe these signals in other objects and react to signal changes.

Actions

`Actions` are structs that conform to the `ActionType` protocol from the `Delta` library. `ActionType` is used when we want to make modifications to the store's `State`. All changes to the `Store` object go through this type. Let's examine one example:

```
import Delta

struct UpdateTodoAction: ActionType {
    let todo: Todo

    func reduce(state: State) -> State {
        state.todos.value = state.todos.value.map {
            todo in
            guard todo == self.todo else { return todo }

            return Todo(todoId: todo.todoId,
                        name: self.todo.name,
                        description: self.todo.description,
                        notes: self.todo.notes,
```

```
                       completed: self.todo.completed,
                       synced: !todo.synced,
                       selected: todo.selected)
        }

        return state
    }
}
```

In our manager, we had a call like this:

```
store.dispatch(UpdateTodoAction(todo: newTodo))
```

The dispatch method call on store with UpdateTodoAction will call the reduce method of UpdateTodoAction. It will also make modifications on the State and return a new version of it. This is the only place where changes to State are permitted; therefore, any changes to State should go through an action.

Let's define other Actions as well:

```
import Delta

struct ClearCompletedTodosAction: DynamicActionType {
    func call() {
        let todos = store.completedTodos.first()?.value ?? []

        todos.forEach {
            todo in
            store.dispatch(DeleteTodoAction(todo: todo))
        }
    }
}

struct CreateTodoAction: ActionType {
    let todoId: Int
    let name: String
    let description: String
    let notes: String

    var todo: Todo {
        return Todo(todoId: todoId,
                    name: name,
                    description: description,
                    notes: notes,
                    completed: false,
                    synced: false,
                    selected: false)
    }
```

```
        func reduce(state: State) -> State {
            state.todos.value = state.todos.value + [todo]

            return state
        }
    }

    struct DeleteTodoAction: ActionType {
        let todo: Todo

        func reduce(state: State) -> State {
            state.todos.value = state.todos.value.filter { $0 != self.todo }

            return state
        }
    }

    struct DetailsTodoAction: ActionType {
        let todo: Todo

        func reduce(state: State) -> State {
            state.todos.value = state.todos.value.map { todo in
                guard todo == self.todo else {

                    return Todo(todoId: todo.todoId,
                                name: todo.name,
                                description: todo.description,
                                notes: todo.notes,
                                completed: todo.completed,
                                synced: todo.synced,
                                selected: false)
                }

                return Todo(todoId: self.todo.todoId,
                            name: self.todo.name,
                            description: self.todo.description,
                            notes: self.todo.notes,
                            completed: self.todo.completed,
                            synced: self.todo.synced,
                            selected: true)
            }

            return state
        }
    }

    struct LoadTodosAction: ActionType {
        let todos: [Todo]
```

```
    func reduce(state: State) -> State {
        state.todos.value = state.todos.value + todos
        return state
    }
}

struct SetFilterAction: ActionType {
    let filter: TodoFilter

    func reduce(state: State) -> State {
        state.filter.value = filter
        return state
    }
}

struct ToggleCompletedAction: ActionType {
    let todo: Todo

    func reduce(state: State) -> State {
        state.todos.value = state.todos.value.map {
            todo in
            guard todo == self.todo else { return todo }

            return Todo(todoId: todo.todoId,
                        name: todo.name,
                        description: todo.description,
                        notes: todo.notes,
                        completed: !todo.completed,
                        synced: !todo.synced,
                        selected: todo.selected)
        }

        return state
    }
}
```

Views

The user will be able to list Todo items from the backend, toggle to mark an item as complete, or swipe left to access functionalities such as **Details** and **Delete**.

Our application will look as shown in the following screenshots:

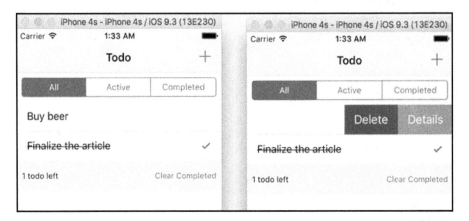

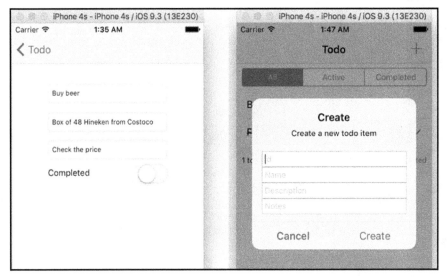

We can design these screens in the storyboard. We will need to implement a custom `UITableViewCell` as shown here to be able to show the proper data on `TableView`:

```
import UIKit

class TodoTableViewCell: UITableViewCell {

    var todo: Todo? {
        didSet {
            updateUI()
        }
```

```
    }

    var attributedText: NSAttributedString {
        guard let todo = todo else { return NSAttributedString() }

        let attributes: [String : AnyObject]
        if todo.completed {
            attributes = [NSStrikethroughStyleAttributeName:
            NSUnderlineStyle.styleSingle.rawValue as AnyObject]
        } else {
            attributes = [:]
        }

        return NSAttributedString(string: todo.name, attributes:
        attributes)
    }
    func configure(_ todo: Todo) {
        store.producerForTodo(todo).startWithValues {
            nextTodo in
            self.todo = nextTodo
        }
    }

    func updateUI() {
        guard let todo = todo else { return }

        textLabel?.attributedText = attributedText
        accessoryType = todo.completed ? .checkmark : .none
    }
}
```

The only interesting piece in this class is the `configure` method. It will be called in our `cellForRowAtIndexPath` method of `TableViewController` to create a `Signal` from the producer, then to add exactly one observer to the `Signal`, which will invoke the given callback when the next events are received.

ViewControllers

We will have two `ViewController` subclasses:

- `MasterViewController`: This will list `Todo` items
- `DetailViewController`: This will present and modify details of each item

Also, we will need `ViewController` scenes in our main storyboard. The following screenshot shows our storyboard:

We are not going to go through the storyboard and related scenes in detail as we assume that the reader is already familiar with these concepts. Storyboards can be downloaded from the GitHub repository of the book (`https://github.com/PacktPublishing/Swift-Functional-Programming`).

MasterViewController

We will present a list of items to the user in `MasterViewController`:

```
import UIKit

class MasterViewController: UITableViewController {

    @IBOutlet weak var filterSegmentedControl: UISegmentedControl!

    var viewModel = TodosViewModel(todos: []) {
        didSet {
            tableView.reloadData()
        }
    }

    override func viewDidLoad() {
        super.viewDidLoad()
```

```
listTodos {
    (response, error) in
    if error == nil {
        store.dispatch(LoadTodosAction(todos: response!))
    } else {
        print("Error: \(error?.localizedDescription)")
    }
}

filterSegmentedControl.addTarget(self, action:
#selector(MasterViewController.filterValueChanged), for:
.valueChanged)

store.activeFilter.producer.startWithValues {
    filter in
    self.filterSegmentedControl.selectedSegmentIndex =
    filter.rawValue
}

store.activeTodos.startWithValues {
    todos in
    self.viewModel = TodosViewModel(todos: todos)
}

store.notSyncedWithBackend.startWithValues {
    todos in
    addOrUpdateTodo(todos) {
        (response, error) in
        if error == nil {
            print("Success")
        } else {
            print("Error: \(error?.localizedDescription)")
        }
    }
}
    }
}
```

We have the viewModel, which is a computed property. In viewDidLoad, we list the Todo items from our backend and we store them in State using LoadTodosAction. Then, we define observations to change our viewModel and to sync changed items with the backend.

IBActions

We will need to define two `IBAction`, one to add a new item to the list and the other to filter the items:

```
// MARK: Actions
extension MasterViewController {
    @IBAction func addTapped(_ sender: UIBarButtonItem) {
        let alertController = UIAlertController(title: "Create",
                                message: "Create a new todo item",
                                preferredStyle: .alert)

        alertController.addTextField {
            textField in
            textField.placeholder = "Id"
        }

        alertController.addTextField {
            textField in
            textField.placeholder = "Name"
        }

        alertController.addTextField {
            textField in
            textField.placeholder = "Description"
        }

        alertController.addTextField {
            textField in
            textField.placeholder = "Notes"
        }

        alertController.addAction(UIAlertAction(title: "Cancel",
        style: .cancel) { _ in })

        alertController.addAction(UIAlertAction(title: "Create",
        style: .default) { _ in
            guard let id = alertController.textFields?[0].text,
                let name = alertController.textFields?[1].text,
                let description = alertController.textFields?[2].text,
                let notes = alertController.textFields?[3].text
                else { return }

            store.dispatch(CreateTodoAction(todoId: Int(id)!,
                                    name: name,
                                    description: description,
                                    notes: notes))
        })
```

```
            present(alertController, animated: false, completion: nil)
    }

    func filterValueChanged() {
        guard let newFilter = TodoFilter(rawValue:
        filterSegmentedControl.selectedSegmentIndex)
            else { return }

        store.dispatch(SetFilterAction(filter: newFilter))
    }
}
```

In the `addTapped` method, we use `createTodoAction` to add an item to the list with the
`completed` and `synced` values as `false`. Therefore,
`store.notSyncedWithBackend.startWithNext` in `viewDidLoad` will view this item as
not synced and will sync it with the backend.

TableView delegates and DataSource

Finally, we need to implement the `delegate` and `datasource` methods for
`UITableViewController`. The code is as follows:

```
// MARK: UITableViewController
extension MasterViewController {
    override func tableView(_ tableView: UITableView,
    numberOfRowsInSection section: Int) -> Int {
        return viewModel.todos.count
    }

    override func tableView(_ tableView: UITableView, cellForRowAt
    indexPath: IndexPath) -> UITableViewCell {
        let cell = tableView.dequeueReusableCell(withIdentifier:
        "todoCell", for: indexPath) as! TodoTableViewCell
        let todo = viewModel.todoForIndexPath(indexPath)
        cell.configure(todo)

        return cell
    }

    override func tableView(_ tableView: UITableView, didSelectRowAt
    indexPath: IndexPath) {
        let todo = viewModel.todoForIndexPath(indexPath)
        store.dispatch(ToggleCompletedAction(todo: todo))
        tableView.deselectRow(at: indexPath, animated: true)
    }

    override func tableView(_ tableView: UITableView, commit
```

```swift
        editingStyle: UITableViewCellEditingStyle, forRowAt indexPath:
        IndexPath) {

    }

    override func tableView(_ tableView: UITableView,
    editActionsForRowAt indexPath: IndexPath) ->
    [UITableViewRowAction]? {
        let delete = UITableViewRowAction(style: .normal,
                                          title: "Delete") {
            action, index in
            let todo = self.viewModel.todoForIndexPath(indexPath)
            store.dispatch(DeleteTodoAction(todo: todo))
        }
        delete.backgroundColor = UIColor.red

        let details = UITableViewRowAction(style: .normal,
                                           title: "Details") {
            action, index in
            let todo = self.viewModel.todoForIndexPath(indexPath)
            store.dispatch(DetailsTodoAction(todo: todo))

            self.performSegue(withIdentifier: "segueShowDetails",
            sender: self)
        }
        details.backgroundColor = UIColor.orange

        return [details, delete]
    }

    override func tableView(_ tableView: UITableView, canEditRowAt
    indexPath: IndexPath) -> Bool {
        // the cells you would like the actions to appear need to be
        editable
        return true
    }
}
```

In the preceding code, we use `DeleteTodoAction` to delete an item by swiping to the left and selecting **Delete**. We use `ToggleCompletedAction` to mark an item as **completed** when we tap on any item on the list, and we use `DetailsTodoAction` to navigate to the details page when we swipe to the left and select **Details**.

DetailsViewController

We will use `DetailsViewController` to present the details of a `Todo` item and modify it. We will have three `textField` and a `switch`. We will observe the changes in the UI and modify the `State` and backend. The code is as follows:

```
import UIKit
import ReactiveCocoa
import ReactiveSwift

class DetailsViewController: UIViewController {

    @IBOutlet weak var txtFieldName: UITextField!
    @IBOutlet weak var txtFieldDescription: UITextField!
    @IBOutlet weak var txtFieldNotes: UITextField!
    @IBOutlet weak var switchCompleted: UISwitch!

    var viewModel = TodoViewModel(todo: nil)

    override func viewDidLoad() {
        super.viewDidLoad()
        store.selectedTodo.startWithValues {
            todos in
            let model = todos.first!
            self.txtFieldName.text = model.name
            self.txtFieldDescription.text = model.description
            self.txtFieldNotes.text = model.notes
            self.switchCompleted.isOn = model.completed
            self.viewModel = TodoViewModel(todo: model)
        }
        setupUpdateSignals()
    }

    func setupUpdateSignals()  {
        txtFieldName.reactive.continuousTextValues.observeValues {
            (values: String?) -> () in
            if let newName = values {
                let newTodo = todoNameLens.set(newName,
                self.viewModel.todo!)
                store.dispatch(UpdateTodoAction(todo: newTodo))
            }
        }

        txtFieldDescription.reactive.continuousTextValues.observeValues {
            (values: String?) -> () in
            if let newDescription = values {
                let newTodo = todoDescriptionLens.set(newDescription,
```

```
                  self.viewModel.todo!)
                  store.dispatch(UpdateTodoAction(todo: newTodo))
            }
      }

      txtFieldNotes.reactive.continuousTextValues.observeValues {
            (values: String?) -> () in
            if let newNotes = values {
                  let newTodo = todoNotesLens.set(newNotes,
                  self.viewModel.todo!)
                  store.dispatch(UpdateTodoAction(todo: newTodo))

            }
      }
      switchCompleted.reactive.isOnValues.observeValues {
            (value: Bool) -> () in
            let newTodo = todoCompletedLens.set(value,
            self.viewModel.todo!)
            store.dispatch(UpdateTodoAction(todo: newTodo))
      }
   }
}
```

In our `viewDidLoad` method, we look for the selected item in `MasterViewController` before navigating to `DetailsViewController`. We also set the `UITextField` and `UISwitch` initial values. We subscribe to changes in the UI, use lenses to update the `Todo` item, and change the `State` via `UpdateTodoAction`. Any item change sets `synced` as `false`. Since this property is observed in `MasterViewController`, any changes to the UI in `DetailsViewController` are synced with the backend without any extra effort.

Summary

In this chapter, we developed a backend with the Swift Vapor library, which handles the `Todo` items `POST`, `GET`, and `DELETE`. Then, we developed a frontend iOS application that leverages functional programming, reactive programming, and `State` management techniques declaratively. We started by developing our `Todo` model in a functional style, and then we developed a `Store` object and its extensions to handle `State` storage, and `Action` to handle `State` changes. We defined and used `Lens` to modify our properties and a `WebServiceManager` with reflection techniques to request for backend resources.

In this case study, we were able to use value types such as `struct` and `enum` and avoid classes. In fact, the only four classes in this case study are related to the iOS SDK (`UIViewController`, `UITableViewController`, `UITableViewCell`, and `UIView` subclasses). We were able to centralize all `State` mutations into the `Store` object, only using `Action` to change the `State` in the `Store` object. Although we did not develop any unit test cases, it is recommended that you explore functional programming unit testing libraries such as Quick (`https://github.com/Quick/Quick`) to ensure the quality of code.

This book has aimed to achieve three goals.

The first goal was to go through functional programming paradigms with Swift in a simple non-mathematical way with code examples.

Some of the concepts are very complex for the first-time functional programmers and sometimes you may have felt that they are not explained in enough depth or detail. In fact, some of details are left out for the sake of applicability and simplicity. After all, Swift is not a purely functional programming language and we always need to deal with Cocoa frameworks that are mostly designed in object-oriented manner. Fighting with frameworks and overcomplicating stuffs in application development is not the preferred way and we are more concerned with getting the best out of Swift functional programming.

The second goal was to compare and combine functional programming with **object-oriented programming (OOP)**, **functional reactive programming (FRP)** and **protocol-oriented programming (POP)** paradigms. This book explains them very briefly and does not aim to be a comprehensive guide for OOP, FRP, and POP. The goal was to explain the level of detail that could be used to compare and to leverage different paradigms.

The third goal was to provide a practical code example of a multi-paradigm iOS application development. Even though it is not a good practice to be dependent on many 3rd-party libraries, we have leveraged them to be able to achieve and demonstrate more in less number of pages.

There are different ways to achieve most of development tasks and we do not claim that our example is representing the best possible way. It serves its purpose to demonstrate some of the techniques.

All the code examples are shared in book's GitHub repository and they will be kept up to date with Swift and Framework changes.

Hopefully, you got a lot out of this book and you will continue to further explore the Swift Functional Programming.

So, what is next?

If you want to learn more about the theory and mathematics behind the functional programming, you should read a book or two about category theory, type theory, and abstract algebra. A Google search on *category theory for computer scientists* will bring up lots of great resources. Also, *Category Theory for Programmers* by *Bartosz Milewski* is a great read.

If you want to experience more with functional programming languages you can read a book on Haskell. *Learn You a Haskell for Great Good* by *Miran Lipovaca* and *Real World Haskell* by *Bryan O'Sullivan et al.* are great resources.

To get more out of Swift Functional Programming, because it is not a simple topic, you should read and rely on multiple resources. *Functional Swift* by *Chris Eidhof et al.* and *Functional Swift Conference* are great resources.

Finally, there are great working examples of open source projects at GitHub such as Kickstarter and thoughtbot repositories that can be examined.

Index